THE BALLET OF THE SECOND EMPIRE

The Gala Performance at the Paris Opéra, in honour of the Visit of the Tsar, on June 4th, 1867.
Angelina Fioretti and Léontine Beaugrand are seen dancing in Act II of *Giselle*

THE BALLET
OF THE
SECOND EMPIRE

Ivor Guest

London: Pitman Publishing
Middletown: Wesleyan University Press

First published (as two volumes) 1953, 1955

First published in this edition 1974 by
Sir Isaac Pitman and Sons Ltd
Pitman House, Parker Street, Kingsway, London WC2B 5PB

Published in the United States 1974 by
Wesleyan University Press
Middletown, Connecticut 06457

Printed by Unwin Brothers Limited
The Gresham Press, Old Woking, Surrey, England
A member of the Staples Printing Group

Library of Congress Catalog Card Number: 73-15010
US ISBN 0 8195 4067 6
UK ISBN 0 273 00496 4
Cat. No. G3547: 13

CONTENTS

v

ILLUSTRATIONS

IN THE TEXT

The caricatures are all by Marcelin, unless otherwise stated. *page*

SOURCES OF ILLUSTRATIONS

PREFACE

WHEN this book was written, between 1946 and 1951, interest in
ballet history was comparatively small, although there existed a
considerable market for books about ballet with a topical
interest. Indeed, that it was published at all was due to the
dogged efforts of the late Cyril Swinson who, despairing of
persuading his fellow directors to take the risk of bringing out
such a specialised work, conceived the idea of publishing it one
half at a time, but without an immediate commitment for the
second half. It would have been logical to put out the first half
first, but the chapters on Emma Livry and *Coppélia* had given me
the greatest pleasure to write and in order to make sure that they
would see the light of day, I requested that the last five chapters
be published first. The book had a very gratifying reception
when it came out in 1953, and two years later the earlier part
followed in an identical format. Now, twenty years on, the work
is being published as a single entity, as it was originally conceived, and I am delighted to have the opportunity of acknowledging the debt I owe to Cyril Swinson, who became one of my
closest friends.

The book—my first incursion into the field of ballet—had
grown out of a passionate, but then fairly recent, interest in the
ballet coupled with an absorbing study of the Second Empire.
My first book had been about Napoleon III, and I doubt if at
that time I foresaw that I was to devote myself exclusively to
the history of ballet and move away from Paris and the Second
Empire. In writing this book it was my aim to chronicle the
events of the ballet and bring to life some of the people involved
in it against the setting of the period. To what extent I succeeded
in this is for others to judge, but in my later books on ballet
history I have set myself this same objective, believing that the
history of an art form is inseparable from contemporary trends
in thought and the social and political conditions of the time, and
worthless if divorced from this setting. Re-reading this early
work, I am very conscious that I wrote it in the full fervour of
Bonapartism!

That I was diverted towards the history of the dance was due in no small part to the thrilling discoveries that awaited me at the Paris Opéra where I have always been received with a warmth that I appreciated more than I can ever express. Gradually a grand design took shape—to extend this chronicle. First this book begat a study of *The Romantic Ballet in Paris*, published in 1966, and I am at present planning to extend my detailed survey of French ballet still further back in time to the pre-Romantic era, spanning the French Revolution and First Empire.

In acknowledging the Paris Opéra Library as the source of so much of the material on which this book is based, I must record my deep gratitude to André Ménétrat, who was its Librarian when this book was being written, and to his ever willing assistants, Mme Marcelle Morillon, the late Mme Carol-Bérard and Mlle Henriette Boschot. I have also to thank the Trustees and Keepers of the Bibliothèque Nationale, the Archives Nationales, the Bibliothèque de l'Arsenal, the Musée Carnavalet, the British Museum and the Victoria and Albert Museum for granting facilities for research and permission to reproduce various items from their collections; and the Brooklyn Museum, of New York, for granting permission to reproduce Degas' oil-painting of Eugénie Fiocre in *La Source*.

Several of those who helped me are no longer alive: Miss O. F. Abbott, who tirelessly undertook research for me in Paris, M. Jean Bozzacchi, who told me all he knew about his aunt Giuseppina, and Dr. Suzanne Dreyfus, who added to my knowledge of her mother, Léontine Beaugrand. My thanks are also due to Mrs. Gladys Weller; to Lady Stirling, who gave me invaluable assistance when the work was in its early stages; and to those friends who read the work in manuscript and generously gave advice—Mr. Cyril Beaumont, with whom I spent many absorbing hours in the inner sanctum of his now legendary shop, the late Mr. W. H. Holden and Miss Lillian Moore, and Messrs. Raymond Mander and Joe Mitchenson.

Dates of events which took place in Russia are all given in the New Style.

IVOR GUEST

London,
April 1974

THE BALLET OF THE SECOND EMPIRE

BALLET IN THE PARIS OF NAPOLEON III

DURING the quarter century spanning the Golden Age of the Romantic Ballet and the ballet of the *fin de siècle* that Degas painted, France passed from the uninspiring reign of Louis Philippe, through the Second Republic and the Second Empire, into the drabness of the Third Republic. When peace came after the tragedy of 1870, little of that Romantic spirit, which had so vitalized the dance in the eighteen-thirties and forties, was left in the ballet: its last flame had died, with the choreographer, Arthur Saint-Léon, in the turmoil of war, and only glowing embers remained to recall glories but recently past.

Marie Taglioni, who had become identified, more than any other dancer of her day, with the Romantic renaissance of ballet, had danced in public for the last time in London in August 1847. With the retirement of its guiding inspiration, the Golden Age of the Romantic Ballet had then come to a close. There followed, however, no abrupt eclipse. The artistic impetus, which had gathered over the years that had produced *La Sylphide*, *Giselle* and *La Esmeralda*, took a quarter of a century to spend itself, and endured throughout the Second Empire, until the death of Saint-Léon, the leading figure in this latter phase of the Romantic Ballet, on the very day of the fateful battle of Sedan.

The production of Saint-Léon's first ballet for the Paris Opéra, *La Fille de marbre*, followed Marie Taglioni's retirement by two months; and his last ballet, *Coppélia*, was given to the public only a few weeks before the outbreak of war in 1870. During the twenty-three years that separate these two works, many other great figures of the Romantic Ballet continued their work at the Opéra. Joseph Mazilier, who had arranged *La Gipsy* for Fanny Elssler and *Le Diable à quatre* for Carlotta Grisi, held the post of *premier maître de ballet* from 1853 until 1859, devising ballets for Cerrito, Priora, Rosati and Ferraris; and in

1867 he came out of retirement to revive *Le Corsaire* for Grant-zow. Lucien Petipa, creator of the rôle of Albrecht in *Giselle*, and brother of Marius Petipa, was dancing until 1862 and *maître de ballet* until 1868, and was to return to the Opéra in 1882 to arrange the choreography of *Namouna*. Jules Perrot, who had appeared at the Opéra in the thirties, returned for a brief period in 1849 to produce *La Filleule des fées* for Carlotta Grisi. Finally, there was Marie Taglioni herself, enticed back to the Opéra in 1858 by the wonderful promise of Emma Livry, for whom she arranged *Le Papillon* and was preparing a second ballet, *Zara*, when tragedy cut short the young dancer's career. These five persons, whose names rank among the greatest of the Romantic Ballet, were responsible for twenty-three of the twenty-eight new ballets mounted at the Opéra between October 1847 and September 1870.

It was nevertheless under their leadership in the fifties and sixties that French ballet began to lose its vitality. These two decades were marked more by progress in the ballerina's technique than by any important evolution in ballet as a theatrical art. The two great technical innovations of the early nineteenth century—the discovery of the *pointe* [1] and the increased elevation in female dancing—were developed and their possibilities explored, often so thoroughly that æsthetic considerations were sacrificed for effect. Choreographers, carried away by the tremendous expansion that the *pointe* had brought to the ballerina's vocabulary, and aware of the public's delight in what was still something of a novelty, were unable to resist taking full advantage of the skill of a Fuoco or a Ferraris. Their preoccupation with feats of technical difficulty found a certain expression in the emergence, during the Second Empire, of the ballet with a ballerina heroine: in 1855, *La Fonti*; in 1861, *L'Étoile de Messine* (which contained a fantastic sequence of *pirouettes sur la pointe*, which Ferraris executed, supported by Mérante, upon an upright tambourine); and, in 1864, *La Maschera*. *La Fonti* was a work by Mazilier, but the choreographers of *L'Étoile de Messine* and *La Maschera* were Italians,

---

[1] It should be remembered that the blocked shoe, as now known, had not been introduced by 1870, the only strengthening employed being the darning of the toe and perhaps the insertion of wadding inside the shoe. *Pointe* work was therefore much less developed technically than it is to-day, although with lighter shoes dancers must have moved more lightly and risen higher in *temps d'élévation*. Whether or not the blocked shoe has proved wholly beneficial is very questionable.

an indication of the still greater emphasis placed on technical prowess on the other side of the Alps.

The discovery of the *pointe* may have made the Romantic Ballet possible, but it also made inevitable the decadence that was to follow. The woman gained thereby an impalpable lightness, with which her male companion was unable to compete; and the appearance of a number of unusually brilliant ballerinas and the corresponding lack of male dancers of equal standard that mark this period hastened the process by which the man tended more and more to become a mere *porteur*, until in the end his rôles were even taken from him and allotted to a female dancer. The practice of casting a woman in a major travesty part became almost general at the end of the Second Empire: in four of the six new ballets produced between 1864 and 1873—*La Maschera, Le Roi d'Yvetot, Coppélia* and *Gretna Green*—the beautiful Eugénie Fiocre played important travesty rôles that enabled her perfect figure to be displayed to wonderful effect. The triumph of the ballerina was complete, but the decline of the Romantic Ballet was made certain, for the eclipse of the male—evidenced by Degas' neglect of him in his pictures—could only lead, as in life itself, to sterility.

While choreographers remained who had known the Golden Age of the Romantic Ballet the dance retained its importance at the Paris Opéra. Indeed, during the Second Empire, Paris regained and kept undisputed her supremacy as the centre of ballet in Western Europe, that had been so seriously challenged by London in the forties. At her opera house, choreographers aspired to mount their works, and ballerinas to crown their reputations. Often ballet more than held its own with its sister-art, opera: in the summer of 1861, when three great dancers—Amalia Ferraris, Marie Petipa and Emma Livry—were numbered among the company, an evening's programme was devoted wholly to ballet for the first time, when, on July 12th, Zina Richard appeared in *La Vivandière*, followed by Ferraris in *Graziosa* and Marie Petipa in *Le Marché des Innocents*.

The decadence, when it came, was very swift. The Opéra closed its doors in the grim days of the Franco-German War, and reopened the following July to distract a public still reeling from the disasters of war and internal revolt. Mazilier and Saint-Léon were dead, and of the other great choreographers of the Second Empire, Lucien Petipa alone was to work again for the Opéra, and he but once; while the two ballerinas who should have been the heritage of the seventies and the eighties, Emma Livry and Giuseppina Bozzacchi, had both died tragically young. Even the theatre, whose boards had known the steps of Taglioni, Elssler, Grisi, Cerrito, Rosati and Livry, was not long to survive the Second Empire.

.   .   .   .

By 1847 the Paris Opéra had occupied, for little more than a quarter of a century, an unpretentious site in the Rue Le Peletier, one of the streets leading off the then fashionable Boulevard des Italiens. It had originally been intended only as a temporary opera house. The previous theatre, in the Rue Richelieu, had been the scene of the assassination of the Duc de Berry, nephew of King Louis XVIII, in February 1820. The Archbishop of Paris, who was called to administer the Last Sacrament to the Duke as he lay dying within the building, would do so only on being given an assurance that the theatre would afterwards be demolished. France was then still recovering from the Napoleonic Wars, and, as a measure of economy, much of the materials from the old building went towards the erection of the new theatre in the Rue Le Peletier, which was intended to serve only until better times permitted a permanent opera house to be built. However, the temporary building was to prove more lasting than most of its predecessors, remaining the home of the *Académie de Musique* for more than fifty years before it was consumed by flames on an October night in 1873.

The theatre had been built in the grounds of the Hôtel Choiseul, which had itself been incorporated to house the administrative offices. The façade, on the Rue Le Peletier, might have been imposing, had the theatre been situated with a large open space before it, but it was marred by an ugly metal awning above the entrance. Unwisely the architect had placed statues of the Muses upon the eight columns that rose up between the windows on the first floor, for it was commonly said that he had forgotten the Muse of Architecture.

Entering the theatre, one passed from an outer into an inner vestibule, on either side of which a wide stairway led to the boxes of the first tier and the *foyer public,* a room stretching the full width of the building, and decorated in white and gold, with hangings of amaranth and orange. Other stairways gave access from the inner vestibule to the pit, the *baignoires* and the orchestra stalls, and to the upper tiers of the house. The auditorium was large enough to seat an audience of nearly two thousand, and, thanks to the large amount of wood used in its construction, was acoustically superior to that of any other theatre in Paris. Behind the curtain, the stage was very spacious, having a proscenium width of more than forty feet and a depth of more than eighty feet; there was ample room at the side of the stage for storage, while backcloths could be flown and set-pieces lowered beneath the stage by means of a complex system of machinery.

.   .   .   .

The strength of the ballet company at the Opéra, exclusive of supers, increased during the Second Empire from about a hundred and twenty to more than a hundred and fifty, representing approximately one-fifth of the total number of persons employed there. The supers, including *écuyers* and *écuyères* for scenes in which horses were used, numbered nearly fifty; and crowd scenes were also, where necessary, augmented by children from the Opéra ballet school, who were given a small fee if they were not yet in receipt of a salary.

That a company of such a size should be organized on a quasi-military basis was hardly surprising. In command was the *maître de ballet en chef*, or *premier maître de ballet*, generally the principal choreographer; a post successively filled, between 1847 and 1870, by Jean Coralli, Saint-Léon, Mazilier, Lucien Petipa, Justament and Mérante. During the last ten of these years the importance of this personage declined as a result of a policy that often subordinated him to a guest choreographer from abroad—such as Marius Petipa, Borri, Rota—or to Marie Taglioni or Saint-Léon, whose prestige entitled them to respect from even the greatest of their contemporaries. By 1870 the duties of the *premier maître de ballet* seemed to have shrunk to conducting the rehearsals of Saint-Léon's ballets during the great man's absence and devising *divertissements* for operas.

To assist the *premier maître de ballet*, there was often a *second maître de ballet*, a post occupied in 1848 by Auguste Mabille, a son of the founder of the Bal Mabille, and later by Lucien Petipa.

Another official was the *régisseur de la danse*, who was responsible for discipline. Throughout the greater part of the Second Empire this office was held by Francisque Garnier Berthier, who had graduated from the Porte-Saint-Martin and specialized in comedy rôles. He was punctuality personified, and ruled his charges with a mixture of severity and kindness.

"I shall go mad!" he was heard to cry one day. "I shall hand in my resignation if this continues! There is little Chatenay eating again on the stage, and Mlle Gaujelin wearing a bouquet of roses in her bodice!"

A friend suggested a fine of half a day's pay on the offenders.

"Half a day's pay!" exclaimed Berthier, his anger suddenly vanishing. "Why not demand their heads, the poor children!"

Berthier was, not unnaturally, very popular, and many dancers—Adeline Plunkett, Mme Dominique, Lucien Petipa, Jules Perrot and Louis Mérante among them—were present at the banquet given after his marriage, in 1857, to a deaf and dumb girl. He retired in 1867, being succeeded as *régisseur* by Eugène Coralli, but resumed his service, as a mime, after the Franco-German War; among the rôles that he then took over was that of Coppélius in *Coppélia*. A paralytic stroke put an end to his career in the summer of 1874, and he died late in December the following year

Eugène Coralli's tenure of office as *régisseur de la danse* was short. In the winter of 1869–70 he let it be known that he wished to retire, but Perrin persuaded him to continue his functions until the rehearsals of *Coppélia* were finished. He was then succeeded by Édouard Pluque, who was to hold the post until well into the nineties. Pluque had been a member of the ballet company in the early fifties, but had interrupted his career to serve for a time in the Cent Gardes, the *élite* bodyguard of the Emperor. Later he had distinguished himself in a brave attempt to save Emma Livry. He was a far less attractive personality than good Berthier: boorish, awkward in speech, obsequious towards his superiors and a bully to the weak, he inspired fear in the hearts of the dancers where Berthier had won their affection.

The dancers of the company, both male and female, were divided into two large groups, known collectively as the *sujets* and the *corps de ballet*.

The path to the *corps de ballet* generally led through the

ballet school attached to the Opéra, the *Conservatoire de danse*, situated at No. 1 Rue Richer, and under the immediate control of the Director and, after the reorganization of 1860, supervised by the principal teacher, the *professeur de la classe de perfectionnement*. The two most prominent *professeurs de la classe de perfectionnement* during the Second Empire were Louis François Gosselin, who was appointed in 1853 and gave lessons to Cerrito, Rosati and Bogdanova, and Marie Taglioni, who succeeded him after his death in 1860. Among the other teachers were Mathieu, Sciot (1848–63) and Adice (who was retired in 1867 [1]).

If not the most famous, certainly the most loved, of all the teachers of this time was Mme Dominique. Born Caroline Lassiat, she had entered the Opéra as a child of ten in 1830, and had danced for many years under the name of Mlle Caroline. She married a violinist in the orchestra, M. Dominique-Venettozza, who was said to be so enamoured of her that he had to be excused from his duty whenever she was dancing. She began to teach in 1853, when she was given charge of the elementary class for girls, and from 1872 until her retirement in 1879, she held the post of *professeur de la classe de perfectionnement*. She formed many of the most promising dancers of the time during her long career as a teacher—Emma Livry, Marie Vernon, Léontine Beaugrand, Giuseppina Bozzacchi—as well as teaching many of the stars who came to the Opéra from abroad, such as Grantzow, Fioretti, Pitteri, Sangalli and Mauri. She died on June 3rd, 1885.

The *Règlement pour le service du Corps des ballets et du Conservatoire de danse de l'Opéra*, which was drawn up in 1860 in the light of recommendations made by Marie Taglioni and Sciot, prescribed the division of the school into seven classes: elementary classes for boys and girls and secondary classes for

[1] Adice harboured bitter grudges against Saint-Léon and Perrin, who was Director of the Opéra at the time of his retirement, and gave full vent to them in his manuscript *Notes sur la direction E. Perrin*, which are now preserved in the Bibliothèque de l'Opéra. Describing his downfall, Adice describes how Perrin unexpectedly ordered an examination. "God! they are ugly!" Perrin was heard to say as four of Adice's male pupils appeared. Instead of letting Adice direct them himself, Saint-Léon bounded on to the stage and gave them absurdly difficult *enchaînements*, for which they were quite unprepared, for example (according to Adice), *préparation et grand rond de jambe en l'air!—assemblé et entrechat sept cambré!—coupé et jeté en tournant!—deux tours en l'air et grande pirouette à la seconde et sur le cou-de-pied!* (The exclamation marks are Adice's.) "Good God! how bad they are!" exclaimed Perrin again. Shortly afterwards Adice was informed that he was to be retired on pension.

men and women—previously the sexes had not been separated
—in which the pupils were initiated into the evolutions of the
corps de ballet, a class for the study of the ballets and *divertisse-*
ments in the repertory, the *classe de perfectionnement* (significantly,
for women only), and a mime class, which was devoted mainly
to studying rôles. Every member of the *corps de ballet* up to the
rank of *coryphée* was obliged to attend the school, and *sujets*
earning not more than 10,000 francs a year had the right to
attend the *classe de perfectionnement*; the teachers also had to give
free personal tuition to *coryphées* who had been excused from
duty to prepare for their promotion to *petit sujet*, until their
débuts.

Pupils were admitted to the school between the ages of seven
and ten, and older only if they showed exceptional promise.
They had to undergo a medical test and also an entrance
examination, which was held three times a year before a com-
mittee consisting of the *maître de ballet*, the teachers, and the
régisseur de la danse. Through their parents, they entered into
articles of apprenticeship with the Opéra, which placed them
under the obligation to serve for five years in the quadrilles of
the *corps de ballet*, when they were ready and a vacancy occurred,
in return for free tuition. The girls were given four pairs of
ballet shoes, two skirts and two bodices annually, and the boys
just four pairs of ballet shoes. Generally the pupils received no
pay until they entered a quadrille, although occasionally one
showing unusual promise might be awarded a small *encourage-*
ment, if admission to the quadrilles was delayed only for want
of a vacancy.

These years of apprenticeship were very hard. Berthe Bernay,
who became a *premier sujet* and a teacher later in the century,
remembered the early stages of her career with justifiable
bitterness.

"I was seven," she wrote, "when, on April 7th, 1863, after
the compulsory medical examination, I began to study dancing
at the Opéra. My parents, who were not well off, lived at
Belleville, on the heights of the Rue du Faubourg-du-Temple,
now near the Buttes-Chaumont. Nearly all my little companions—I might even say, all—lived, like me, with their
parents at a similar distance from the Opéra, and in the same
sort of district. I have said that I was seven years old. Winter
and summer, my mother used to wake me up at half past seven

in the morning to go to work, and I had to leave home so as to be dressed and ready to dance in the scenery-store in the Rue Richer, where the classes were then held, on the stroke of nine o'clock. Needless to say, omnibus fares were beyond my small means, and I had to walk. What journeys those were, the reader can judge for himself!

"The morning lesson lasted from nine o'clock until half past ten. Afterwards, I changed and returned home for lunch at midday. But I was not always sure that I would be finished after my lesson. I was not always so lucky as to get back so early. Often I had to take part in rehearsals at the Opéra itself, for the young pupils such as myself were employed as supers. When this happened, I used to have lunch in the Rue Richer with my mother off the modest ration we had brought in our basket—never have I forgotten that basket!—and afterwards we went to the Rue Drouot to attend the rehearsal, which lasted until two o'clock. Only then was I free to make my return journey to Belleville. Then, if I was appearing on the stage in the evening, we walked back once again to be in time for the call at eight o'clock. Finally, when the performance had finished at midnight, I set out for home. My poor mother literally used to drag me along on her arm, and at one o'clock in the morning, worn out, we arrived home, where my father was waiting up for us. We slept hastily, and set out once again for my class at eight o'clock the next morning.

"I used to earn a fee of one franc for the rehearsal, and the same for the performance in the evening. I followed this calling, at this price and in these conditions, from the age of seven to the age of thirteen."

After entering the third quadrille, which comprised sixteen pupils and carried with it an *encouragement* of 300 francs a year, a girl might hope to be promoted through the various grades of the *corps de ballet*: through the second quadrille, composed of two classes each of eight dancers, and the first quadrille, which was similarly constituted, to the rank of *coryphée*. There were sixteen *coryphées* too, and these also were divided into two classes; a *coryphée* of the first class could in time earn 1,500 francs a year.

From *coryphée*, she would be promoted *sujet*, and as such make her official début: being first a *petit sujet*, earning up to about 2,500 francs a year; then rising to *grand sujet*, with a

salary mounting to about 5,000 francs; and finally becoming
a *première danseuse*, when she might receive between 10,000 and
20,000 francs a year. Higher still in the hierarchy was the *étoile*
(the term was not yet in official use), almost without exception
a foreign dancer, and generally Italian, earning a salary
correspondingly higher: seldom less than 30,000 francs a year,
and often much more, and sometimes, before the Opéra was
taken over by the State in 1854, augmented by a fixed bonus
given for each performance. Carolina Rosati was being paid at
the rate of more than 60,000 francs a year when she left the
Opéra in 1859, a figure never exceeded nor even approached
during the Second Empire and for very many years afterwards.

The male dancers, who were less in number, were organized
on a somewhat similar basis, but the annual salary of the best
seldom exceeded 10,000 francs. When Saint-Léon was simultaneously fulfilling the duties of *premier danseur, premier maître de
ballet* and *professeur de la classe de perfectionnement*, he only received
24,000 francs a year, inclusive of all royalties on his ballets.

Not only did the organization of the company have a military
flavour, but so also did the discipline to which the *corps de
ballet* was subjected. The rules were codified in the *Règlement*
of 1860:—

"21. Unpunctuality, insubordination and breaches of the
regulations are punishable according to the general
rules and customs of the Opéra. In the cases specified
hereunder, offending artistes incur the following
disciplinary penalties:—
Reprimand and posting up in the Foyer.
Exclusion from the Foyer for a specified time.
Loss of rank or place, and replacement by an
artiste of a lower rank for one or more performances.

"22. These penalties will be imposed, according to the
seriousness of the offence, on every artiste of the
corps de ballet who creates a disturbance during the
performance by talking or laughing in the theatre,
distracting the attention of persons on the stage, or
applauding or showing disapproval in any manner
whatsoever; who interferes with the stage management by causing an obstruction in the wings, arriving

before the call, or talking too loudly; who interferes with the scene-shifting; who comes into view of the audience; who makes a noise behind the curtain; in short, who shows lack in any way whatsoever of consideration towards others, of the respect owed to the public, of decency, and of discipline at performance or rehearsal.

"23. The same penalties will be imposed on artistes who miss their entrances, appear untidily dressed on the stage, or are negligent or careless in their duties.

"24. Suspension from duty with loss of salary and exclusion from the Opéra may be pronounced in the case of a serious misdeed.

Recurrence of the offence in the same month is an aggravating circumstance.

Three suspensions in the same year may involve reduction in rank and salary, and even termination of contract and expulsion.

"25. Unpunctuality at performances and rehearsals and absence are punishable by fine.

The presence of the artistes will be attested by a nominal roll which each must sign at the time indicated according to his or her duty.

Arrival after the removal of the nominal roll entails a fine of one day's salary.

"26. Absence during part of a performance, whether due to late arrival or early departure, entails a fine of three day's salary.

The fine is ten days' salary if, without just cause, the artiste neglects his or her duty entirely.

"27. Fines are doubled if an offence is repeated in the same month.

Any artiste who is fined three times in the same month incurs . . . termination of engagement and expulsion from the theatre."

The *Règlement* of 1860 also inaugurated the system of examinations, on the results of which depended the promotion from one rank in the *corps de ballet* to another. It laid down that the examining Jury should consist of the Director, the stage manager, the *maître de ballet*, the *professeur de la classe de per-fectionnement*, the *régisseur de la danse*, and several *sujets* selected by the Director. The first of these examinations was held on April 13th, 1860, before a Jury which included Alphonse Royer, Marie Taglioni, Amalia Ferraris, Emma Livry, Lucien Petipa and Louis Mérante.

The scene at such an examination, that of 1870, has been described by Ludovic Halévy. The Jury was seated in the orchestra stalls. Émile Perrin, the Director of the Opéra, was presiding; on one side of him was Saint-Léon, and on the other, Marie Taglioni, dressed "in a black striped Havana costume, grey-haired, taking notes on a large sheet of paper, just like an old University professor," [1] Among the other members were Mérante, Eugène Coralli, Beauchet, Mathieu, Mme Domini-que, Léontine Beaugrand and Laure Fonta. Standing at the side of the stage, violin in hand, was M. Dominique-Venettozza.

There was a great commotion before the examination began at half past ten. "Moving hither and thither about the stage, in a state of nervous agitation, are the *coryphées* and the members of the quadrilles, all in short white skirts, with large coloured sashes tied in small bows behind them. Then, all around, restless, bewildered, breathless and purple-faced, are mothers, mothers, and yet more mothers—more, I am sure, than there are dancers! Jostling the firemen and the stage hands in the wings in their anxiety to be near their daughters until the great moment, they are making their last-minute inspection. What serious and delicate matters there are to be considered: that the ribbons of their ballet shoes are securely tied, that their tights have no creases and are firmly fixed about the hips, that the seams are straight, the bows properly tied, and the tarlatan skirts puffed out prettily. The inspection over, the mothers energetically rub chalk on the soles of their daughters' ballet shoes, before embracing them with the words, 'Go, my child, take care of your *pointes*, hold your shoulders back, think of

---

[1] In her memoirs, Anna Bicknell, the governess of the children of the First Chamberlain of the Empress's Household, described Taglioni as she appeared during a visit to the Tuileries in the winter of 1862–63 to watch Mérante rehearsing twelve noble ladies in a *divertissement* for a costume ball. "I took the opportunity of turning round," she wrote, "and there I saw a remarkably stiff-looking person, with pursed-up mouth and very prim appearance, absolutely the conventional type of a pedantic school-mistress. I never was more astonished. Mérante had wished to have her opinion of the dance; but she spoke very little, and seemed the reverse of agreeable or natural."

your mother, and of your father too, who will curse me and box your ears if you do not get your 800 francs to-day.'

"There are mothers also in the corridors, mothers in the pit, mothers in the back of the *baignoires*, mothers too in the little corner of the orchestra stalls beneath the Aguado box. The air is filled with the odour of sausages, Eau de Javel and Eau de Cologne.

"'*Allons, mesdemoiselles*, let us begin,' says Mérante, and tall M. Pluque, *régisseur de la danse*, calls out the first *coryphées* . . . Mérante then gracefully dances before them a little *variation* which might be translated thus: *développé, tour à la seconde, petit rond de jambe en tournant, jeté, assemblé et changement de pied*. The first *coryphées* watch him very intently, at the same time working out the variation where they stand. They shuffle their feet, flutter their arms, arch their backs, pull back their shoulders; nothing could be prettier. The signal is given. M. Dominique scrapes away. The *coryphées* start off together, and come to a stop at the same time, with the regulation smile, on the last note from M. Dominique's violin. Now the second *coryphées*. . . . Mérante again racks his brains to find something new. He decides on this: *temps de cuisse, cabriole, temps de cuisse, cabriole, quatre temps de pointe en tournant*. . . . M. Dominique takes up his violin, and at a sign from Mérante, the girls dart forward. The Jury gravely studies the *cabrioles*, observes the *temps de pointe*, weighs up the *temps de cuisse*. Mlle Fonta scribbles away interminably.

"The examination continues. Mérante makes the first class of the first quadrille execute a little *adage*: *passez par un coupé en attitude, développez à la seconde, passez à la quatrième devant, ballonnez et entrechat huit*. For the second class: *pas de bourrée, fouetté derrière, glissade, cabriole*. Then come the little ones of the second quadrille, earning 600 or 700 francs, who, still new to the art, are a little confused by the *pirouettes* and *fouettés derrière*."

Saint-Léon occasionally shouts encouragement from his seat in the stalls. "*Allez, mes enfants*," he cries, when some of the girls, called upon to execute *temps ballonnés*, appear nervous, "there's no need to be afraid. Higher than that!" Then, waving his hand towards the flies, he adds, "There's plenty of room."

"The Jury picks out little Mlle Dupuis [who had recently played one of the flowers in the last scene of *Coppélia*], and keeps her back after the examination is over," continued

Halévy. "Mme Taglioni makes her work a little on her own in the centre of the stage, and the little dancer does all that Mme Taglioni tells her with much strength, grace and correctness. . . ." It was probably the one great moment in her career.

.   .   .   .   .   .

A not unimportant factor in the decline of ballet as an art during the latter half of the nineteenth century was to be found in the attitude of an important section of the Opéra audience. "The man of fashion at the Opéra," wrote Charles Yriarte in 1867, "with his box or his stall, his favourite dancer, his opera-glasses, and his right of entry backstage, has a horror of anything which remains on the bills for a long time, of anything artistic, which must be listened to, respected, or requires an effort to be understood. The man of fashion . . . has little use for the sublime strophes of the great Gluck; he wants the brisk and lively melodies of M. Auber, the adorable flutterings of Mlle Fioretti or Mlle Fonta, the fairylike effects of Giselle and the ethereal *pirouettes* of the Wilis, the *ballonné* of Mlle Baratte, the alluring shape of Mlle Morando in travesty. There is no need to go further. I wager that eight out of every ten *abonnés* prefer *Pierre de Médicis* to the fourth act of *Les Huguenots*, and *Néméa* to *Guillaume Tell*. And why? Simply because Louise Fiocre shows her limbs in *Pierre*, and her younger sister Eugénie shows much more than that in *Néméa*. And because, when you are a man of fashion with your box at the Opéra, and have listened to *Les Huguenots* and *Guillaume Tell* a hundred times, you would much rather attend the Opéra peaceably and without going through violent musical emotions, recline in an excellent seat, equipped with excellent opera-glasses, and indulge in the cult of the *plastique*. To the soothing strains of sweet and lively music your attention can wander from the calves of Mlle Brach or Mlle Carabin to the shoulders of Mme de N——; and during the interval, you can visit every box, or receive visitors in your own. That is the real Opéra, the only Opéra possible for this brilliant, light-hearted society."

The attraction, to many people, was in fact the *danseuses* rather than the dance itself. To be the protector of an Opéra dancer was then one of the most coveted hallmarks of fashion,

for it was one that could generally be obtained only by the
select few who had the right of entry into the Foyer de la
Danse. This room, situated immediately behind the stage, was
very unpretentious, having originally been designed merely for
the use of the dancers. Modestly decorated and not very
brightly lit, its principal, and almost only, ornament was a
bust of Guimard which had been bequeathed to the Opéra by
the dancer Nivelon; the floor sloped gently down towards a
mirror, and a *barre* ran round the other three walls. Since the
Revolution of 1830, a few of the most distinguished *abonnés* had
been granted the privilege of admission backstage during the
performance, with the result that by the Second Empire, the
Foyer de la Danse had become an important centre of fashionable life. How this social institution came to affect the ballet
can well be judged from an observation of Léo Lespès in 1864.
"It is since [the Restoration]," he wrote, "that Swiss village
girls, peasants from the Abruzzi, and flower-girls from the
Marché des Innocents [1] have been seen with 6,000 francs
glittering at the tips of their ears and emerald rings more
numerous than those worn on her fingers by the beauty
imprisoned in the depths of the sea."

The proficiency of the company certainly suffered, for some
dancers considered it more important to gratify the *abonnés* in
the Foyer de la Danse and elsewhere, than the public. "What's
the use of doing yourself so much harm, when you can please
just as well with much less effort," exclaimed an exasperated
ballet girl who had tried to perform *doubles tours sur la pointe* and
had finished in an undignified position on the floor. "If you
haven't a good figure, you must use your talent, but if you are
pretty and well formed, that makes up for everything."

A visit to the Foyer de la Danse was said to be one of the four
things than an ordinary tourist in Paris could not hope to
enjoy. "Admission to this inner shrine of Grace and Beauty
could not be obtained by money—that is, by money unaided
by influence." It was reserved exclusively for the men who held
the reins of fashion, and in particular for the members of the
select Jockey Club, who occupied seven of the proscenium boxes
and one large *baignoire*, and who regarded the Opéra as a sort

---

[1] The allusion is to three ballets mounted since that time at the Opéra, Filippo
Taglioni's *Nathalie* (1832), Cerrito's *Gemma* (1854) and the Petipas' *Le Marché des
Innocents* (1861).

of fief. The President of the Jockey, the Vicomte Paul Daru, irreproachable alike in manners and dress, would stride about the Foyer de la Danse like a Sultan in a seraglio, having a word or a smile for everyone, even the little *rats* and the *marcheuses*, and charming them all with his nonchalant good-humour. Here, too, many of the great figures of the day would gather to find relaxation in the company of the dancers: the Duc de Morny, the Duc de Persigny, Comte Walewski; the Marquis de Caux, who was to marry Adelina Patti; the Duke of Hamilton; Prosper Mérimée, Théophile Gautier, Jules Janin, Albéric Second, Eugène Scribe; Meyerbeer, Adam, Thomas and—most familiar and popular of all—Auber, who was invariably to be found on a velvet-cushioned bench by the mirror. There the old man—he was sixty-five in 1847, and lived long enough to survive the Second Empire—delighted in the chatter of the girls surrounding him. "This is the only room I am fond of," he would say happily. "Pretty heads, pretty shoulders, pretty legs. As much as one could wish for. More than one could wish for. . . ."

The forgathering in the Foyer de la Danse before the ballet was no less a ritual for the dancers, who never thought of remaining in their dressing-rooms, but came to show themselves to the *abonnés*, to talk and joke and flirt and receive the homage that was their due. Most of them had been brought up from childhood in the Opéra, and knew its traditions almost by instinct. "Independently of their intrinsic beauty," wrote the Comte de Maugny, "they had a professional stamp, an originality of appearance, an art of pleasing, a bearing at once free and reserved, which came from being accustomed to mixing with men of fashion." Rarely did one of them take as a lover someone who had not the right of entry backstage.

Those almost legendary creatures, the dancers' mothers, were not allowed in the Foyer de la Danse, but they were never very far away. When the performance was over, they collected in a formidable band by the stage-door. "Epic scenes took place there," recalled de Maugny. "I have seen damsels departing triumphantly on an admirer's arm after a good quarter of an hour's parley with *maman*. I have seen some disappear surreptitiously behind their duenna's back, leaving her prey to an epileptic agitation; and others carrying on brazenly beneath their very nose and receiving a volley of

The Façade of the Paris Opéra on the
Rue Le Peletier (1869)

The Foyer de la Danse, c. 1860

Irma Carabin in
La Maschera

Pauline Mercier in
L'Étoile de Messine

Francine Cellier

Clara Pilvois

blows that would have frightened a street-porter." It was often prudent to negotiate with the mother before laying siege to the daughter. For they were not all so careful of their children's honour as the creature nicknamed *La Guenon*, the she-monkey, by a certain *abonné* whose designs were effectively thwarted by her vigilance. Many quite openly encouraged their daughters to accept the presents and proposals that were offered them in the Foyer de la Danse. A friend of Ludovic Halévy knew one such family well, and calling at their apartment one afternoon, was met at the door by the mother in a state of violent excitement. "Ah, *monsieur*, we cannot receive you to-day!" she exclaimed before he could utter a word. "If you only knew!" She paused to take breath, and then burst out afresh. "We have a King in there, a King!"

The wish of a visiting monarch to be entertained by one of the dancers had naturally to be respected, although the extent of the hospitality was left to the parties concerned. When the notoriously coarse King Victor Emmanuel II of Piedmont visited Paris in the winter of 1855, he said to the Empress, "*On me dit que les danseuses françaises ne portent pas de caleçons. Si c'est comme cela, ce sera pour moi le paradis terrestre.*" He soon had an opportunity to learn for himself, for on November 26th, Napoleon III took him to the Opéra to see *Jovita*, and the following conversation was supposed to have taken place in the Imperial Box. The King of Piedmont, carried away by the beauty of one of the dancers, asked the Emperor what price the lady commanded. After inquiring of his suite, Napoleon told him, fifty louis. In a powerful voice, which could be heard by many of the audience, Victor Emmanuel protested indignantly at such an exorbitant figure. The Emperor, ever the perfect host, would not hear his guest troubling himself about such a matter. "Charge it to my account," he said good-humouredly, and the King of Piedmont sat through the remainder of the ballet in a pleasurable state of anticipation.

The Comte de Maugny, the authority on the *demi-monde* of the Second Empire, described the dancers of the Opéra as "the Faubourg Saint-Germain, the cream of the *demi-monde*," and the Foyer de la Danse as a place of contact between the two worlds into which Parisian society was divided. The exigences of their profession of course placed the dancers on a very different plane from that of the great courtesans, such as

Cora Pearl, Anna Deslion and Giulia Barrucci, who devoted their whole lives to gallantry; and it should be said at once that the breath of scandal very seldom touched the great ballerinas and indeed many of the lesser known dancers. "The life of a dancer," explained de Maugny, "was in fact far less wild than was commonly supposed. Classes, rehearsals and performances took up most of their days and evenings. Thus gallantry could only be a secondary pastime, and in most cases necessarily took a reasonable form. . . . The ballerina is fated to be the steadiest and most tranquil of the *demi-mondaines*."

Only a few had any real contact with the *haute bicherie*. One of these was Pauline Mercier, whose name was mentioned with those of Cora Pearl, Adèle Courtois, Léonide Leblanc and Émilie Williams among the guests at a ball given by Antonia Sary in 1865. She was blonde, very pretty, and inclined to be buxom, qualities which greatly attracted the discerning Vicomte Paul Daru, whose mistress she was for a number of years. She stirred the Goncourt brothers too, who noticed her one evening at the Opéra, bathed in a reddish glow of light that brought out the clear whiteness of her skin; they were reminded of the girl in Rembrandt's *Night Watch*, and began to ponder over the lighting effects the great artist must have used in his studio. Another dancer who frequented the circles of the *demi-monde* was Éline Volter, who was known for missing her entrances; and no doubt her younger sister, Henriette, often accompanied her, for the two were inseparable. Yet another was Irma Carabin, who threw gay parties, at which young men of fashion, if they were fortunate enough to receive an invitation, could gain acquaintance with the *demi-monde*.

More intimately linked with the *demi-monde* than any other Opéra dancer was undoubtedly Amélie Hairivau. She was a sister of Esther Duparc, one of the most renowned *cocottes* in Paris, whom de Maugny described as "the eldest of five sisters, all devoted to gallantry." A younger sister, Clémentine, was also a dancer at the Opéra. Amélie was very beautiful, tall, slender and perfectly proportioned, with hips "worthy of an Andalusian" and very small feet; her profile was faultless, and a slight cast in her eye only added to her attraction, giving her features a bizarre and unusual expression. No other dancer possessed more verve or a greater power of repartee, and no other dancer had been fined more often for answering back the *régisseur*. Amélie Hairivau was incorrigible and impenitent. "She loved good-looking men, and did not hide the fact," wrote de Maugny. "If she did not absolutely loathe civilians, she adored soldiers, always provided they were not weaklings or imbeciles, two categories of males that she held in equal scorn. . . . She was really in her element in male company, when she would give full rein to her sallies and let herself go freely, without restraint, and with all the vivacity of her temperament. No woman, in my opinion, among all that I have known, was in similar circumstances more amusing, more captivating, more charming. . . . I met her again last year," —the Comte is writing in about 1891—"still pretty (God forgive me!), although enormously round and stout. And do you know what this pitiless joker said to me? 'My dear, I hardly recognized you. You were not so . . . dilapidated as I imagined you would be. Between ourselves, all our contemporaries are ruins that should be razed to the ground, like the Tuileries, for the embellishment of Paris.'"

Another frail member of the *corps de ballet* was Francine Cellier, who first tasted fame in 1857, when scandal linked her name with that of Baron Haussmann, the Prefect of the Seine responsible for so much of the rebuilding of Paris. The Baron discreetly took precautions to prevent publicity, such as having Francine dress exactly like his daughter when they were out driving together, but Mme Haussmann discovered his escapade in the end, and left him, taking her daughter with her. The scandal was quickly hushed up—by the Emperor's order, it was said—and Mme Haussmann persuaded to return. Francine deserted ballet for the legitimate stage when her adventure was still being talked about, and the success of her début as an actress was no doubt stimulated by the jingle:—

> Du premier rang au dernier
> De l'orchestre, on se démène
> Pour voir l'effet que Cellier
> De plus près fait de la scène.

Paul Mahalin said in 1887 that it was well known that she "lived on the fruit of her successive household removals."

The amorous adventures of ballet girls was a very popular theme during the Second Empire, and it often escaped notice that many dancers were in fact highly principled women and followed serious pursuits in their hours of leisure. "What a paltry opinion novelists have of the ballet girl's virtue," commented *Le Figaro* in 1859. "There is not one Parisian novel which does not introduce a banker or a man of fashion who keeps a ballet girl of the Opéra. But the *Académie de Musique* barely contains thirty *danseuses*, so that even if the *rats* and supers were included, there would be at least a thousand happy admirers for each of them."

Two years before these words were written, a young *sujet*, Zilia Michelet, had surprisingly produced a little book of religious reflections, written from a Protestant viewpoint, called *Bluettes antimondaines d'une danseuse*. "The discussion has been penned in answer to the various attempts made to convert her by the Abbé Théobald," it was explained. "The work is of a most remarkable tendency and has excited the greatest interest amongst the writers of *L'Univers* and other religious publications." Albéric Second reviewed the book at length in *L'Entr'acte*, and declared that it was quite incomprehensible. Zilia made a valiant reply, but she counted without his malice, for Second published her letter, "after," as he pointed out, "having rectified the somewhat fantastic punctuation," though having taken care not to correct the numerous grammatical errors.

Zilia Michelet was not so eccentric as many would have believed, for some of her companions were equally studious. The red-haired Blanche Montaubry, for instance, was well versed in medicine. The wisdom of Anna Rust was such that even the stage hands were said to be polite to her. Héloïse Lamy was seldom seen without a political journal, and after the performance was over, would return home, shut herself up in her room and write poetry, inspired by the ballet she had been dancing in only a few hours before. It was she, incidentally, who subjected herself to such a rigorous diet to retain her slim figure that someone said of her, "Lamy never spits for fear of getting thirsty."

Others were homely rather than studious. Julie Stoïkoff, who was called *La Niagara* because of her falls, was well known for her piety and her love for her mother; and there were many, of course, who married and became model wives and mothers: Angelina Fatou and Marie Sanlaville, for instance, and Carlotta Morando, who had borne eight children by 1887.

Such qualities, however, commendable and appreciated though they no doubt were, had little appeal to the popular imagination. The public's ideal of an Opéra dancer was probably more closely approached by the high-spirited Clara Pilvois and the voluptuous, good-tempered Eugénie Schlosser.

Clara Pilvois—known in the Foyer de la Danse as "Célimène des Batignolles"—was the heroine of many anecdotes. Although she had a ready wit and was never at a loss for a reply, her knowledge was very limited: according to de Maugny, she once admitted that she thought the Edict of Nantes was an important English lady, and another time, when someone mentioned the name of Garibaldi in her hearing, she innocently enquired, "Is that gentleman a member of the Jockey?" (It is only fair to add that this saying was almost legendary, and that its origin was attributed by Paul Mahalin to Irma Carabin.)

It was Clara Pilvois who once dared to introduce the wild gyrations of the cancan into one of Mazilier's rehearsals. The *maître de ballet* was horrified and threatened to give her *pas* to someone else if she persisted in such behaviour. The admonition was ignored, and she was ordered to leave. She left haughtily, but very soon came back imploring to be forgiven.

"Please, please give me back my *pas*," she begged. "If you don't, my mother will die when she hears of it."

Mazilier had not the heart to refuse, but the following evening nevertheless the audience were treated to the curious spectacle of one of the nuns in *Robert le Diable* dancing the cancan.

Some time later, Clara slipped and fell during a performance of *La Muette de Portici*. As she remained prostrate on the stage, the *pas* was interrupted while some of her companions carried her off into the wings, where she regained consciousness surprisingly quickly.

"You frightened us," they told her. "Why didn't you get up?"

"Why, the *abonnés* would have laughed at me," Clara pointed out. "As it is, my re-engagement is now a foregone conclusion."

Clara Pilvois liked to give the impression that she received more jewellery than was in fact given her, and nearly ruined herself by constantly changing the settings. Her companions soon discovered her subterfuge, and whenever she arrived at the Opéra wearing what appeared to be a new piece of jewellery they would cluster round her and chant unmercifully:—

> "*Ces bijoux, je gage,*
> *Lui coûtent beaucoup,*
> *Encore un montage . . .*
> *Montage du coup.*"

She even wore her diamonds when she appeared for class at nine o'clock in the morning.

Eugénie Schlosser adopted another ruse to give a similar impression, mixing false gems with real in the same setting. But she was no more successful in deceiving the other dancers.

'My poor Schlosser," one of them said to her one day, "your liqueurs must all be evaporating."

"Why?"

"You seem to be wearing all the corks round your neck," came back the cruel reply.

Eugénie Schlosser was the daughter of a drummer in the Montmartre National Guard, and entered the *corps de ballet* at the age of fourteen in the summer of 1852. She first attracted notice nearly three years later, when she created the little rôle of Cupid in *La Fonti*, and by 1857, had so matured as to be classed by *Le Figaro* as the prettiest girl in the *corps de ballet* and the third prettiest actress in Paris. "Mlle Schlosser, as is well known," wrote Albéric Second that same year, "is at the moment the eighth wonder of the world and the first wonder of the Opéra." The following year, Albéric Second noticed another aspect of her character. On a bleak November day, he recognized her sitting alone in an omnibus, and moved by curiosity and having some time to spare, he descended from the vehicle at the same stop and followed her as she walked quickly to the Church of Saint-Étienne du Mont. He stood in the church and watched her go to the tomb of Sainte-Geneviève, where she lit a candle and knelt in prayer for fully quarter of an hour. That evening, he saw her again, on the stage of the Opéra, and never before had she looked more beautiful or danced more gracefully.

In the spring of 1862, the former Secretary-General of the Opéra, Gustave Vaëz, who had helped her at the time of her début, became seriously ill. As soon as she learnt of his plight, she left everything to go to his bedside, remaining with him till the end, and for two days afterwards keeping vigil, with his sister, by the deathbed.

There were two very different sides to her character. She was, wrote de Maugny, "sensual pleasure personified, with an ideal blonde head, eyes of a troubling eloquence, a mouth thirsting for love and crying out to be kissed, and the most delicious, the most diabolically exciting body in the five corners of the earth. A beautiful, captivating creature! Too captivating, perhaps, since much was asked of her, and she knew not how to refuse. . . . She let herself go freely, according to the whim of the moment, thinking neither of her strength nor of her health, in love with pleasure for pleasure's sake, making merry without rest or thought for the morrow: a Manon Lescaut, whose Des Grieux were not all chivalrous—far from it. So was she withered, aged, and destroyed before her time."

She danced for the last time in 1863, when she was only twenty-five, and that summer went to Eaux-Bonnes, in the Pyrenees, hoping the altitude and rest would dispel the consumption that had attacked her lungs. Shortly before, she had fallen deeply in love with the dancer, Alfred Chapuy. She could not hope to marry him, for he was already married: his wife was Louise Monnier, who had herself been a dancer, and by her he had a daughter, Marguerite, who later was to create the rôle of Micaëla in Bizet's opera, Carmen. Not a day passed when Eugénie did not write to her lover, always signing herself by the pet-name he had given her, "Nounou," and often enclosing with her letter a forget-me-not or some other flower she had worn in her hair. Hope and despair alternated as her malady ran its course. In the autumn of 1865, she returned to Paris with only a few months to live. She died in her apartment at No. 28 Boulevard Poissonnière in the morning of November 18th. Shortly afterwards, her letters to Chapuy were read in open court, when her father contested her will, by which she had devised her small property in Nogent-sur-Marne to her lover. The simple sincerity of their language formed a more touching epitaph than could ever have been inscribed on stone. "Voilà," commented a writer in L'Entr'acte, "voilà, comment on aime encore aujourd'hui! et cela à l'Opéra!"

Theatre critics fulfil a dual purpose: they are at the same time arbiters of contemporary taste and chroniclers. To future generations, their contribution is almost as important as that of the dancers themselves, for such is the ephemeral nature of a theatrical art that its history must largely be written from their accounts.

The Second Empire was very fortunate in its possession of ballet critics. Seldom, before or since, has such a profusion of literary talent been gathered together in the service of the dance. Among them were Jules Janin, *le prince de la critique*, who contributed to the *Journal des Débats* for some forty years . . . genial, good-natured Théophile Gautier, poet and novelist as well as critic, and in later life appointed to the sinecure of librarian to the Princesse Mathilde . . . Pier Angelo Fiorentino, the translator of Dante's *Divina Commedia* . . . Nestor Roqueplan, who at one time was himself Director of the Opéra . . . Amédée Achard, a prolific novelist . . . Théodore de Banville, the poet . . . Paul de Saint-Victor . . . Charles Maurice . . . Albéric Second . . . B. Jouvin . . . the eccentric Paul Scudo . . . and many others hardly less gifted.

Of all these, Théophile Gautier rightly commanded the greatest respect as a critic of the dance, for few had a more intimate understanding than he of the meaning and possibilities of ballet as an art. He also had the advantage of collaborating, as scenarist, in five ballets mounted at the Opéra—*Giselle, La Péri, Pâquerette, Gemma* and *Sacountala*—and another given at the Porte-Saint-Martin, *Yanko le bandit*; and to these was nearly added a seventh, *Le Preneur des rats de Hameln*, with choreography by Mérante and a score by Massenet, which the Opéra was considering in the autumn of 1872 but abandoned after the poet's death in October. "No dramatic work presents more difficulties than a ballet," Gautier once wrote. "The best ballet scenario would surely be an album of scenes designed in outline, like the illustrations by Retsch for Gœthe's *Faust*, from which a child can understand the story without reading one word of the text. . . . The animation of plastic art, that is the real element of choreography, and an author writing a ballet would do well to collaborate with a painter or a sculptor, whose silent art has accustomed him to giving form to an idea."

Gautier had been theatre critic of *La Presse* for some ten

years when Cerrito made her début in 1847, and was to remain with that paper until the spring of 1855. He then became theatre critic of *Le Moniteur*, but operas and ballets came within the orbit of the music critic, Fiorentino, and it was not until the latter's death in 1864 that Gautier resumed his regular reports on performances at the Opéra. In the New Year of 1869, he moved to the staff of the newly-formed *Journal Officiel*.

Though he may not have been so well versed in the technique of ballet as some of his fellows, Gautier's reviews were unique for the impeccability of their style and the wonderful imagery of their descriptions. So sure was his command of syntax and vocabulary that he seldom needed to correct his copy. " I throw my phrases into the air," he said, "and, like cats, I know they will land on their feet."

He was a great conversationalist too, and much of his talk was recorded by the Goncourts in their Journal. But he seems seldom to have spoken to them about the ballet, for they only once mention a discussion on this subject. They were spending a few weeks with the Princesse Mathilde at her château of Saint-Gratien in the summer of 1868, when Gautier arrived to join them. One evening, he began to talk about the dancers of the Opéra. "He described," recorded the Goncourts, "their white satin ballet shoes, each of which is reinforced by silk darning at the point where the dancer feels her weight is concentrated. An expert can tell, by a glance at this darning, the name of the dancer. This work, by the way, is always done by the girl herself." What more might have been said that was deemed by the Goncourts unworthy of record!

Gautier and nearly all his colleagues had lived through the Golden Age of the Romantic Ballet. Their judgments were the judgments of men who had seen Taglioni, Elssler and Carlotta Grisi at the summit of their careers, cherished experiences that must ever have remained deeply impressed upon their memories, losing only any roughness with the passing of time. Remembering the best of the past, they took up their pens to record the present, and through their eyes, that saw so much, the voluptuous sparkle of Cerrito, the tremendous dramatic fire of Rosati, the lofty flight of Ferraris, the gentle grace of Emma Livry, and the childlike charm of Bozzacchi can be enjoyed for all time.

II

THE COMING OF CERRITO AND THE
DEPARTURE OF CARLOTTA GRISI

When Nestor Roqueplan and Henri Duponchel assumed the management of the Paris Opéra in the summer of 1847, they directed their attention almost at once to the ballet company. Within a few weeks the whole of the *corps de ballet* had been reviewed by Duponchel and the *régisseur de la danse*, Desplaces *père*, and terms had been agreed with Fanny Cerrito, whom the Parisians had been waiting to see for seven or eight years, and her husband, Saint-Léon. Now at last it was settled that they would give three series of performances at the Opéra in the winters of 1847, 1848–49 and 1849–50 at a joint salary of 6,500 francs or, in the event of any of the series being extended to five months, 6,000 francs a month.

The elder of the two, Fanny Cerrito, was born in Naples, at No. 6 Pedamentina San Martino, on May 11th, 1817, and baptized shortly afterwards with the names, Francesca Teresa Giuseppa Raffaela, at the Church of Santa Maria Ognibene: she was the daughter of Don Raffaele Cerrito and his wife, Donna Marianna D'Alife, the former a Second Lieutenant in the Fanteriola Regiment who had fought in the armies of Napoleon under Murat and Macdonald.[1] The child was wonderfully supple and graceful in her movements and possessed an unusual strength; and as she grew older other rare qualities developed, a sprightly personality, a vivid imagination, and such a power of fascination that all who knew her predicted a future bright with success. She began to study dancing at an early age, but at first showed little talent. When her doting father sought an opinion from Fiorentino, the critic said to him: "I can only tell you what her teachers have told me. She is an incorrigible

---

[1] For this information, I am indebted to the management of the Teatro di San Carlo, Naples, in whose archives Fanny Cerrito's birth certificate is preserved. Later in life, Cerrito adopted the name of Marianna.

child, and will never learn to place her feet correctly, nor will she ever be able to raise her leg to the level of her nose." Fiorentino was soon to be proved wrong, for he had failed to take note of the child's unusual tenacity and determination. He could not have known, for instance, of the many hours she spent patiently massaging her face·before the little pocket-mirror she always carried, until she was at last to succeed in softening her naturally somewhat heavy features into a beauty that none could deny her.

The *angioletta gentile*, as she was to be called, made a successful début in her native city, and was soon being applauded with equal enthusiasm throughout Italy and in Vienna. She was hailed as the fourth Grace, *la quarta Grazia*: "*non di danzar*," it was said of her, "*ma di volare è dato*." Costly presents were lavished upon her; great personages came to do her homage; and the experience of being drawn through the streets in her carriage by a delirious throng of admirers soon became to her almost commonplace.

In 1840, Fanny Cerrito danced in London for the first time, and thereafter, for many years, no season in the English capital was complete without her; at Her Majesty's Theatre in the Haymarket, she created leading rôles in many of Perrot's ballets and *divertissements*, and counted almost from the beginning as vociferous a body of champions as did any of the other great ballerinas who appeared there. She was adored. One evening, the ribbon of one of her ballet shoes having broken off, a gentleman leapt from the omnibus box to pick it up and kiss it reverently before returning to his place; on another occasion, she received a magnificent jewelled brooch from Queen Adelaide.

It was in London too that she fell in love with Arthur Saint-Léon, with whom she had first danced in Vienna in the winter of 1841. They planned to marry in Paris, at the fashionable church of Saint-Roch in the Rue Saint-Honoré, where the French Royal Family attended divine service; but because the priest there considered it beneath his dignity to marry theatrical folk, the ceremony had to be held, on April 17th, 1845, in humbler surroundings, at Batignolles, where the bridegroom's parents lived.

Saint-Léon was some four years younger than his wife. He was born in Paris on September 17th, 1821, his real names being Charles Victor Arthur Michel [1]; the name of Saint-Léon was adopted as a *nom de théâtre* at the start of his professional career. The son of a male dancer of the Opéra, he was destined from childhood to follow his father's calling, but he also showed a precocious aptitude for the violin. Both Paganini and Mayseder, his teachers, were astonished by his virtuosity, which was such that he appeared in public as a violinist when he was thirteen, some years before he was seen as a dancer; his first engagement in Paris was in March 1837, when he played the violin at two concerts in the Rue de Rivoli.

Nevertheless, his ruling ambition was to become a dancer. After studying first under his father in Stuttgart, and later under Albert, who considered him one of his best pupils, he made his début at the Théâtre de la Monnaie, Brussels, on November 19th, 1838, as *premier danseur de demi-caractère*, and within a few years won a considerable reputation in Germany, Italy and Belgium. In 1843, he first appeared in London, being immediately acclaimed as a "phenomenon" for the vigour and ease with which he turned and for his remarkable elevation. It is possible that he acquired that rarest of gifts among dancers, a hovering quality in his elevation, for one writer described how "for some moments he would appear suspended in mid-air by invisible wires."

He and Cerrito soon realized the advantages of a partnership. Wherever they appeared, they were acclaimed with enthusiasm and showered with presents and honours; and now, in the summer of 1847, with an unbroken sequence of successes behind them, they were looking to Paris for the supreme triumph to crown their careers.

---

[1] Saint-Léon's birth certificate, preserved in the Archives of the Opéra, reads as follows:—

"Du 19 septembre 1821 à midi. Devant nous, Frédéric Pierre Baron Lecordier, maire du 1er arrondissement de Paris, officier de la légion, chevalier de l'ordre de St. Michel, est comparu Sieur *Léon Michel*, artiste de l'Académie Royale de Musique, âgé de 44 ans, demeurant rue St. Marc 21, lequel nous a présenté un enfant du sexe masculin, qu'il nous a déclaré être né allée des Veuves no. 11, le 17 du présent à 3 heures du soir, de lui et de Dame *Adèle Joséphine Nicolau*, son épouse, demeure susdite, auquel enfant il a donné les prénoms de *Charles Victor Arthur*.

"La dite déclaration faite en présence des sieurs Jacob Gard, propriétaire, âgé de 51 ans, allée des Veuves 13, Pierre Gaspard Forestier, docteur en médecine, âgé de 60 ans, rue Montesquieu no. 4, et ont le père et les témoins signé avec nous, après lecture faite. Ainsi signé Léon Michel, Gard aîné, Forestier et Lecordier."

Saint-Léon was baptized in the Reformed Church of Paris on October 24th, 1821. His godparents were his mother's sister, Victoire, and her husband, Jacob Gard.

That August, Saint-Léon was corresponding regularly with Duponchel and Deligny, the Secretary-General of the Opéra, making the necessary arrangements for the approaching début. The ballet he had in mind from the beginning was *Alma*, for which Deshayes, Perrot and Cerrito had devised the choreography when it was first given in London five years previously, and which he had himself revived several times in a shortened version. No other ballet, in his opinion, better displayed his wife's talents.

His letters to Duponchel contained meticulous instructions. "I beg you," he wrote on August 2nd, "to direct your attention and your good taste to something which has always been badly contrived, namely the statue hiding the *danseuse* in Act I. This statue is placed on its own in the centre of the stage, and at a stroke of the gong, it separates to reveal Alma coming to life; and at the end, this action is reversed when she turns back into a statue. As Alma is coming to life, a light from above must focus on her, first green, then gradually changing to yellow, and ending in a vivid red." Later letters gave descriptions of the scenery required, instructions for the interpretation of the characters, and details of the arrangements he was making concerning the music. "Regarding Costa's music [for *Alma*]," he wrote from Bath on September 1st, "it is very good, and I will try to retain as much of it as possible. M. Deligny tells me there are some very distinguished musicians in Paris, which I do not in the least doubt, but I have already reached an agreement with Pugni, who will be coming with me to Paris. . . . In any case, I doubt whether any composer in Paris would have been willing to make the adjustments necessary."

Saint-Léon arrived in Paris with Cerrito early in the second week of September, and set to work with such energy that the new ballet, re-entitled *La Fille de marbre*, was given its first performance less than six weeks later, on October 20th. During the rehearsals, the ballet had been shortened still further by the omission of a ballroom scene, and by the suppression, at the last moment, of a singing rôle (that of the Genie of Fire) and a chorus in the first scene.

Saint-Léon's scenario for *La Fille de marbre* bore a considerable resemblance to that of *Alma*. The ballet opens in the Palace of the Genie of Fire. Manasses (Saint-Léon), a sculptor, has fallen in love with his statue of Fatma (Cerrito), and is willing to barter his soul that life be given to it. Belphegor (Quériau), the leader of the salamanders, makes a sign with his sceptre, and the statue rises out of a rock. Flames flare round it, as it comes to life. When Manasses learns of the condition imposed that Fatma is forever to remain insensible to love, he wishes to retract the bargain, but it is too late. The scene changes to a public place in Seville, where a notice announces that dancing is forbidden. Manasses arrives with Fatma, who ignores this prohibition and by her impetuous dancing charms everyone, including the Moorish prince, Alyatar (H. Desplaces), who has seen her in his dreams and has fallen deeply in love with her. The second act takes place in the Alhambra, where the King of Spain (Monet) is celebrating a victory over the Moors. Fatma dances before him. Seeing Alyatar concealed behind a curtain, she feels her heart stirring with emotion for the first time. Suddenly the Moors break into the palace, and for a while all is confusion. The Spaniards are routed, and Alyatar is proclaimed King of Granada. Fatma consents to become his queen, but as he leads her to the throne, the scene darkens, thunder peals, and she is turned back into a statue. Alyatar hurls down his crown in grief. Manasses is struck dead: Belphegor has claimed his price.

The critics appreciated that this ballet—"this strange faery, this incoherent dream, this hurly-burly of genii, demons, salamanders, Turks, Moors, Spaniards, penitents and arquebusiers," as Fiorentino described it—had of necessity been hastily mounted, and few voices were heard in censure of the banality of its plot. As a theatrical work, it certainly compared unfavourably with the more skilfully contrived ballets in the repertory, but it served its purpose well of introducing Saint-Léon and Cerrito to Paris with the minimum of delay, and was greeted at the fall of the curtain with whole-hearted applause.

Though Fanny Cerrito had already acquired an international reputation, her task in upholding it in Paris was by no means simple, for the French considered themselves as the final arbiters in all matters appertaining to the dance. Fortunately, she enjoyed the unquestionable advantage of being physically very well endowed. Small and compact of build, she was well proportioned and graced with beautifully rounded shoulders and arms, and a wonderfully clear skin; her legs were slender, and her feet, though wide, were small and delicate. A smile that was irresistible and blue eyes that could be tender, provoking, ingenuous and merry in turn gave brilliance and mobility to her attractive features; and in her fair hair shone glints of gold.

All were agreed on the charms of her person, but opinions were divided on the question of her technique. "Cerrito's dancing," declared Fiorentino, who was completely under her charm, "resembles nothing that has been seen or done before; she bewilders the connoisseurs, confounds the savants. . . . Now there are chaste, meditative poses and lowered, modest glances . . . and now amazing bounds, voluptuous *écarts*, diabolical *développements*. You have only just seen her twisting and turning like a snake round her dancer, and whirling with him like a leaf carried away by a gale, when, a moment later, you see her walking with a superb, nonchalant step, happy to show you her beautiful arms and shoulders, her marble-like bust, her supple, shapely figure. Then she darts anew into space, and falls drooping, quivering, writhing in one supreme convulsion, her head touching the ground, her eyes bathed in light, as the sound of the castanets in her hands slowly dies away. . . . And in all these movements, in all these attitudes, in the groups especially, there is always that same grace, that same harmony, that same charm, that same unexpectedness, that something which can be learnt from no teacher and in no school."

Gautier, while praising her vivacity and her graceful artlessness, detected signs of lack of training, but did not reinforce his observation with details of her technical shortcomings. Charles Maurice, of the *Coureur des Spectacles*, however, was not so considerate. He had been impressed neither by the ballet nor by the dancers. "It is clear from Mlle Fanny Cerrito's manner, from her style of dancing and the forceful expression of her miming, that she has been schooled in Italy," he wrote. "She runs with affectation, jumps to excess, and performs steps that show lack of training. We have even observed turned-up toes, the last word in negligence or rebellion. She has seductive poses and a fantastic lack of conventionality, in which a pleasing vivacity takes the place of correctness, and the second failing of which is to savour of toil. Only in *adage* is she completely successful, for she gets out of breath after a few bars. As a mime, she is a nullity, although she makes up for it by her zeal." A day or two later, Charles Maurice was complaining again. In the Spanish dance, *L'Aldéana*, he accused her of affecting "contortions and bendings that would be better performed elsewhere than in a theatre. . . . Her *pointes* are weak," he continued, "and that of her left foot well nigh powerless. . . . We would mention a *sissonne en tournant* that this lady executed, first omitting the beat, with turned-up toes and sagging knees, and then, when she did beat it, with her body tilted to one side to maintain her balance—incontestable proofs of weakness and the absence of all training."

Fanny Cerrito succeeded in spite of these failings. Though she fitted into neither of the two categories into which *danseuses* were still placed in the popular mind—the *danseuses nobles* and the *danseuses de demi-caractère*—her cajolery, her coquetry and her bewitching manner won her a triumph that the Parisians could only explain by assigning her to a third category, of which she was the sole and ideal example, that of the *danseuse de fantaisie*. Her style was quite unique, for no other dancer was to take up her rôles with any conspicuous success after her.

No less astonishment was caused by the feats of her husband. "He is the most amazing, the most extraordinary, the most aerial dancer that has ever been seen," wrote the delighted Fiorentino. "I would call him a living aerostat, were I not afraid of over-flattering balloons. He reaches prodigious heights, hovers and balances himself in space, and if ever he consents to come to earth, it is merely through courtesy or simple curiosity on his part." Jules Janin was left breathless by the very sight of Saint-Léon's jumps and turns, and other critics voiced their pleasure at his masculine style and manner.

Charles Maurice was, of course, harder to please. Saint-Léon, he wrote, "is still a young man, whose body presents a double aspect of definition which . . . equally justifies praise for a dancer who is ably overcoming a great obstacle and at the same time putting his unfortunate build to good use by his strength. . . . His head is always inclined to the left. . . . He has what is called a prominent shoulder. On the other hand, his legs are of a dimension perfectly served by their strength, and very favourable to the brilliance of his *entrechats*, whether open or closed. His great elevation fires the spectator; it is . . . the principal cause of the success of M. Saint-Léon, whose dancing is otherwise very commonplace and also somewhat Italian, as,

Théophile Gautier

Jules Janin

Paul de Saint-Victor

B. Jouvin

Albéric Second

Pier Angelo Fiorentino

Nestor Roqueplan   Paul Scudo

too, is his miming." But, "if he lacks distinguished features and a pleasing form, and if his physique has a stiffness reminiscent of the dancers of another age, he is at least vigorous, he jumps with ease, and his movements, though affected, have a certain brilliance. He even has *ballon*."

"To sum up," Maurice concluded, "there is, in the appearance of the honest and, by many standards, interesting couple, all that is necessary to promote an appetite for a certain number of performances, after which satiety will follow because variety is not among their merits; though there are merits enough to furnish pretexts for the praises of those false connoisseurs who are always inclined to find that everything that glitters is gold. Our school and the artistes who cultivate it have nothing to learn, nothing to forget or fear from the passage of this travelling couple; and if there is profit for anyone, it will be for them."

Profit indeed there was, for shortly after their début, Saint-Léon and Cerrito were summoned by King Louis Philippe to give the new ballet at the Palace of Saint-Cloud, and were rewarded, Cerrito with a magnificent bracelet, and Saint-Léon with a purse containing 3,000 francs.

.   .   .   .

For those who could not accustom themselves to Saint-Léon and Cerrito, there was still Carlotta Grisi, who for seven years had maintained the reputation she had first earned when creating the title-rôle in *Giselle*, and whose supremacy, now that Marie Taglioni had retired, might well have seemed unchallengeable. Her contract with the Opéra assured her a salary of 24,000 francs a year, augmented by at least 1,330 francs monthly in bonuses, which was much more than was paid to any other member of the company. Relations between her and the Opéra were, however, at this moment somewhat strained. As a result of her having prolonged her holiday early in 1847 without permission, the production of the ballet *Ozaï* had been delayed, and the management had thereupon sued her for breach of contract, claiming 10,000 francs damages. The Court of First Instance had found against her, and this decision had later been upheld on appeal. Nevertheless, the Opéra could not afford to dispense with her services, and as soon as the Saint-Léons' engagement terminated, preparations for a new ballet for Carlotta Grisi, with a scenario by Dumanoir, score

by Adam, and choreography by Mazilier, were pressed
vigorously forward.

This ballet, *Griseldis, ou les Cinq sens,* told of the adventures
that befell Elfrid, the Crown Prince of Bohemia (L. Petipa), on
his journey to meet his prospective bride, a princess of Moldavia. Elfrid shows no enthusiasm when the marriage is decided
upon by his father (Mazilier), and when Griseldis (Grisi), in
the guise of a shepherdess, has appeared to him, awakening his
sense of sight, and given him a simple crown of flowers concealing her portrait, only his father's anger restrains him from

CARLOTTA GRISI AND LUCIEN PETIPA IN ''GRISELDIS''
Caricature by Lorentz

refusing to go to Moldavia. The second scene finds him on his
journey, being entertained by peasants, among whom is
Griseldis; and when he is about to continue on his way, his
sense of hearing is stimulated by a lovely voice singing. The
scene changes to the palace of the Governor of Belgrade.
Elfrid awakes from his sleep at the touch of a kiss, but searches
the harem in vain for Griseldis. The fourth scene passes in a
forest. A hunting party rides through the trees; a woman
dismounts and gathers some flowers before disappearing after
the others. Elfrid then arrives with Jacobus (Berthier), his
companion. As they partake of a meal sitting on the grass, they
are interrupted by the *fête des jardinières.* Elfrid is insensible to
the sweet-scented flowers that are offered him; only a small
bouquet thrown at his feet by some unknown hand arouses his
sense of smell. Night falls. While Elfrid tries to sleep, Griseldis

appears to him again. Passing her hands before his eyes, she sends him into a deep trance, conjuring up beautiful visions at which he gazes in wonder. Then she fills a cup and places it to his lips, and he has experienced the joys of taste. In the fifth and final scene, Elfrid has arrived at his destination, the Moldavian court. Here he meets Griseldis again, and, clasping her in his arms, places upon her finger the ring given to him by the Moldavian ambassador. At the sound of a fanfare, Griseldis breaks away from his embrace and flees. The wedding procession approaches. Elfrid is resolved to refuse the hand of the princess, but as she reaches him, she sings a familiar refrain, lets fall her veil and reveals herself as Griseldis.

For many weeks, the attention of the public was directed to the progress of the rehearsals, and in particular to the hunt that Duponchel was arranging, with *écuyères* from the Hippodrome, in the fourth scene. When *Griseldis* was first given on February 16th, 1848, there was disappointment that this hunt was not more spectacular—there were horses, to be sure, but where were the hounds, the deer, the outriders, the carriages, the guests? asked the more fastidious critics—but for this there was ample compensation in the appearance of Carlotta Grisi on horseback. "A *première danseuse* on horseback!" exclaimed Fiorentino. "What temerity! What impudent daring! . . . Suppose that the noble animal that then carried the Opéra and its fortune had fallen or stumbled! God protect France! But have no fear: Mlle Griseldis is as firm in her stirrups as she is on her *pointes*." [1]

The hunt, the *fête des jardinières*, the hypnotism scene and the visions that followed it—in short, all the principal features of the ballet—occurred in the same scene, with the result that the ballet lacked balance. Great care had been lavished on the flying visions, and in fact the first night had been postponed by forty-eight hours to perfect them. Artistically, they were considered a great improvement on the flying in earlier productions, for instead of the usual skinny children uncomfortably strung up on wires, they were composed of mature beauties arranged in picturesque groups.

Another point of interest was the refrain that Carlotta Grisi

[1] Sir Francis Burnand, in his *Records and Reminiscences*, recalled Carlotta Grisi, whom he had seen riding in Hyde Park, as "a dazzling equestrienne. . . . As a boy, I remember I was . . . utterly astonished at Carlotta being able to ride, and actually cantering about the Row."

sang at the end of the ballet in a pure and true soprano voice, trembling slightly with emotion. It was by no means her first experience of singing in public. She was a cousin of the eminent soprano Giulia Grisi, and both Malibran and Pasta had tried to persuade her to forsake dancing for singing; she had sung an aria from *Lucia di Lammermoor* at Perrot's benefit in London in the summer of 1836, and the first rôle she had played in Paris—

CARLOTTA GRISI IN "GRISELDIS"
Caricature by Bertall

in *Le Zingaro* at the Renaissance in 1840—had contained singing as well as dancing.

If further justification had been needed for her decision to continue as a dancer, it would have been found in the brilliant *pas* by Mazilier that she danced at the end of *Griseldis*. "It embodies strength with grace, suddenness without abruptness, a chronometer's precision that yet allows suppleness and elegance, a marvellous brilliance and *brio* which realize the dream of the accomplished *danseuse*, Elssler and Taglioni in one person," wrote Gautier. "There is, in particular, a movement turned on one *pointe* alone, in which she flashes forward, flung by that vigorous leg as by a bow of steel—the most audaciously charming impossibility that a dancer who is mistress of the resources of her art can dare."

Little fault could have been found with Carlotta Grisi, but the other members of the cast were open to much criticism, particularly to that of Charles Maurice. Lucien Petipa, who was on the stage almost incessantly from the first rise of the curtain to its final fall, was allotted only one *pas*. Though a competent dancer, he was becoming careless, possibly through the little work he was given to do. "He affects a most disgraceful stoop," wrote Maurice. "His elevation is taken too visibly from the muscles of the back, which causes him to land heavily. His *entrechats* are beaten neither exactly nor quickly. He pirouettes without balance, and allows his leg, which should remain by the other, to float about. The manner in which he holds his hands (the right one especially) is unbearable, the form he gives them when jumping resembling a scoop." Adèle Dumilâtre, who took the leading rôle in the *fête des jardinières*, also came in for criticism: her strength and talent were failing, her *pointes* were becoming feeble, her stereotyped smile was exasperating.

The success of *Griseldis*—for initial success it certainly achieved—was compromised by the outbreak of revolution in Paris only a week after its first performance. In three days of confused street fighting, Louis Philippe fled the country and a Republican Government was set up under the leadership of the poet Lamartine. During the Revolution, the armoury of the Opéra was broken into and rifled by the mob, and its motley collection of arms of all ages and all countries was requisitioned for service at the barricades. For a week, no performances were given. Then, on February 29th, the theatre was reopened with a programme that included *La Muette de Portici* and patriotic songs. Under the new régime, the Opéra reflected the temper of the moment: the inscription, ACADÉMIE ROYALE DE MUSIQUE, on the front of the building was hastily obliterated and replaced by the words, THÉÂTRE DE LA NATION; and a Tree of Liberty was ceremoniously planted in the courtyard, only to be quietly removed a few years later as the country settled into an age of prosperity under Louis Napoleon.

For the Opéra, the most serious consequences of the Revolution were the temporary suspension of the Government Subsidy and the fall in receipts resulting from the apprehension of the public. Though the Subsidy was restored, and an advance allowed on the following winter's instalments, the crisis still remained, and Duponchel was only able to balance his budget by reducing salaries. The sacrifices were accepted with few demurs.

.   .   .   .

The whole of that summer was a lean period for the theatres of Paris, for there was further cause for alarm at the end of June, when heavy street fighting broke out afresh in the city. However, the Revolution had now spent itself. The revolt was quickly put down by the Army, and thereafter the elections of the new Deputies proceeded more quietly and the popularity of Louis Napoleon, who was to become President of the Republic the following December, increased as the desire for order grew stronger.

These difficult months saw the last performances of Adèle Dumilâtre and the début on May 22nd of Louis Mérante in *La Jolie fille de Gand*. Adèle Dumilâtre was the younger of the two daughters of Michel Dumilâtre, a *pensionnaire* of the Comédie-Française, both of whom had been engaged at the Opéra, where they were known, on account of their thinness, as "*les sœurs Demi-Lattes.*" Their father was very proud of them, and while watching them dance, was in the habit of turning to his neighbour and making such a remark as, "Who is that light and elegant dancer who is so like Taglioni . . . and that other one, so correct and vigorous, the one with the tip-tilted nose?" Should his neighbour be able to inform him that they were the Dumilâtre sisters, the old man would murmur a satisfied "Ah!" and sit back smugly in his seat. For several years, Adèle Dumilâtre was the mistress of a rich landowner from Havana, but after she left the Opéra she married an equally wealthy gentleman by the name of Francisco Drake del Castillo. Being left a widow some years later, she then went to live with her sister Sophie at Pau, and later moved, with her two sons and daughter, to a château in Touraine. She died in Paris, at her home in the Rue Cler, on May 4th, 1909, shortly before her eighty-eighth birthday.

Louis Mérante, who came from a well-known dancing family, was to remain an important member of the Opéra ballet —first as a dancer, and later as *maître de ballet* and choreographer—from his début, at the age of twenty, in the summer of 1848 until shortly before his death in July 1887. He had made his first stage appearance at Liége when he was six, and in 1846 had been appointed *premier danseur* at Marseilles; now, after a short but successful engagement at the Scala, Milan, he had joined the Opéra to understudy Lucien Petipa.

Carlotta Grisi's leave commenced in May 1848, and for a few months the Opéra had to rely on its lesser luminaries: on Maria, who played Fenella in *La Muette de Portici*; on Sofia Fuoco, the great technician of the *pointe*; on Flora Fabbri, who in June appeared in the second act of *La Sylphide*; and on Adeline Plunkett, who took over Grisi's rôle in *Le Diable à quatre*.

Adeline Plunkett's disadvantage lay in her coming from a family, part Irish and part Flemish in descent, when it was fashionable for a prima ballerina to be of Italian stock. She had appeared in London, at Her Majesty's, in the summers of 1843 and 1844, but, despite influential protection, her engagement there had been terminated after the scandalous culmination of her feud with another dancer, Elisa Scheffer. One evening, as Cerrito was about to dance her famous *pas de l'ombre* from *Ondine*, Adeline Plunkett aimed a kick at her enemy, but unfortunately missed, and instead knocked over the lamp that provided the light for the moon. That winter, she had moved to Drury Lane, where she had the unnerving experience of witnessing the fatal burning of Clara Webster during a performance of *The Revolt of the Harem*. Her début at the Opéra followed in March 1845, when, with great pluck but perhaps little wisdom, she appeared in Carlotta Grisi's part in *La Péri*.

Since then she had made steady progress. In April 1847 she had been given the title-rôle in Jean Coralli's *Ozaï* to create, and a year later, her popularity and prestige being considered sufficient to warrant another creation, a new ballet was put into rehearsal, with a view to its being given some weeks before the Saint-Léons returned in the autumn. It was called *Nisida, ou les Amazones des Açores*, and its scenario, written by Deligny, the Secretary-General of the Opéra, was inspired by the founding in the Azores, during the fourteenth century, of the Republic of Graciosa by a group of unhappy, betrayed women. As the ballet begins, galleons are approaching the island bearing a cargo of young Spaniards, it being the custom to admit men for one day in each year. Before their arrival, the Queen, Joséfa

(Maria), offers to proclaim Nisida (Plunkett), the most intrepid of her warriors, general-in-chief of her army. Nisida at first refuses, and confesses that she is haunted by the memory of a young man; but begged to reconsider, she agrees to accept the honour. The galleons arrive, and the young men are led blindfold down the gangplanks and the bandages are removed from their eyes. A barrel begins to move on the deck of one of the ships, and from it emerges the ridiculous and repellently ugly figure of Don Oscar (Berthier). Meanwhile, as the men file past the Amazons, Nisida has recognized him whose memory haunts her, Don Éthur (L. Petipa). Joséfa is also charmed by him, and when the time comes for the men to sail away, she approaches him and asks him to hide in her tent. But when she has gone, he enters Nisida's tent, and it is Don Oscar whom Joséfa finds in the dwindling light on her return and leads, deliriously kissing her hand, into her own tent, under the impression that he is Don Éthur.

The second act opens in a grotto, chosen by both Joséfa and Nisida, unknown to each other, as a safe haven for their lovers. As day breaks, Joséfa discovers that she has been deceived and draws her sword on Don Oscar, but, softening, hides him, commanding him to leave the island at nightfall. The Amazons enter and bathe in the waters, until they discover the presence of Don Oscar and chase him from the grotto. Nisida then arrives to tell Don Éthur that he must find a safer hiding place, but they are surprised by Joséfa, who, incensed, tells him to choose between her and Nisida. Don Éthur declares his passion for Nisida. Joséfa scornfully insults Nisida, who draws her sword and, in the fight that ensues, strikes the Queen's weapon from her hand. Generously, Nisida returns it, but Joséfa summons her subjects by a blast on her trumpet and commands them to pass judgment on Nisida and her lover. With one accord, they demand that they die. The scene changes, and the Amazon army is seen coming down from a high mountain in the sunlight. Nisida and Don Éthur listen calmly as Joséfa pronounces their fate, but no sooner has this been done than galleons bearing men are seen approaching the island. The invasion is successful, the young men countering the women's blows with bouquets of flowers, and after Joséfa has called down a curse upon her unworthy subjects, she takes flight, followed by a few faithful Amazons, as the curtain falls.

Fanny Cerrito

Oil-painting by Laure

La Fille de marbre, Act I, Scene I

La Fille de marbre, Act I, Scene II

La Fille de marbre, Act II

Sketch for the setting of the last scene of *Griseldis*

La Vivandière

Mlle Maria's mishap

Nisida, which was presented to the public on August 21st, 1848, was the first ballet to be arranged by Auguste Mabille. "The clarity of his lines, the true feeling in his groups, his facility in handling masses are very promising," wrote Gautier of the choreography. "The dancing itself lacks neither novelty nor grace, but it is a pity that he had to work on such an insignificant theme." Another critic described Mabille's work as "the orchestration of choreography," explaining, "Groups occupy the stage almost continually; the whole of the first act is composed of figures executed with a precision that cannot be too much praised."

Adeline Plunkett, for whom the ballet had been produced, just lacked that final distinction necessary to stand out above all others. Criticized by Gautier for neglecting her legs and concentrating too much on the voluptuous effect of her poses, she enjoyed only a shared success with Maria, a very haughty Joséfa, and Sofia Fuoco, who astounded Gautier by performing what he described as "*une pointe avec pirouette en spirale ascendante la plus étonnante du monde*" in the *pas de treize* in Act I. In the second act, Louise Taglioni, a cousin of the great Taglioni, made her début at the Opéra in a *pas seul*: she displayed much grace, but it was said that she had two obstacles to overcome—the great name she bore and the English cast of her features.

In Gautier's judgment, apart from Benoist's carefully composed score and the setting for the bathing scene, which was "decidedly original," the production of *Nisida* was "not worthy of the usual splendours of the Rue Le Peletier."

. . . .

That summer, Saint-Léon and Cerrito were appearing with their customary success in London. As the time for their return to Paris approached, Saint-Léon wrote to Deligny: "I shall be in Paris at the end of [August] unless I stay a week in some spa to make war on the rheumatism that has paid me a visit, encouraged by the Siberian weather dogging us in this charming town. It will not be long before we see each other again, no longer now as Royalists but as Nationalists, and I hope that our feeble talents, added to our zeal, will recapture as much as possible of the good receipts of autumn of '47. My wife is very well in spite of the 'steeple-chase' that Lumley is pleased to

make these ladies dance in the name of ballet; she asks me to
send thousands and thousands of good wishes to you as well
as to MM. Duponchel and Roqueplan, and, looking forward
to our little chats, with you rolling your cigarettes and me filling
my pipe, remember me to those gentlemen and believe me,
your sincere friend, A. Saint-Léon."

They arrived in Paris in September, and reappeared at the
Opéra early in October in *La Fille de marbre*. "She is as
voluptuous and as much an enchantress as ever," wrote
Gautier of Cerrito, "and as for correctness, she has gained much
since last year." A few weeks later, on October 20th, the first
Paris performance was given of Saint-Léon's *La Vivandière*, a
one-act ballet, to a score by Pugni, which had been first
produced at the Teatro Alibert, Rome, on November 22nd,
1843, under the title, *La Vivandiera ed il Postiglione*. The haste
with which it had been revived at the Opéra was evident from
the costumes, many of which had been seen before in *Griseldis*
and other ballets.

The slight plot told of a *vivandière*, Kathi (Cerrito), returning
to her village and her lover, Hans (Saint-Léon). Hans's father
disapproves of the match and refuses his consent, because she
has no dowry. So she compromises a young Baron (Fuchs) and
an elderly Burgomaster (Berthier) by her coquetry, with the
result that both contribute towards a dowry, which leads to
the happy conclusion of the ballet.

Saint-Léon's choreography was very animated, too much
so in Gautier's opinion. "We believe that *La Vivandière* would
achieve a greater effect," he wrote some three years later, " if
everybody were not in a perpetual state of trepidation. It is as
though the stage were on fire and nobody can put his foot down
for longer than a second. This false animation is tiring, and the
eye longs to rest on a few quiet groups. Among this dizzy swarm,
it is impossible to focus one's glasses on a dancer or *danseuse* for
one moment; they are ever eluding you, carried away by the
volubility of the movement. A few *pas sur place* would form a
happy contrast; Saint-Léon, we feel, is a little too fond of
making his dancers move about the stage." Another critic
remarked that Saint-Léon's *pas*, "instead of being, like so
many others, incoherent mixtures of jumps, *pointes*, *entrechats*,
pirouettes, etc., are small scenes full of feeling, and by means of a
very ingenious use of mime, their significance is always clear."

Saint-Léon was less successful in his arrangement of larger groups, which were somewhat confused in structure, due possibly to the haste of the production.

The success of *La Vivandière* was largely a personal triumph for Cerrito, who had been dancing the rôle of Kathi regularly for nearly five years. The ballet contained many of her most effective *pas*: the martial *pas de la vivandière* and the graceful *pas de l'inconstance*; a *pas de six*, adapted from Antonio Guerra's ballet, *Le Lac des fées*; and a spirited *pas de caractère*, *La Redowot-schka*, in which she was partnered by her husband.

Saint-Léon himself received the expected harsh treatment from Charles Maurice, who spoke of his "jumping in the manner of the *Grotteschi*,[1]" and told his readers, "If you want *doubles tours en l'air*, there you will find them! M. Saint-Léon is lavish with them, as though that were dancing." Gautier was more appreciative and perhaps more just. "Not for a long time,' he observed, "has a genuine male dancer been seen in France. The marked decline in popularity of the male dancer has considerably reduced his choreographic portion in ballets. . . . Since Perrot's retirement, Saint-Léon is the only man who has dared to dance at the Opéra for the sake of dancing, and everyone has been surprised at his success."

This short ballet was not to be Saint-Léon's only contribution that winter, for it was followed three months later by *Le Violon du Diable*, a more elaborate work than either of those he had already arranged in Paris. Once again, however, a hurried production was betrayed by the appearance of familiar costumes, this time from the ballet *Ozaï*. *Le Violon du Diable* was a revival of *Tartini il Violinista*, which had been created at the Gran Teatro la Fenice, Venice, on February 29th, 1848; Adice went so far as to suggest that it was a complete copy of a ballet by Emmanuele Viotti. The playbill of the Venice production had credited the music to "Saint-Léon and Felis, with the exception of the second act, which is by Cesare Pugni;" but in the Paris production Pugni alone was named as the composer.

The ballet was successfully given its first performance at the Opéra on January 19th, 1849. Saint-Léon took the rôle of Urbain, a young violinist, madly in love with the beautiful

---

[1] Possibly an allusion to the Kobler troupe of "Italian" dancers who had visited Paris at the end of 1812. They were noted for their technical virtuosity. The story of this company is told in Marian Hannah Winter's *The Pre-Romantic Ballet* (London. 1974).

Hélène de Vardeck (Cerrito), who herself loves a rival suitor, Saint-Ybars (Fuchs). The sinister Dr. Mathéus (E. Coralli) gives Urbain's violin such a tone as to have an irresistible effect on Hélène's heart, and, as the price of his assistance, demands Urbain's soul. Urbain refuses, whereupon the doctor breaks the magic instrument. All is finally retrieved by the intervention of the saintly Father Anselme (H. Cornet), who brings another violin, instilled with beneficent magic, and no less potent. When it is discovered that Urbain is really of noble birth, Hélène's father gives his consent to the marriage. The ballet ends with a *divertissement* inspired by the drawings of Grandville: flowers in a hot-house come to life and bear away their gardener (Saint-Léon) to the Kingdom of the Dew, whose Queen (Cerrito) he weds.

The main interest of the ballet lay in the unprecedented feat of Saint-Léon's appearance as choreographer, dancer and violinist. "Oh thrice supreme Saint-Léon!" murmured Janin in admiration. Of Saint Léon's ability as a violinist, Adolphe Adam wrote: "Saint-Léon belongs to the Paganini school. He seeks his principal effects in the eccentricities and the difficulties of harmonics and the succession of *pizzicato* and *col arco*, which does not prevent him from playing with infinite style and elegance the *air varié* and the various *andante* passages of which his musical rôle is composed. Account must also be taken of the extreme difficulty of taking up the violin in the middle of a scene and playing it at a given moment, without time to make all the preparations that a musician never neglects before commencing his solo."

Once again Saint-Léon and Cerrito came in for criticism from Charles Maurice, who, needless to say, had not enjoyed himself at all that evening. Annoyed by the bad taste of all around him who were applauding what he considered to be a poor ballet and miserable execution, he felt an increasing revulsion as he watched Saint-Léon; he noted that his head was placed too low on his body, that his legs were of an unnatural length, and—worse still!—that he had a paunch. Cerrito he liked little better: she held her herself badly, he thought, and her miming was not only Italian, but, in his opinion, outmoded. But he was certainly prejudiced, for Gautier said that Cerrito danced like a Grace, and Janin thought he had never seen her more charming, while the achievement of Saint-Léon in his triple capacity allowed of little exaggeration.

.   .   .   .

For some time, the better-informed *habitués* of the Foyer de la Danse had known that the stage career of Mlle Maria was drawing to its close and that she had accepted a proposal of marriage from the Baron d'Henneville. It was like the climax to a novel. Born of a Jewish family named Jacob in one of the poorest quarters of Paris, Maria had risen, with great patience and perseverance, from figuring as a child in processions at a few sous a night to the rank of *première danseuse*; and now she was to become a Baroness. Her stage career might well have ended a few weeks earlier than it did and in unhappier circumstances, for one evening in February, while dancing in the opera *Jérusalem*, she had approached too close to the footlights and, for fear of her costume catching fire, and unable, by her momentum, to hold herself back, she leapt over them, landing on the shoulders of one of the musicians in the orchestra pit, fortunately without sustaining injury.

For her farewell performance on April 9th, 1849, she appeared in two rôles which she had created, Joséfa in *Nisida* and the Countess in *Le Diable à quatre*. At the end there were prolonged cheers, and at least fifty bouquets must have fallen at her feet as she stood weeping with emotion before the audience. "*Adieu*, Maria the dancer, and *bonjour, madame la baronne*," wrote Janin. "You have been all you should have been, good, simple, not over-vain, nor ambitious, nor clamorous —in short, charming; and your bounding companions will not fill your place for some time to come."

.   .   .   .

Just a week later, on April 16th, a musical event of the greatest importance took place, the first performance of Meyerbeer's *Le Prophète* at the Opéra.

Meyerbeer was, above all, a practical man of the theatre and fully appreciated the importance of spectacle and production in the ultimate success of an opera. His *Robert le Diable*, for instance, had owed much of its popularity to Filippo Taglioni's Ballet of the Nuns, in which the choreographer's famous daughter Marie had played the leading rôle, and in conceiving *Le Prophète*, Meyerbeer had devoted much care and attention not only to composing the ballet music, but also to planning the actual form of the *divertissement*. He retained a vivid recollection of a successful ballet by Paul Taglioni called *Liebeshändel*, first produced in Potsdam in 1840 and since given at many other German theatres and in Warsaw, which had included a sensational ice scene, for which roller-skates had been used. Envisaging a somewhat similar scene for his opera, Meyerbeer had written to his friend Paul Taglioni who was to be passing through Paris on his way to London early in 1849, to ask him if he would bring with him the plans and models used in *Liebeshändel*. Paul Taglioni had obligingly done so and to Meyerbeer's satisfaction, had permitted the Opéra to make use of them in *Le Prophète*.

The *divertissement*, which was arranged by Auguste Mabille, was inserted in the third act of the opera, the scene showing the Anabaptist camp by the side of a frozen lake. Youths and girls were seen skating across the ice bearing provisions for the Anabaptists, and then, while the soldiers were eating, removed their skates and began to dance. All joined in a waltz; then followed a lively *redowa* by Adeline Plunkett and Lucien Petipa, and after a *quadrille des patineurs*, the *divertissement* ended with a *galop*. At the close of the scene, the sun was seen to rise over the lake, a historic effect, for it marked the first occasion on which electricity was used in stage-lighting.

For the additional difficulties involved in the use of roller-skates, the *corps de ballet* were rewarded with a bonus of 5 francs a performance. No inefficiency was tolerated, and the slightest fault entailed the withdrawal of both skates and emolument. The use of roller-skates, limited as it was to the *entrée*, may well have horrified the purists, although far worse outrages were perpetrated in productions of this opera elsewhere. In Antwerp in 1852, for instance, an unusual piece of business was introduced: two of the skaters detached themselves from the *corps de ballet*, disappeared down the prompter's box, as though through a hole in the ice, and emerged a moment later with an enormous fish, alive and wriggling.

.   .   .   .

It was a happy coincidence that the Opéra's choice of choreographer for what proved to be Carlotta Grisi's last

ballet in Paris should be Jules Perrot, to whom she owed her
first successes. Perrot was an established favourite in Paris. In
the thirties he had often partnered Taglioni at the Opéra, and
many people had been surprised that he was not re-engaged in
1841, at the same time that Carlotta Grisi made her début.
From 1842 to 1848, he had been *maître de ballet* at Her Majesty's
Theatre in London, where he had earned renown as the greatest
living choreographer by producing a series of grand ballets and
divertissements for the most eminent ballerinas of the day. In
October 1848, he had made his début at St. Petersburg, whence
he had now returned to Paris to fulfil a brief engagement at the
Opéra. This contract was to expire less than a month after the
first performance of his new ballet, after which he was to
journey back to Russia, there to be joined early in 1850 by
Carlotta Grisi.

Carlotta Grisi's contract with the Opéra had terminated
at the end of January 1849, but, in order to dance in Perrot's
ballet, she had agreed to extend her engagement on a temporary
basis, from May until the end of the year, at a monthly salary
of 3,000 francs, to which were to be added at least seven
bonuses of 100 francs. Her reappearance was delayed for
many weeks when she fell ill with cholera in the summer, but
she had recovered sufficiently by September to take over her
rôles in *Le Diable à quatre* and *Giselle*, and on October 8th,
created the leading part of Ysaure in the first performance of
La Filleule des fées.

This ballet was one of the most ambitious ever to have been
produced at the Opéra, being divided into three acts, compris-
ing seven scenes and a prologue. The story centred round the
character of Ysaure (Grisi), the godchild of the White and
Pink fairies (Emarot and L. Taglioni), against whose magic
is pitted that of the Black fairy (L. Marquet), who was turned
away from the christening festivities to avoid the guests numbering thirteen. Ysaure's hand is sought by two rivals: Alain
(Perrot), her foster-brother, whose suit is favoured by the Black
fairy, and the Prince Hugues (L. Petipa), who is assisted by
the two good fairies. Ysaure prefers the high-born Hugues,
and after he has proposed marriage, her humble room is
transformed, by the agency of the good fairies, into a palatial
chamber, her small mirror grows to several times its original
size, and rich clothes appear from nowhere. But the Black

fairy, whose influence is stronger, ordains that any man setting eyes on Ysaure shall lose his reason. The good fairies then bear Ysaure away to a wooded lakeside, although not before the unlucky Alain has looked upon her. To make up for her misfortune, they transform her into a fairy. With her newly bestowed power, Ysaure makes Hugues appear to her in his sleep. The deranged Alain then arrives, bent on mischief, but Ysaure is once again spirited away, this time to a grotto, the home of the springs. Meanwhile, Alain has obtained Ysaure's magic wand, and walls of rock open before him as he makes his way with Hugues into the grotto. Before Hugues can set his eyes on Ysaure, the good fairies strike him blind. The Black fairy at last consents to allow Hugues to recover his sight, on the condition that he picks Ysaure out from among the naiads, a test which he accomplishes with ease; and the ballet ends with the magnificent apotheosis of Ysaure's wedding in the Fairy Paradise.

Most particularly, the ballet brought into relief Perrot's great facility in devising evolutions for large numbers of dancers on the stage at once: the quality which, more than any other, marked his superiority to Mazilier, whose *pas d'ensemble* were often ineffective, and to Saint-Léon, who until then had never had time to devote much attention to crowd scenes. During the rehearsals of *La Filleule des fées*, the *corps de ballet* discovered that Perrot was a man of unusual methods when composing a *ballabile*. When the inspiration came, he would squat down on the floor with his head in his hands, an indication, as everyone soon learnt, that he was to remain in that position for some considerable time. So the girls whiled away their time, some embroidering, some reading, others eating their lunch. The sound of snoring from the motionless choreographer was the signal that the scheme of the *ballabile* was formed in his mind. Someone then woke him up, and the rehearsal proceeded. Of the finished result, Gautier wrote: "The *danses d'ensemble* are arranged with unusual intelligence and care. The master's eye has obviously penetrated everywhere; nothing has been left to chance. No one can handle large numbers choreographically with more assurance than Perrot; the whole of this crowd is dancing, from the footlights to the backcloth, and each dancer is performing a movement pleasing to watch and well designed."

Le Violon du Diable, Act I, Scene I

Arthur Saint-Léon in
Le Violon du Diable

Joseph Mazilier

La Filleule des fées, Act II

Lucien Petipa and Carlotta Grisi
in *La Filleule des fées*

Gautier was enraptured both by the ballet and by its heroine. "*La Filleule des fées*," he explained, "is danced by Carlotta Grisi to a choreography by Perrot . . . a double perfection complete in itself, the execution being on a level with the conception, and the conception never eluding the execution, with harmony and grace going hand in hand—the ideal in ballet realized! Never perhaps has the charming dancer been more correct, more graceful, stronger and lighter than in *La Filleule des fées*. It seemed as though she were flying, as though some invisible hand held her in the air; and the tip of her white satin ballet shoe alighted on the ground making no more sound than a snowflake. What charming poses, what modest, naïve enjoyment, what poetic simplicity are to be found throughout this rôle played on the *pointe* from one end to the other; and what abandon there is in her *tours de force*, what grace in her strength, what facility in her performance of impossibilities! A *pas* by Perrot danced by Carlotta! Nothing better could be imagined! Terpsichore herself . . . muse that she is, could not do as much with her antique buskin as can our young Italian with her little satin slipper.

"Perrot, cast in the rôle of Alain, interpreted it with that charming feeling that is peculiarly his own. There is no better actor and dancer than he, even when he is not dancing, for the *pas* in a ballet belong to the beloved, and in *La Filleule des fées*, Perrot, left unmarried at the end, is reduced to the state of a comic opera bass. . . . The pleasure of lifting the heroine and making her float for a moment in a haze of gas-light four feet from the ground is reserved for what might be called the tenor of the dance, for Petipa, who admirably acquits himself of this task with an ardent and chivalrous grace which is the secret of his constant success."

The scale of the production of *La Filleule des fées* was reflected in the severe test of the machinist's ingenuity that it entailed. In one scene, the wall of Ysaure's cottage had suddenly to become transparent to show her sitting at her dressing-table, and a little later the whole cottage had to vanish and reappear on a distant hill; in the next scene, he had to devise a means of transforming Ysaure's humble room into a palatial chamber in full view of the audience. The sets were very magnificent. Gautier gave special praise to the lakeside scene, designed by Despléchin, in which the sound of water from real fountains mingled with Adam's melodies, and the electric light gave the impression that the roof of the theatre had been removed to let in the moonlight. Only the inscriptions that appeared on the scenery to convey the Black fairy's pronouncements seemed lacking in taste.

It was in *La Filleule des fées* that Carlotta Grisi danced in Paris for the last time, on December 21st, 1849. Late in the summer of 1853, there were rumours that she was to return to the Opéra, but they were unfounded, for shortly afterwards she retired from the stage to spend the rest of her days quietly near Geneva, where she was to die on May 20th, 1899. In the seclusion of her retirement, her name was seldom brought to the public's notice, for others had taken her place in their affections. But in the summer of 1866, Jules Janin published in his *feuilleton* a letter he had received from her to inform his readers how their pet of yesterday was faring. "My friend," she had written. "If ever you should see a fine herd of beautiful milch cows, turn your thoughts to the Swiss maid, Carlotta Grisi. Of all the poems I have danced, of all my dreams, I am left with a herd that browses in my pastures and in exchange gives me a tub of milk each evening. I am fortunate, believe me. I tread real turf with those light feet that the romancing critics said never touch the ground. But I certainly do touch the ground, and, with my feet in sabots, I am now going out to contemplate this rustic opulence. *Adieu*, kind friend, love me always. . . ."

III

CERRITO AND PRIORA

A few days before Carlotta Grisi's last appearance at the Opéra, Saint-Léon and Cerrito began their third season in Paris with a revival of *Le Violon du Diable*, amid an enthusiasm expressed in flowers: the stage was so littered with bouquets at the end of the performance that Cerrito "had to make three journeys to carry them all away in her arms, and each time she seemed to give way under the burden."

Before two months were out, Saint-Léon had prepared a new ballet in which he and his wife appeared for the first time on February 22nd, 1850: *Stella, ou les Contrebandiers*, both scenario and choreography being by himself, and the score, which introduced many popular Neapolitan melodies, by the faithful Pugni. Like Saint-Léon's earlier ballets, it was a light work, seemingly designed principally as a framework for the display of his wife's and his own brilliant technique. "It is sad," commented Gautier, "to see so ingenious a mind as that of M. Roqueplan [who was now sole Director of the Opéra] neglecting as he does the intellectual side of ballets performed at this theatre. More than any other work, a ballet must have a poem, or, should this word seem too ambitious, a plot, which is worked out very clearly and can be understood without effort. . . . Speech is naturally forbidden in a silent drama; no allusion can be made to the past or to the future, but everything takes place in the present, and the subject must explain itself."

The ballet opened with the capture of Gennaro (Saint-Léon), the son of a revenue officer (Lenfant), by a band of smugglers in the mountains. They believe him to be a spy and are about to shoot him when Stella (Cerrito), the daughter of their chief, declares that she loves him. Her father (E. Coralli) places her ring on Gennaro's finger. However, Gennaro seizes the first opportunity to escape and return to his *fiancée*, Louiselle (L. Taglioni). He is followed by Stella, who takes employment as Louiselle's maidservant, but after making as much mischief as

51

she can—breaking crockery, upsetting macaroni over the notary, holding the candle so near the marriage contract that it catches fire—she is dismissed. She next appears as Gennaro and Louiselle are on the way to their wedding, and shows Louiselle that Gennaro is still wearing her ring. The ballet ends happily, if artificially, by Louiselle releasing Gennaro from his vows, Stella's father turning out to be not only rich, but an old friend of Gennaro's father, and Stella entering the church with Gennaro in Louiselle's place.

The applause at the fall of the curtain was a demonstration in favour of Saint-Léon and Cerrito as dancers, rather than an expression of approval of the ballet. But Roqueplan was very satisfied. "Cerrito is my lucky star," he was heard to say happily.

If Gautier had criticised the structure of the ballet, he had nothing but praise for the performers. "In the servant scene," he wrote, "Mme Cerrito's sulky rebelliousness and graceful provocation are charming. She knows exactly how to stop at the limit beyond which a comedian becomes a clown . . . and how to keep all her charm while raising a laugh, a difficult thing for a woman. In the *tarantella* [i.e. the *Sicilienne*], she displays a brilliant verve and petulance; nothing could be livelier, gayer, prettier, more loveable or more charming. This *pas*, in which Saint-Léon partners her admirably, will be all the rage. In particular, there is one moment of delightful grace and originality, when he places his foot against hers and they move together without separating, as though joined at the toes. Saint-Léon . . . rises so high that you can read the evening paper before he alights; beneath his feet, every plank becomes a spring-board, propelling him heavenwards. Well does he deserve the name of 'india-rubber man' that the English have bestowed upon him, for no rubber ball ever bounced more lightly."

The climax of the ballet, both scenically and dramatically, was the fourth and last scene, representing the fair at Piedigrotta, a quarter of Naples. Its atmosphere was sufficiently authentic to delight even a Neapolitan like Fiorentino. There were street hawkers selling their wares, *lazzaroni*, *zampognari*, clowns; and the air was filled with the chatter of castanets, the beating of tambourines, the ringing of bells, the splutter of rattles, and the Angelus pealing from a church tower. This was the background to the *Sicilienne* which had so charmed Gautier, one of the most brilliant *pas de caractère* in Cerrito's repertory which Saint-Léon had interpolated into this last scene.

Saint-Léon's enemies would have their listeners believe that there were other instances of plagiarism, no less flagrant for being less patent, in *Stella*: the ill-disposed Adice declared that he recognized two *ensembles* from Paolo Samengo's *Il Conte Pini*, as well as two extracts from a ballet by Perrot.

.   .   .   .

That summer, the Saint-Léons rented the Villa des Jardies, a country house a few miles outside Paris that had once belonged to Balzac, and where, more than thirty years later, another eminent Frenchman, Gambetta, was to die. One Sunday while they were there, the two dancers, at the request of the mayor and the *curé*, assisted at a High Mass for the poor of the parish, Saint-Léon accompanying the organist on his violin, and his wife helping to take the collection. When Cerrito was congratulated on her good work, she replied, "Oh, I am very happy! This is my finest success!"

Their holiday at last came to an end, and in the middle of September they again appeared at the Opéra, in *Le Violon du Diable*. While Cerrito was waiting for the performance to begin she went into the Director's private box behind the curtain. A gentleman with Roqueplan kissed her hand, and, as he did so, a button fell from his glove.

"A souvenir!" cried Cerrito, picking it from the floor. "I shall keep it!"

"A fine souvenir!" laughed the gentleman. "What will you do with it?"

"It will be my lucky charm. I am not an Italian for nothing," she said. "You have never given me anything before, not even a bouquet, and I am sure your first present will bring me luck."

When the gentleman saw her next, she was brimming over with excitement. Another of Roqueplan's guests that evening had been the Nepalese Ambassador, who had presented her with two magnificent bracelets sparkling with diamonds and other precious stones, a stroke of good fortune which she attributed to the little button.

Meanwhile her husband was preparing a new ballet for her, as well as finding time to rearrange the *divertissement* in *Guillaume*

Tell and to devise the dances for Auber's new opéra, *L'Enfant prodigue*. A man of decided opinions, Saint-Léon firmly believed that a choreographer, to merit being so called, should always write his own scenarios, but the French public had found the plots of his previous ballets so weakly constructed that the management had persuaded him to collaborate with Gautier in this new work. There was also to be a change of composer; in place of Saint-Léon's friend, Pugni, whose scores had found little more favour with the public than the scenarios, Benoist, the *chef de chant* at the Opéra and the composer of *Nisida*, had been chosen to write the music.

When Janin saw the first performance of the new ballet, *Pâquerette*, on January 15th, 1851, he found it hard to believe that the scenario had come from Gautier's pen, "so primitively is it stamped with that unbelievable nonsense and miraculous stupidity which characterize Italian ballets." It was certainly little better than Saint-Léon's previous efforts: perhaps Gautier had found it difficult to resist the exacting demands of the dynamic choreographer. The ballet traced the adventures of Pâquerette (Cerrito) and the two rivals for her hand, François (Saint-Léon) whom she favours, and Job (E. Coralli). Job's father is pressing François' father for the repayment of a loan, and when Job is unlucky in the draw for conscription, François enlists in his place to discharge the debt. Pâquerette follows the soldiers and herself tries to enlist, but Sergeant Bridoux (Berthier) sees through her ruse. After an altercation with the Sergeant, François is placed under arrest, but Pâquerette obtains the keys of his cell and rescues him. Bridoux, furious at being outwitted, orders the unfortunate Job, who has followed Pâquerette, to don uniform in François' place. The lovers escape to a tavern, where François falls asleep and dreams of Pâquerette. The soldiers arrive in search of the fugitives, but François throws snuff in their faces and escapes with Pâquerette once again. Finally all ends happily: François and Pâquerette have married and settled in Hungary, where François is pardoned after Pâquerette has uncovered a plot against the French commander.

A few days later, an apologia appeared above Gautier's signature in *La Presse*. "All the *pas* of Cerrito and Saint-Léon— we can say this without blushing—were greeted with enthusiastic applause. In the first scene, she is seen in a charming peasant costume, all lace and satin and flowers, which has the merit of being most adorably make-believe; in the second, she wears male clothes with the greatest of ease and grace; in the third, she appears in a haze of white gauze shimmering with golden spangles; and in the fourth, a smart Hungarian jacket clings tightly to her trim figure, and boots with resonant heels imprison her pretty feet. . . .

FANNY CERRITO AND ARTHUR SAINT-LÉON IN "PÂQUERETTE"
Caricature by Marcelin

"The action follows the dancer, and in three bounds Cerrito is far away. We start in French Flanders and finish in Hungary. Why Hungary? There seem to be two or three reasons, none of them very good, for this, but when one has seen that *pas*, sparkling like a dragonfly waltzing in a sunbeam, who can say that we were wrong to follow Cerrito to a town with a difficult spelling and which perhaps exists no more than the Bohemian sea-ports of which Shakespeare speaks? . . . There is also a dream scene which is not perhaps very logical, but it is no worse produced than the dreams in tragedies crowned by the *Institut*, and instead of being displayed in hexameters, is written in white tarlatan, in pink tights, in garlands of May lilies, in the gentle movements of pretty heads and beautifully rounded arms, in reeds that part to show charming smiles by the glow of an electric sun sprinkling a trail of rubies on a lake. . . ."

But neither Cerrito's wiles nor Saint-Leon's feats could remedy the weakness of the plot, and the ballet was dropped from the repertory after nine performances. It was remembered only by the famous *pirouette sur place* of Saint-Léon, taken very slowly, and the moving trap on which Cerrito slowly descended while crossing the stage in the dream scene. Another scenic effect, which would have been no less memorable, had to be abandoned before the first performance. Despléchin had planned to represent a lake by means of mirrors so placed that the dancers would appear to the audience to be gliding on the

ARTHUR SAINT-LÉON IN "PÂQUERETTE
Caricature by Marcelin

water, but the difficulties of manœuvring them proved too great. Twelve years later, the problem was to be solved and a similar arrangement of mirrors used in the second act of *Giselle*.

In March 1851, the Saint-Léons left Paris and travelled south to Madrid, to add yet another triumph to their career. They returned to Paris together in June, but a few weeks later Cerrito journeyed on to London alone, while her husband, who had signed an engagement as *premier maître de ballet* at the Opéra, remained behind in the French capital. Their marriage, and with it their stage partnership, had finally foundered.

.   .   .   .

Saint-Léon's first task on taking up his new appointment was to arrange a *divertissement* for the allegorical cantata, *Les*

Nations, which was first given on August 6th, 1851, in honour of the visit of the Lord Mayor of London and a deputation from the Great Exhibition. The ten dances of which it was made up were designed to show all the great nations united by Peace before a backcloth, painted by Despléchin, depicting the Crystal Palace in Hyde Park. Flora Fabbri, who shortly before had taken over the title-rôle in *Paquita*, was chosen for the principal character of Glory, recalling to France the military triumphs of her past and indicating Peace as the ideal now to be sought. It was a prophetic foreshadowing of the declaration that Louis Napoleon was to make the following year, on the eve of the Second Empire—"*L'Empire, c'est la paix!*"

On October 20th, four years to the day since he and Cerrito had made their début at the Opéra, Saint-Léon introduced to Paris the Russian dancer, Nadezhda Bogdanova, as Kathi in *La Vivandière*. Nadezhda, now a girl of seventeen, had come to Paris with her father on the recommendation of Fanny Elssler, who had seen her dance in Moscow. Shortly after their arrival, her young sister had fallen ill, and the doctor who called to attend her had been able to arrange for Nadezhda to dance at one of the Princesse Caroline Murat's *soirées*. This had led to an audition at the Opéra before Roqueplan, who had decided that she should study under Mazilier for a year before making her début in a *pas de deux*. Then Saint-Léon had seen her on his return from Spain and had taken her at once under his personal tuition to prepare her for taking over his wife's rôle in *La Vivandière*.

"The young Russian dancer," wrote Gautier after her début, "is small, well formed, with trim legs and dainty feet. Her expression is gay, refined, intelligent, with something arch and roguish that contrasts with the cold, stereotyped smile of commonplace *danseuses*. She is remarkably nimble, rapid, precise. Everything she does is clean, lively and correct; she darts and bounds hither and thither, then stops suddenly and turns back her head like a hunted gazelle, but one that well knows it can never be caught. Judging her in this ballet, and to borrow a musical term, Mlle Nadezhda is more successful in *presto* than in *adagio*. She is an alert, light and lively dancer, with an impish rather than a voluptuous grace, and who, while keeping within her nature, could cultivate a charming originality. She recalls neither Elssler, Taglioni nor Carlotta Grisi, but perhaps a little of Cerrito, which is doubtless due to the coaching of Saint-Léon. She is also a clever mime, with a keen feeling for a situation. Her success was not for a moment in doubt."

.   .   .   .   .   .

Despite Bogdanova's privilege of being the first to take over one of Cerrito's rôles at the Opéra, she was considered still too inexperienced to don the mantie that the great dancer had relinquished. The Opéra's choice of a successor had in fact already rested on a fifteen-year-old Italian prodigy, Olimpia Priora. The pupil of her father, Egidio Priora, a well-known *maître de ballet*, Olimpia had been acclaimed in Italy as a *danseuse noble* of rare distinction, combining the great qualities of both Taglioni and Elssler; her elevation was reputed to be loftier even than that of the first Sylphide.

She made her début at the Opéra on November 24th, 1851, in Mazilier's *Vert-Vert*, a ballet that had been in preparation for some considerable time, at the end of which Saint-Léon had intervened to revise the production and to arrange the concluding ball scene. The score, which contained a profusion of good melodies, was the work of two musicians in the Opéra orchestra, Deldevez who wrote the first half and was named first and Jean Baptiste Tolbecque. Deldevez had originally been asked to write the whole of the score, but Girard, the conductor, had prevailed upon Roqueplan to give his *protégé*, Tolbecque, an opportunity to show his worth. Deldevez had to accept this arrangement, but apparently did so with bad grace, for, to his disgust, Girard refused to excuse him from his normal duties with the orchestra on the first night.

The scenario had been written by Leuven, one of the authors of the popular *vaudeville* of the same name (first produced with Déjazet in 1841) on which the ballet was based; both works were inspired by Gresset's poem. The action of the ballet takes place in eighteenth-century France. The curtain rises on a merry flirtation between the Queen's maids of honour and the pages, but a sad note is soon introduced when Blanche (Priora), one of the maids, finds their pet parrot, Vert-Vert, dead in his cage. After the poor bird has been buried with mock solemnity in the garden, the question arises, who is to take its place in their affections? Their choice falls on the young nephew of their governess (Plunkett), a pretty lad, but all too soon comes word from his mother summoning him home. Accompanied by his tutor (Berthier), the new Vert-Vert sets out on his journey, followed at a distance by Blanche, who has fallen in love with him.

The old tutor and his charge reach an inn, where they find a troupe of strolling players preparing to present a harlequinade.

ADELINE PLUNKETT IN "VERT-VERT"
Caricature by Marcelin

Soon Blanche arrives, and the lovers are reunited. Meanwhile, the troupe is in a state of consternation, for their leading dancer has injured her leg. At Vert-Vert's suggestion, Blanche takes the lamed dancer's place, until her escapade is brought to an end by the arrival of the police to arrest her.

Blanche is taken back to Fontainebleau in disgrace. Her companions beg their governess to forgive her, and when she refuses, become rebellious. Distant strains of music are heard, announcing the opening of the ball at which they were to dance the quadrille, but which now, as a punishment, they have been forbidden to attend. When their governess has left them, Vert-Vert steals into the dormitory with the pages, and a gay, mock battle ensues. Suddenly the governess returns. But her anger is at last appeased and the maids forgiven, and the curtain finally falls on the brilliant scene of the ball.

The ballet scarcely flagged during the whole three and a half hours of its first performance. Its whimsical little plot sufficed to connect the series of vivid scenes and amusing episodes—the mock funeral procession, the harlequinade, the entrance of Vert-Vert and the pages into the maids' dormitory, the ball—giving the effect, not of a smoothly developing story, but rather of the brilliant but fleeting impressions of a dream. The interest was sustained still further by the mounting intensity, both in quantity and spirit, of the dancing. The first act contained a *pas seul* by Priora; the second the harlequinade, with *pas de deux* by Priora and Lucien Petipa, and Plunkett and Beauchet; while the ball scene of the last act contained the most animated choreography of all, including a *valse hongroise* by Bogdanova and Fuchs, and a charming choreographic episode, *Le Fruit défendu*, in which Plunkett and Priora danced in the guise of a shepherd and shepherdess.

The object of the greatest curiosity that evening was, of course, Olimpia Priora. She was a striking girl in appearance, tall and well proportioned, and wonderfully supple and elegant in her movements. She was not strictly beautiful: her features were too semitic in their mould, the set of her eyes too oriental, and the jet-black abundance of her hair was unfortunately repeated in her eyebrows, which were so thick as to appear artificially darkened, and in a silky down that shaded her upper lip. Though the rôle of Blanche suited neither her serious temperament nor her classical style, she awakened great enthusiasm among the critics. "Her dancing," wrote Gautier, "is vigorous, precise, correct. In particular, she has an extraordinary elevation and rises very high without gathering force with her arms and solely by her spring. Her *entrechats* are beaten cleanly; her *pointes* stab the stage like arrow-heads. In *temps penchés*, she never trembles; her body might be supported by a marble pillar. And she makes the three *tours* as quickly and freely as a man. The originality of her style consists of a certain masculine vigour, tempered by an extreme flexibility in 'renversements' and 'poses contrariés.' Her success was decided from the first *pas*, and grew act by act to finish with a real ovation. It is the most brilliant ballet début that we have seen for a long time, and we believe that the pleiad of Taglioni, Elssler, Carlotta Grisi and Cerrito is about to be enriched by a new star."

Adeline Plunkett was much more happily cast in the rôle of Vert-Vert, and her interpretation noticeably improved after

OLIMPIA PRIORA IN "VERT-VERT"
Caricature by Marcelin

the first few performances. "She belongs to the pier-glass and the gouache fan," wrote Gautier. "She was charming. . . . Impossible to dream of a little fellow daintier, more roguish, more arch, more prettily petulant than she." Gautier's observant eye was also caught by the *corps de ballet*, which he noticed had been rejuvenated. "In the absence of talent," he recorded with a certain satisfaction, "one at least sees fresh faces and pretty figures."

.   .   .   .

To augment Priora's reputation as a dancer in the Taglioni manner, Saint-Léon revived *La Sylphide* for her on March 5th,

1852, taking himself the rôle of James Reuben, with Louise Taglioni as Effie and Berthier as Gurn. Priora's assumption of the title-rôle, so inseparably associated with Marie Taglioni, was unfortunate, for it dulled the favourable impression she had created in *Vert-Vert*. She lacked the lightness and the delicacy of feature and figure of her illustrious predecessor; and as Fiorentino watched her, he seemed to see another Sylphide hovering above her, "an apparition, a memory, a dream," and he begged her not to disturb his illusions.

It was Saint-Léon who was most at fault. Because the original choreography afforded the male dancer little opportunity for display, he made several innovations which shocked those to whom this ballet was sacrosanct. He introduced *pirouettes* of astonishing duration and rigidity, such as only he could perform, and leapt to incalculable heights. Also, he lightened the interpretation of his rôle, particularly in the *pas de trois* for the Sylphide, Effie and James in Act I—one of the most poetical passages in the ballet—in which he expressed, almost comically, the confusion and embarrassment of a man buffeted hither and thither between two women, instead of the inner struggle between reality and the ideal, which was what the *pas* was originally designed to convey. There were other causes for complaint too. "When the dancer is on the stage, the *maître de ballet* should remain in the wings," Fiorentino remarked. "Through force of habit and excess of zeal, Saint-Léon continues to command the crowd, muttering rebukes and restraining the high-spirited; he is everywhere giving orders, holding his class in public."

It was indeed almost a parody, and the illusion was further shattered in the second act, when, as a result of a faulty wire, an unfortunate sylphide was kept suspended for several minutes many feet above the stage. The audience were far more terrified than she, for while they were clamouring for the curtain to be lowered, she was smiling broadly back at them, apparently quite in her element.

A few months after this revival, Schneitzhœffer, who had composed the score of the ballet, and whose name was so difficult for the Parisians to pronounce, died in an asylum in Montmartre.

·   ·   ·   ·   ·   ·   ·

Meanwhile, another pupil of Saint-Léon, Héloïse Guérinot, using the stage name of Regina Forli, had appeared in the leading rôle of *Le Violon du Diable* on February 6th, 1852. Though billed as a début, this was not her first appearance on the Opéra stage, for, as a child, she had taken part in *La Gipsy* thirteen years before, appearing in the first act as Sarah Campbell, the rôle which Fanny Elssler played in the second and third acts. Jules Janin now saw her as "a bounding, roguish little girl with an alert mien, a small bust, and a beguiling smile. She is very young, very Italian looking, and very artful, with a thousand fond ways intended for the gentlemen of the pit." "Mlle Regina," wrote another observer, "appears to run or walk, as she pleases, very dexterously on the tips of her toes. She was much applauded for that, which we consequently took to be one of the beauties of the art of dancing."

Within the next twelve months, she added three of the greatest rôles in ballet to her small repertory: the title-rôle of *La Sylphide*, which she danced with some success during a short engagement in London in the summer; Giselle, which she danced at the Opéra for the first time on August 11th; and, on February 2nd, 1853, the leading rôle in *La Péri*. In all three parts she had to contend with memories, still fresh in the minds of the audience, of their illustrious creators, Taglioni and Carlotta Grisi; but it was a distinction nevertheless to be chosen as Grisi's successor in her greatest rôle, that of Giselle, for only one other dancer had shared it with her at the Opéra—Élisa Bellon, who had played it on two occasions only in 1842.

Ciceri's scenery, which had been in use for eleven years, was now showing signs of wear. "The sky needs a touch of the broom," wrote Gautier, "the yellow vine leaves have fallen and whirl around like the golden dust of Dantzig brandy, and the castle stands precariously on its rock and will soon tumble headlong into the valley if not repaired with a few strokes of the brush. Giselle has only three or four pieces of straw to her roof, and what straw! . . . The water of the lake is nearly dry, the reeds are becoming discoloured thongs; the moonlight has lost its mystery. But all this is forgotten when the young dancer, lively and quick, darts forward from the faded wings.

"Mlle Regina Forli has features of a charming refinement, skin of an opal transparency, a slender and delicate body, and a chaste and aerial style of dancing, which allows her to attack this rôle that Carlotta Grisi's interpretation rendered almost impossible. Also, she mimes the scenes that demand passion with great intelligence and sensitiveness. We were glad to see Petipa again, and regretted the absence of Adèle Dumilâtre, that beautiful Queen of the Wilis, a moonbeam shaded with gauze, and of Mlle Forster, who was so noble and charming a huntress [in the rôle of Bathilde]."

Unfortunately, Regina Forli had already reached the summit of her ability. Although her engagement was renewed for a further year in the winter of 1854, no further opportunities came her way. In time she became disheartened, and one day in the summer of 1855, she failed to appear at rehearsal and sent a sad little note to tell Mazilier she had decided to abandon her career as a dancer.

.   .   .   .

Next, Saint-Léon concentrated his attention on the *divertissement* in Halévy's grand opera, *Le Juif errant*, which was presented at the Opéra, after many months of preparation, on April 23rd, 1852. The production was on a gigantic scale: the eight scenes ranged from Antwerp and Constantinople in this world to the Valley of Jehoshaphet in the next, where the Destroying Angel shows visions of both Heaven and Hell to the Wandering Jew. The *divertissement* was set in Act III, in the Imperial Palace of Constantinople, the dances being woven into a slight episode of a shepherd trying to escape from a swarm of bees and charming them by the tones of his pipe. The rôle of the shepherd Aristée was created by Mérante, and Louise Taglioni and Bogdanova led the bees. *Les Abeilles*, as it was called, was one of Saint-Léon's most successful *divertissements*; later he produced it in St. Petersburg, Vienna, Budapest, Lisbon, Dresden, Königsberg and Magdeburg, and in the summer of 1866 brought it back to the Opéra, interpolating it into a revival of Halévy's *La Juive*, with Eugénie Fiocre as Aristée and Fioretti and Annette Mérante as the principal bees.

.   .   .   .

Saint-Léon's energy knew no bounds. In addition to his triple duties at the Opéra as dancer, *maître de ballet* and *professeur de la classe de perfectionnement*, he was preparing a

Stella, Act II, Scene II
La Sicilienne

Stella, Act II, Scene II
The Fair at Piedigrotta

Nadezhda Bogdanova in *La Vivandière*

learned treatise on a method of dance notation. The work was published in the winter of 1852, under the title of *La Sténochorégraphie*, and was dedicated to the Tsar, who showed his appreciation the following spring by giving the author a

PART OF THE PAS DE SIX FROM "LA VIVANDIÈRE", RECORDED IN SAINT-LÉON'S STENOCHOREOGRAPHIC SYSTEM OF DANCE NOTATION

diamond ring. Though no acknowledgment was made, Saint-Léon may have founded his method on one used by his teacher, Albert: Adice, for what his word may be worth, contended that Albert realized the deficiences of his system and abandoned it, and that Saint-Léon, wishing to add to his reputation by a display of erudition, resurrected it and published it as an original work. In spite of his declared intention of using it to record all his ballets, Saint-Léon seems never to have found time to commit to paper more than the *pas de six* from *La Vivandière*, which was published in the book to illustrate the application of the method. It was not immediately abandoned, however, for in his proposal to set up a *Conservatoire de la Danse*, which he expounded in a pamphlet published in Lisbon in 1856, Saint-Léon suggested that the pupils should all learn *sténochorégraphie* in an intermediate class before passing to the *classe de perfectionnement*.

. . . .

After an absence of more than eighteen months, Fanny Cerrito reappeared at the Opéra towards the end of October 1852, dancing with her husband in the brilliant last scene of *Stella* at a gala performance attended by Louis Napoleon and the Arab chieftain, Abd-el-Kader. Louis Napoleon had seen her often before, not only during his Presidency in Paris, but earlier when he was an exile in London; once, in the summer of 1847, he had figured with her in a quadrille at one of Mr. Lumley's *fêtes champêtres* in Fulham. At that time, Louis Napoleon had been regarded, by all save his staunch followers, as a ridiculous adventurer, but now, little more than five years later, the ambition towards which he had striven so purposefully was on the point of being realized. Only a few days before, he had made a triumphant entry into Paris after a tour of the provinces, during which he had everywhere been acclaimed as the saviour of the country and, although the official proclamation was not to come until December 1st, Emperor of the French. He thus had every reason to be pleased on this evening of Cerrito's return, and after the performance was over, sent gifts to the principal dancers: jewelled brooches for Cerrito, Priora and Plunkett, and bracelets for Louise Taglioni and Bogdanova.

Cerrito owed her re-engagement largely to the influence of Louis Véron and Auguste Romieu, the Director of Fine Arts. She had so set her heart on reappearing at the Opéra, that she had vowed to present a silver chalice to the chapel of the Blessed Virgin at the church of Notre-Dame de Lorette when her wish was granted. She kept her promise, and it was Romieu himself who visited the *curé* to arrange for the gift to be accepted.

Under the terms of her new contract, she was to dance at the Opéra for eight months in each of the two following years, at a monthly salary of 3,000 francs, with bonuses of 200 francs for all performances after the sixth in any one month. There was little delay in presenting her in a new ballet. On December 29th, 1852, she created the title-rôle in *Orfa*, a ballet arranged, not by her husband, but by Mazilier, to a scenario by Henry Trianon and a score by Adolphe Adam.

Gautier was delighted at the original choice of Iceland as the setting. The curtain rose on a snowy plain near Reykjavic, with Mount Hecla in the distance, and in the foreground the altar and statue of Loki (Berthier), the God of Fire, whose cult is being superseded by the more advanced creed of Odin. Orfa (Cerrito) and her *fiancé*, Lodbrog (L. Petipa), come to celebrate their approaching wedding around a welcoming fire. Seeing an old man (Lenfant) being teased by the crowd, Lodbrog invites him to sit by the fire and join in their rejoicing. The sound of a harp is heard, as the old man gratefully extends his hand over Lodbrog's head and vanishes. The priests of Loki emerge to perform the marriage ceremony. As they are about to give their blessing, the statue hurls shafts of lightning into the air. The priests refuse to continue under such an augury. Lodbrog angrily shakes his fist at the statue, which begins to glow. Orfa is irresistibly drawn to the pedestal, and is swallowed into the earth with the statue amid a burst of flames. The old man suddenly reappears, and gives Lodbrog a golden arrow to enable him to rescue his beloved, pointing the way to the distant mountain.

The second act is laid in the palace of Loki in the heart of the mountain. A magnificent stairway leads to the crater; all around are flowers and trees glittering with jewels and precious metals. Loki enters carrying Orfa, whom he lays on a couch encrusted with diamonds. At a sign from him, she regains consciousness. The Seven Passions and Vices (Bogdanova, L. Marquet, M. Marquet, Rousseau, Mathé, Jendron, Féneux) are then summoned to break down her resistance. While they are exercising their wiles, Lodbrog appears at the top of the stairway and descends, scattering the guards with the magic arrow. Loki retaliates by imprisoning Orfa in a tuft of golden reeds; then, cursing angrily, vanishes into the ground. The mysterious old man reappears, and makes the despairing Lodbrog touch the reeds with his arrow. As he does so, they part and Orfa is released. Orfa then herself takes the arrow, with which she restores to their natural shape many young girls whom Loki had transformed into rocks and flowers. After the old man has revealed himself as the god Odin, the backcloth rises on the apotheosis of Valhalla, lit by electric light. Odin mounts the stairway to his throne, where he sits surrounded by his family and lesser deities to give his blessing to the two lovers.

When Fanny Cerrito made her first entrance, reclining indolently in her sleigh amid a sea of furs, her golden hair glinting in the bright gas-light, a spontaneous burst of applause broke out from all parts of the house. Never had she looked lovelier; "never," wrote her admirer, Fiorentino, "did Canova, Pradier or Tenerani chisel a more perfect or more voluptuous beauty." Her powers and her charm certainly showed no diminution. Those distinctive qualities which so characterized her style—her nonchalance and her petulance, her softness, her languor, her purity of line—were unimpaired by the absence of her usual choreographer and partner. *Orfa*, however, was of a very different nature, both choreographically and structurally, to the ballets that Saint-Léon had invented for her, and at times she seemed a little ill at ease in her part. Janin noticed this, and wrote: "Mme Cerrito is certainly not a dancer to turn up one's nose at, but she does not quite grasp the meaning of these great works. She is an Italian, a little plump and pretty, and better made for dancing a light *pas de deux* with a strong partner, who can support her at difficult moments, than to bear the heavy burden of such a powerful composition."

This was the first time that Cerrito had danced at the Opéra to the music of Adolphe Adam, whose latest score went far to assure the ballet's success. The sets were as magnificent as the audiences of the Opéra had come to expect. The scenery for the second act, the subterranean palace, with its wide golden stairway descending from the heights, and the sparkling of jewels amid clusters of exotic foliage, dazzled and at the same time shocked Jules Janin. "Twenty years ago," he remarked, "all Paris swore by *La Sylphide*, and yet there were not twenty-four sous' worth of diamonds in *La Sylphide*, nor in *La Fille du Danube* either! Oh! the blunderers that bring the Bourse and California to the Opéra!"

.　　.　　.　　.　　.　　.

While Cerrito was accustoming herself to Mazilier's choreography, Saint-Léon was preparing another of his pupils, Mathilde Besson, for her début in a revival of the old ballet, *La Fille mal gardée*. Mathilde Besson, a slender girl with delicate features and light brown hair, who might have stepped from a picture by Greuze, made her appearance in the rôle of Lise on February 23rd, 1853, and found herself faced with the almost impossible task of contending with the memory of Fanny Elssler, who had once played it with a depth and mystery which had accorded strangely with the apparent frivolity of the ballet's subject. Mathilde Besson, however, made a good showing: one critic compared her style to that of Adèle Dumilâtre, and Gautier praised her interpretation. "She is the *fille mal gardée* herself," he wrote. "She has everything the rôle requires—youth, a simple coquetry, modest boldness, charming impudence, a light and rapid step. Even her emotions served her well, and if she did not die of fright at her début, as she told me she would when she came to see me, her uneasiness was visible to all and gained her general indulgence, particularly since she held herself firmly on her *pointes*, made no blunders, and betrayed her anxiety only by the pallor of her features."

She was well supported in her ordeal. Lucien Petipa, in the rôle of Colin, partnered her with the assurance of the experienced dancer he was, although a certain heaviness in physique and movement was beginning to be noticed, such as creeps on men with the approach of middle age. Berthier's interpretation of the rôle of Mère Simon as a peevish, fidgety old woman was very comical, if a trifle exaggerated, yet it by no means overshadowed Louis Petit's rendering of that of Alain. "M. Petit," wrote Gautier, "whose name seems to be an antiphrase, for he is one of the tallest of mortals, gave to the character of the imbecile who is borne skywards by his umbrella, the drollest aspect of a cardboard figure. His every joint seemed retained only by a knot of thread, so incredible were the antics of which he delivered himself."

This revival of *La Fille mal gardée* was not entirely successful. "Sometimes," explained Gautier, "time imparts to the light works of another age an old-fashioned grace that is full of charm, an atmosphere of the past that is very pleasing to the eye and the heart. *La Fille mal gardée* is a case in point. By present choreographic standards, this ballet errs because of the in-genuousness of its theme, the poverty of its spectacle, the childish puerility of its dancing, which almost border on the ridiculous, but it nevertheless gives pleasure, and one likes to see it now and again, just as one does the aquatints of Demarne and Carle Vernet."

.   .   .   .

In the spring of 1853, Mazilier began to prepare a new ballet for Priora, but almost at once had to suspend his rehearsals to comply with Roqueplan's instructions to add another major feminine rôle for Marie Guy-Stéphan, who had just been engaged, it was reported, "*par ordre supérieur.*" The newcomer had danced for many seasons in Madrid and had made a study of Spanish dancing, which Mazilier had to incorporate as best he could in a choreography already partly conceived and designed to accord with a setting of Rome in the reign of Nero. Fortunately there was time enough for this revision, and for a most thorough preparation too, for the Opéra closed its doors for three months in the summer for redecoration of the interior. When the first performance of the new ballet, *Aelia et Mysis*, was at length given on September 21st, 1853, three Spanish ladies of the very highest distinction were present in the theatre to witness the début of Marie Guy-Stéphan: Queen María Cristina of Spain; the Empress Eugénie, whom Napoleon III had married the previous January; and Eugénie's sister, the Duchess of Alba.

The first act of the ballet was set in the *atrium* of the Consul Messala's villa in Ostia, overlooking the sea. Messala's daughter, Aelia (Priora), is discovered reclining on an ivory couch, sad at heart ("like a vapid English miss," said Gautier) and unamused by the clowning of the slave Scurra (Berthier). Costly presents are brought, sent by Tigrane, Prince of Pontus, whom her father has chosen as her future husband, but these awaken no interest or pleasure in her. A beat of the gong then summons Euclio (L. Petipa) and his company of musicians and dancers, who are to take part in the *atellana* during the betrothal ceremony. Euclio bids his company to leave him, but Mysis (Guy-Stéphan), a Thessalian dancer, hesitates, as though apprehensive, before obeying her master's command. Left alone, Euclio and Aelia begin to rehearse the dance they are to perform together at the coming ceremony. Aelia is disturbed at first by its passionate nature, then gradually responds in the realization of her love for Euclio. Mysis, watching them unobserved, divines their secret. She interrupts their dance, and in her jealousy threatens to betray them unless Euclio promises to return with her to Thessaly immediately after the *atellana*. The company then assembles: Messala (Lenfant), Tigrane (L. Mérante) and his suite, the High Priestess (L. Marquet), and finally Scurra, who is merry with wine. After Mysis has danced (with Beauchet) her *pas gaditan*, the *atellana*, entitled *Veneris Nuptiae*, the wedding of Venus, is announced.

It is a mythological *divertissement*, opening with the rising of massive volcanic rocks slowly from the ground. Out of one of these appears Vulcan (Berthier), who summons the Cyclops, and then, tired of the life he leads, begs Jupiter to allow him to take a wife. Jupiter descends from the skies on an eagle and throws a handful of roses into the waves, from which Venus (Priora) emerges in a shell, attended by Cupid (Letourneur) and the Graces (L. Taglioni, Forli, Bogdanova). Cupid, seeing that the grotesque Vulcan holds no attraction for Venus, summons the virile Mars (L. Petipa). Then follows the *pas de Mars et Vénus*, which Aelia and Euclio have been seen rehearsing. Its significance is so striking that Tigrane rises from his chair in anger, and Mysis reveals the lovers' secret. Ordered to explain, Aelia declares her love for Euclio. Messala flies into a rage. Amid a hail of stones and arrows, Euclio dives into the sea, while Aelia is commanded by her father to become a Vestal Virgin.

The second act takes place in the sacred forest of the Vestals, which no man may enter on pain of death. Despléchin's set for this act was a masterpiece. "Neither Poussin nor Bellel, the great masters of landscape painting, could have produced a nobler composition," wrote Gautier. "Here is antiquity in all its unfathomable mystery." After the High Priestess has reminded Aelia of her father's command, Mysis appears bearing magic herbs which inform the Vestals that she is initiated into the sacred mysteries. She tells them that Euclio has perished. Invited to participate in the evening's festival, she shows them the dances of her country. Aelia suddenly sees Scurra's head appear above the surrounding wall, and from a note which he throws to her, learns that Euclio lives. Overjoyed, she joins in the dancing. Euclio and Scurra enter the holy place by a rope ladder, but they are observed by Mysis, who cuts the cords, thus destroying all hope of their escape. Euclio seizes a sacrificial knife to kill Mysis, but Aelia restrains him and, giving the weapon to Mysis, offers to die herself, so that Mysis and Euclio can escape together. Moved by Aelia's unselfish devotion, Mysis conceals the men in the *sacellum* and then dances before the Vestals to distract their attention. The High Priestess seizes a torch to light the sacred fire, and discovers the intruders. She invokes the anger of the goddess Vesta. Amid thunder and lightning, flames appear,[1] towards which the two men are dragged to be put to death. Aelia begs for mercy to be shown to them, then runs to the altar, dons the sacred veil, and, taking the pontifical branch from the High Priestess's hand, holds it above their heads, as they walk through the great bronze gates, which open before them, to freedom. Exhausted by her sacrifice, Aelia falls lifeless at the foot of the altar as the curtain falls.

Olimpia Priora and Marie Guy-Stéphan were both seen to good advantage in this strong drama. The rôle of Aelia suited Priora much better than had those in *Vert-Vert* and *La Sylphide*. With her classic profile, such as might have adorned an antique cameo, her marble-smooth complexion and her hair shining brilliantly as a raven's wing, she gave a deeply moving interpretation of the tragic young patrician girl. Her miming was more expressive, more impassioned than had been seen at the Opéra for a long time, and her dancing was distinguished by the soft grace of her poses, her elevation, her *ballon* and her precision. Marie Guy-Stéphan was no less applauded, and the number of bouquets which were thrown at her feet bore witness to her triumph. The only concession Mazilier had made to her particular style was in the *pas gaditan*, to which he had imparted a certain Spanish flavour; in the remainder of the ballet, she took the opportunity of displaying a no less remarkable talent as a *danseuse noble*. Her speed and agility were extraordinary. "The eye can hardly follow her," wrote

---

[1] It was in *Aelia et Mysis* that the effect known as luminous fountains was employed for the first time at the Opéra. Electric light was focussed down a stream of water, which, when broken, appeared to sparkle with little flashes of light. The apparatus to achieve this effect is described in J. Duboscq's *Catalogue des appareils employés pour la production des phénomènes physiques au théâtre* (Paris, 1877).

Caterina Beretta in *Les Vêpres siciliennes*

Olimpia Priora

Sketch for the setting of *Vert-Vert*,
Act III, Scene I

Orfa, Act I

Aelia et Mysis, Act II

Design by Despléchin for *Jovita*,
Scene I

Fanny Cerrito as Fenella in
La Muette de Portici

Fiorentino. "She is a whirlwind, a flame, a flash of lightning. She dazzles, fascinates, triumphs, before there is time to realize the charm she exercises and the unbelievable movements of her small fairy feet."

Aelia et Mysis was considered by many contemporaries to be one of Mazilier's finest ballets. For Gautier, it was a welcome departure from the standardized type of Romantic ballet, with its preoccupation with Germanic legend, while Janin, a real lover of the classics, found the subject one after his own heart and declared that a more moving climax had not been seen since *La Sylphide*. *Aelia et Mysis* was to be one of the first of several ballets devised by Mazilier in the grand manner. Its emphasis lay on the mimed drama, the dances being introduced only as occasion offered, in the *atellana* in the first act and in the dances of Aelia and Mysis before the Vestals in the second. In this, Mazilier was perhaps influenced by contemporary Italian choreography, which was ambitiously striving to express in dance and mime plots of a complexity unknown in French ballet, but at the same time debasing the dance, for in Italy the dramatic portion of these grand ballets was often confided to mimes. Guided by French taste, Mazilier was to be more moderate, and more successful, in his approach. The more exaggerated Italian style of mime would never have found favour in Paris, while the separation of the functions of mime and dancer in France was certainly unthinkable when the Opéra secured the services of Carolina Rosati, whose talent as an actress equalled, if it did not exceed, her quality as a dancer.

THE ADVENT OF ROSATI

CAROLINA ROSATI was in her prime as a dancer when Roqueplan succeeded in engaging her, at his third attempt, in the
spring of 1853. Born at Bologna on December 13th, 1826, and
taught by some of the finest masters in Italy, Antonia Torelli,
Giovanni Briol and Carlo Blasis, she had gained a reputation
throughout the peninsula at an early age, first under her
maiden name of Galletti, and later, becoming the wife of the
dancer Francesco Rosati, under her married name. During
her first London season in the summer of 1847, Escudier, the
music agent, wrote from the English capital, urging Roqueplan
to cross the Channel at once to see her. As a result, Duponchel,
Roqueplan's partner, who was in London coming to terms
with Saint-Léon and Cerrito, sounded Lumley about engaging
Rosati too. Lumley received Duponchel's proposals with little
enthusiasm, and, by pleading pressure of business, managed
to postpone discussion until Duponchel returned to Paris. The
matter was then continued somewhat half-heartedly by
correspondence. But Lumley's insistence that he should be
given full details of the rôle chosen for Rosati's début, and that
she should make her appearance before Cerrito, were considered
unreasonable, and negotiations languished. She was not
forgotten, however, for when she happened to be in Paris in
1849, Roqueplan approached her a second time, offering her a
pas in the opera *Jérusalem*, but she sensibly refused and instead
devoted her visit to studying under Gosselin.

Rosati's Paris début took place little more than a year later,
on February 25th, 1851, at the Théâtre Italien, at that time
under Lumley's management, where she played Ariele, the
mime rôle created by Carlotta Grisi in London the summer
before, in Halévy's opera, *La Tempesta*. Luck seemed against
her, for at the first performance she caught her foot in a trap
and badly bruised her knee in falling, while the opera itself was
received coolly and given only eight times. Now, in 1853,
she had once again returned to Paris, but this time well provided

with amulets to ward off the influence of the "evil eye" which she suspected to have been the cause of her former misfortune. Apparently, however, her superstition had its limits, for her début at the Opéra, in Mazilier's ballet, *Jovita*, took place, of all days, on a Friday—November 11th, 1853.

Mazilier had chosen Mexico in the seventeenth century as the setting for his new ballet. Jovita (Rosati), the daughter of a rich planter, and Don Altamirano (L. Mérante), a young

CAROLINA ROSATI IN "LA TEMPESTA"
Caricature by Marcelin

lieutenant, are in love, but the girl's father (Lenfant) will not consent to their marriage until Altamirano has been promoted. To earn his captaincy, therefore, Altamirano plans to capture the brigand chief Zubillaga, and agrees to accompany an old man who offers to lead him to the villain's retreat. As they are setting out, the old man suddenly throws off his disguise and reveals himself as none other than Zubillaga (L. Petipa). After plundering the plantation, the brigands carry off Altamirano to hold him to ransom. Bent on rescuing her lover, and disguised as a gipsy, Jovita follows the brigands to the mountain grotto which they have made their camp. She manages to allay their suspicions until the opportunity arises of cutting Altamirano's cords. Then she sets fire to the store of gunpowder. There is a terrific explosion as the rock face collapses, carrying with it Zubillaga and his brigands. In the last scene, Jovita and Altamirano are received in triumph by the Viceroy, who finally grants her request by promoting her lover to the rank of captain.

The merits of the ballet and the efforts of the supporting cast were quite overshadowed by the triumphant début of Rosati, and received only scant attention from the critics. The action was simple and easily understood; the music, by Théodore Labarre, the harpist, carefully orchestrated and containing many charming melodies; the sets, designed, painted and constructed in the usual masterly fashion. An important contribution to the theatrical appeal of the work was made by Victor Sacré, the chief machinist,[1] who devised the collapse of the grotto at the end of the second scene, producing a most realistic and terrifying effect. Mazilier's choreography was also praised, particularly a very original and comic kicking dance performed by Mme Dominique and Berthier, and the ensembles, so often before the weakness of his choreographic compositions.

It was Rosati's evening. "La Rosati," wrote Gautier "(let us say so at once, for the thing is becoming a rarity) is an excellent mime, recalling Elssler in the expressive mobility of her features, the precision of her gestures, the rightness of her attitudes. Her miming is clear, lively, impassioned, and always easily intelligible; she knows how to render her thoughts visible, and what is passing through her mind is at once reflected in her expression. As for her person, she is an Italian in every sense of the word: abundant black hair, black eyes, black eyebrows, an olive complexion that whitens in a strong light, and something savouring of antiquity in the sinews of her neck and the full, firm lines of her bust and arms; her legs, somewhat strongly built, end in small, sensitive feet, well made and well arched, with delicate ankles and toes of steel that, in temps de pointe, pierce the ground like javelins. And she has a sort of robust, vivacious elegance that bears no resemblance to the arch graces and mincing airs of the danseuse d'école. As a dancer,

[1] The position of chief machinist was a very important one. He not only was in command of all the machinists and stage hands, but often had to invent novel and spectacular stage effects and be responsible for their smooth and safe working. The collapse of the grotto in Jovita (1853), the shipwreck in Le Corsaire (1856), the two-tier set in Marco Spada (1857), and the lake in Giselle (1863 revival), were examples of the demands made upon him. Sacré was chief machinist at the Opéra from 1847 to 1872.

she has not much elevation, but all she does is quick and precise, and rendered with a sure touch and an execution beyond reproach. Her *pas* in the first scene, which in style is related to the *Jaleo* and the *Cachucha*, includes two or three very quick and difficult movements that are admirably performed; the *pas de fusil*, consisting mainly of contrasted poses and attitudes, furnished her with a happy opportunity to develop her qualities of speed and precision. In the very pretty, very captivating and very brilliant *pas du tambour de basque*, we would have liked more *brio* and bustle. She was not altogether at ease in the manipulation of the *tambour de basque*. . . . A dancer as agile and sensitive to rhythm as she should have flashed like lightning amid that tornado of noise; but the *pas*, such as it is, gave pleasure none the less, and the purely Spanish regret which we express here was not shared by the public. You must have seen the *pandero* vibrating in the hands of a *gitana* from Albaicín or the Barrio de Triana for my allusion to be fully understood. La Rosati received the most gratifying welcome from the Parisian public, and was recalled with loud cries after the fall of the curtain."

Even the critics were carried away. Fiorentino spoke of "her sprightly vivacity and a lightness of a bird skimming over the ground," and, like Gautier, was reminded of Fanny Elssler. In Rosati's style he remarked "energy and vigour in her *pointe* work, grace, harmony and suppleness in the movements of her body, amplitude and lightness in covering the stage, cleanly beaten *entrechats* and rapid *pirouettes*, and, in the final *stretta* [a sequence of *cabrioles*], a fury, a bravura, a turbulence such as to make one giddy." As a mime, she impressed him most of all in the concluding moments of the first scene, when she conveyed her anguish and sadness at the loss of her lover, her courageous resolution to rescue him, and the joy she anticipated in having him back—"a masterpiece of truth and passion; mobility of features and eloquence of regard could not possibly be carried further."

Only Janin was at all critical. "La Rosati," he wrote, "has succeeded by her very daring and her disregard of convention. She is beyond all analogy. She dances at our risk and peril. And so much the worse for us if we are taken in, for it is just another step towards the ruin and decadence of that fine art of the dance as it was understood in the days of our great *danseuses*."

Roqueplan lost no time in securing Rosati's services at the

Opéra for a further two years. Under her current engagement, which was due to expire at the end of November 1854, she stood to receive 3,500 francs a month in salary and bonuses, a figure which was increased to 5,000 francs for the term of her new contract. Such generosity must have made it impossible for her to refuse his request that she should stay on in Paris until the middle of December, although she was under contract to appear in Turin, in a new ballet, early in the New Year.

Her farewell performance at the Opéra, just before her departure for Italy, was such a triumph that it seemed incredible that she had made her début there only one month before. "The bouquets fell in avalanches," wrote Gautier, "and the dancer would have remained entombed beneath this scented shower, had not a swarm of supers been occupied in clearing the stage and making lanes amid this thick bed of flowers. . . . In a few performances, this charming artiste has captivated the public, for she combines her qualities as a dancer—clarity, precision, quickness—with a classical perfection of detail and the most expressive miming. She acts even better than she dances. She renders to perfection love, joy, surprise, terror, the whole gamut of human emotions. . . . With La Rosati, the spectator never loses sight of the theme, and follows the action through the delicate tracery of her *entrechats* and *pirouettes*."

.   .   .   .

Fanny Cerrito soon discovered how seriously her supremacy was threatened by the appearance of this new star when, in the spring of 1854, she learnt that the Prefect of the Seine had engaged Rosati to play the leading rôle in a *divertissement* to be given during a fête at the Hôtel de Ville. Deeply offended at being passed over, Cerrito appealed to the Minister of State, and it was only as a result of his intervention that she was given a part in this entertainment of equal importance to that of her more youthful colleague.

She had on more than one occasion in her career given proof of her talents as a choreographer, but she had not so far had the honour of staging a ballet at the Opéra. When Roqueplan suggested that she should both produce and appear in the next new ballet, she assented very readily, not only because of the renown which it might bring her, but also perhaps because she would be treading ground where she need not fear the rivalry of Rosati. Again, with Saint-Léon's services no longer available she may well have thought that only she could do herself justice by bringing her qualities as a dancer into full relief.

The task before her, as she soon found out, was far from easy. Unaccustomed to working under a woman, the company showed themselves obviously reluctant to accept her authority, and the two months of preparation was a time of great trial for her. Often a pose had to be rehearsed ten or twenty times before anything like the desired result was achieved.

"But *madame*," they would cry, "it is impossible to dance this *pas*! We cannot raise our legs so high!"

"That is because you do not want to," retorted Cerrito.

"Then let us see you do it yourself," came back the insolent reply.

To play the leading rôle of a sinister nobleman with hypnotic powers, Cerrito had brought with her from London Girolamo di Mattia, an Italian mime who was then at liberty as a result of Lumley's failure and the closing of Her Majesty's Theatre. At rehearsal di Mattia was punctual and conscientious, and always trying to be useful, in the hope of being offered a permanent engagement at the Opéra. He also helped Cerrito to arrange the spectacular duel scene, which, at his suggestion, was taken from Galzerani's ballet, *Irene di Herstall*, in which he had danced many times at Naples, and once with such realism that he had broken his shoulder and dislocated his wrist.

Progress was slow, for Cerrito was ever begging Gautier to incorporate novel effects in the scenario, or remembering some brilliant and successful passage from an earlier ballet— from Perrot's *Le Délire d'un peintre*, or her husband's *La Fille de marbre* or *Stella*—which she wished to adapt and insert into her choreography. She conceived the idea of an enormous mirror reflecting the movements of those dancing before it. Then she wished to leap through a window, and ordered a tree to be constructed so that its foliage would break her fall. Next it was a magic circle that was required, to enclose her while the duel was being fought.

All these ideas Gautier good-humouredly fitted as best he could into his scenario. He was often present at the rehearsals. One day, feeling that di Mattia was not making enough of his hypnotic passes, he remonstrated with him. "But *monsieur*, you make your arms seem too short," he said.

"*Monsieur*," di Mattia replied, "these are the arms I rehearse with. I have others for the performance.

Di Mattia kept his patience for a long time, but soon he could stand no more of Cerrito's whims. "*Madame*," he said to her, "I am here as a mime, not a harlequin." It was his first outburst of temper. Not long before the first performance, which was given on May 31st, 1854, he was seen no more at rehearsals, and the rôle of the hypnotist was hurriedly learnt by Louis Mérante.

The action of the ballet, which was entitled *Gemma*, passed in southern Italy early in the seventeenth century. The Countess Gemma (Cerrito) is about to leave a convent, and, as the curtain rises, is discovered in her boudoir, trying on the dress that she is to wear at her farewell ball. She is eagerly awaiting the arrival of the man with whom she has fallen in love, Massimo (L. Petipa), an artist who is coming to finish painting her portrait. The Marquis of Santa Croce (L. Mérante), a dissolute nobleman possessing hypnotic powers who burns with a passion for her which is not returned, enters the room. Under his strange influence, Gemma is induced to make love to him. When Massimo is announced, Santa Croce hides. Then, when the artist has left, he casts a spell upon a rose which earlier she had contemptuously refused but which she now places tenderly to her bosom. At the ball, Santa Croce again mesmerizes Gemma, and finally dances with her out of the room to the terrace outside, where, amid flashes of lightning, his men seize her and carry her away.

The second act finds Gemma a prisoner in Santa Croce's castle. She is wearing a wedding-dress and is still under his evil influence, but Santa Croce, realizing that she cannot remain forever entranced if she is to become his wife, allows her to regain her senses. But she again repulses him, and, in despair, leaps through the open window. She escapes to Massimo's studio, and discovering the artist demented from worry at her disappearance, restores his reason by removing her portrait and herself stepping into the frame. Santa Croce arrives in pursuit, but seeing what he takes to be only a picture, leaves to continue his search elsewhere. He at last recognizes Gemma at a wedding festival in the mountains. Again he hypnotizes

Carolina Rosati in *La Fonti*

Carolina Rosati in *Le Corsaire*

Sketch for the setting of *Le Corsaire*,
Act I, Scene I

Sketch for the setting of *Le Corsaire*,
Act I, Scene II

her. As she meekly follows him up the mountain slope, the enraged Massimo attacks him with a sword. They fight. Suddenly Santa Croce staggers, fatally wounded, and falls headlong into the swift torrent below. As the final chords of the score are heard, Gemma is carried to the foot of the mountain and Massimo takes her in his arms.

"It is a severe task," wrote Gautier in his review of *Gemma*, "to arrange five large scenes in which often there are more than a hundred persons on the stage, whose every movement must be designed and co-ordinated from the *coryphée* placed near the footlights to the least important super fluttering obscurely at the back of the stage. The choreographer must, at the same time, be poet, painter, musician and drill-sergeant to discipline and manœuvre these crowds; qualities rarely found in one person. Fanny Cerrito has accomplished this difficult task in a manner that will surprise those who had any doubts about her talent." Her choreography was remarkable, not for its flow or consistency of texture, so much as for the brilliance of a few isolated passages, such as the mirror scene, a *pas de deux* danced by Louise Taglioni and Beauchet, and the *Abruzzaise*. The mirror scene, though not a new effect, had seldom before been attempted on so large a scale. Gemma and her ladies, numbering about a dozen, were seen preparing for the ball before a large mirror, behind which a similar number of dancers portrayed their reflections, reproducing their move-ments with admirable precision. Pauline Mercier, a pretty blonde of sixteen, appeared as Cerrito's reflection. Between such inspired passages, however, there were dull moments. "With so many twists," commented Fiorentino, "it is difficult not to entangle the skein."

It was principally as a dancer that Cerrito was welcomed back that evening. "Twenty years of success," wrote Fiorentino, "have not placed one wrinkle upon her alabaster forehead, nor changed by one imperceptible shade the gold of her hair." Although her style and execution were by no means faultless, although she was now becoming short of breath, her womanly charm and her soft, warm grace were such that no invidious comparisons came to mind when watching her dancing. In the scene in Massimo's studio, which had been adapted from *Le Délire d'un peintre*, her poses forcibly reminded Gautier of the figure of Psyche in Canova's statue, *Amor e Psyche*, and in the

Abruzzaise she showed a fire and an attack that contrasted sharply and effectively with her gentler moments.

Her interpretation of her rôle was masterly and proved the existence of a power of mime that had never been fully brought out before. She extracted every poignancy from Gemma's very helplessness before Santa Croce's sinister power. Nor was it easy to forget her in the ball scene, as, to the lilting melody of a waltz, she whirled round and round in the arms of the evil nobleman, in complete subservience to his will; and again in the scene in Santa Croce's castle, which contained no dancing at all, when bewilderment at finding herself in strange surroundings gave place first to terror, then to desperation.

Louis Mérante was very fortunate in taking over the rôle of Santa Croce, for it gave him an opportunity of displaying his talent as a mime that might otherwise have remained undetected until much later. "He knew," wrote Gautier, "how to assume a sinister and fatal expression by cleverly accentuating his delicate and youthful features, which are more suited to express tender sentiments than ferocious passions. His gestures have authority; his look, fascination." The death leap in the final scene could have been no less effective had di Mattia performed it. Not within living memory had such a feat been seen at the Opéra; some said that the ballet owed its success to its fall.

That *Gemma* was performed only seven times was not so much an indication of failure, as due to Cerrito's departure from the Opéra shortly afterwards. Its reception on the first night could hardly have been warmer: there were cheers for Cerrito, cheers for Gautier, and cheers for Count Gabrielli, the young Italian composer. All this enthusiasm, however, seemed exaggerated and artificial to Jouvin of *Le Figaro*. "Just a word about the rain of bouquets which inundated the stage during the whole performance of the new ballet," he commented. "I believe that the limits of the possible and the ridiculous have just been reached. No attempt was even made to deceive the public by throwing the official bouquets from different parts of the house. The proscenium box on the third tier, to the right of the players, was filled with dancers' mothers. One of our colleagues counted forty-three bouquets falling from that box. They were all hurled in profusion and at random, and when the venerable Ferdinand Prévost, whose duty consists in putting on evening dress and announcing the names of the authors, came forward to make the customary acknowledgments, a magnificent bouquet of white roses fell at his feet. All this farce of enthusiasm, arranged in the morning at the flower shop, is a scandal, and it is high time that it stopped, for it could become dangerous to the public. In future, no dancer will want to be outdone by Cerrito, and at the next ballet you will run the risk of having pots of flowers and tubs of orange trees falling on your head."

.　　.　　.　　.　　.　　.　　₃

On June 29th, 1854, by Imperial decree, the Opéra became a department of the Emperor's household. The deficit of nearly a million francs that had accumulated over the past few years was paid off, and Roqueplan confirmed in his position as administrator, although subordinated to the superior authority of the Minister of State. That inveterate scandal-monger, the Comte Horace de Viel-Castel, commented that the salary of 25,000 francs a year that the Director was now to receive would hardly be sufficient, since Louise Marquet alone must cost him something very near that figure.[1] Not long afterwards indeed, Roqueplan tendered his resignation, and was succeeded, on November 11th, by François Louis Crosnier. Perhaps he had wearied of the heavy responsibilities he had borne for more than seven years; perhaps he resented the interference of the Minister of State in putting his own house in order.

For during that year, he had fallen out with two of his dancers. He had allowed Priora's engagement to lapse, because she had refused to dance in the opera, La Vestale, and his dispute with Guy-Stéphan, over alleged breaches of contract

---

[1] Louise Marquet's career as a dancer at the Opéra covered a period of nearly forty years. Her first contract, entitling her to a salary of 200 francs a year, commenced on January 8th, 1841; she made her début as a sujet in 1851, playing Fenella in La Muette de Portici; and retired in 1879, shortly after creating the rôle of the Princess in Mérante's Yedda. After leaving the Opéra, she took over the deportment class at the Conservatoire, and later became maîtresse de ballet at the Opéra-Comique. Suffering from cancer, she endured much pain during the last two years of her life, but bravely continued her work. An operation in the summer of 1890 was not wholly successful. On December 3rd of that year, she attended the first performance at the Opéra-Comique of Diaz's Benvenuto, for which she had arranged the dances, but the effort greatly fatigued her. She was never seen at the theatre again, for she died not three weeks later, on December 22nd, 1890. She was the youngest of three sisters, all of whom were at one time engaged at the Opéra. The eldest, Delphine, abandoned ballet for the legitimate stage, while Mathilde, who was the least talented, forsook the theatre altogether when still a young woman.

by the Opéra, had been taken to the Courts. The Minister soon intervened to stop this litigation and negotiated a settlement markedly in Guy-Stéphan's favour. He next invited Roqueplan to give him his views on prolonging Cerrito's engagement, which was due to expire at the end of October. Roqueplan suggested a year's extension on the same terms as before, but the Minister considered that an increase of salary could be afforded, and Cerrito was re-engaged until the end of October 1855 at 3,500 francs a month.

On December 13th, 1854, at the request of Auber, Cerrito appeared as Fenella in his opera, *La Muette de Portici*, for the first time in Paris. Although she had played it elsewhere before, she was obviously unequal to the heavy demands of the rôle, which Rosati, who was incontestably the stronger mime, would have interpreted so much more effectively; and she was doubly unfortunate in having to contend directly with her rival, who, dancing the leading part in the *divertissement*, was acclaimed with the wildest applause. Marie Guy-Stéphan also appeared in the *divertissement*, performing a Spanish dance with such abandon that she nearly caused a scandal by twice stopping short directly below the Emperor's box with her full skirt held up to the level of her eyes.

A mutual antipathy had arisen between Cerrito and the new Director, and soon there began a series of bitter disputes that poisoned their relations still further. Cerrito accused Crosnier of unjustly restricting the number of her appearances, and laid claim to the half-benefit performance which was due to her under a term of her previous contract. That she had not insisted before on this term being fulfilled was due mainly to Roqueplan's gentle persuasiveness; she had in fact originally agreed to produce *Gemma* on the understanding that the first performance would be given for her benefit, but she had been won over by his reasoning and agreed to waive this condition. Crosnier had none of Roqueplan's great charm. Soon there could be only one solution, and Cerrito's engagement at the Opéra was terminated from September 15th, 1855, her right to a benefit being expressly reserved.

In the spring of the following year, she returned to Paris specially to settle the outstanding matter of her benefit with Crosnier, but although she remained in the city for two months, he refused to see her. Eighteen months later, being in Paris again, she broached the subject with Alphonse Royer, who by then had succeeded Crosnier as Director. Appreciating that the ballets in which she had danced had been out of the repertory for several years and could only be produced with considerable difficulty, she suggested that she might accept a reasonable sum in full settlement of her claim. Shortly afterwards, the Minister of State approved the payment to her of 6,000 francs, and the matter was at last closed.

After her break with the Opéra in 1855, Fanny Cerrito had gone to Russia, where she became a great favourite of the Tsar Alexander II. One evening in the autumn of 1856, while she was appearing at Moscow in *La Fille de marbre*, a burning piece of scenery fell on her shoulder. Her costume was alight for a few seconds, and, although the flames were extinguished before she suffered any serious injury, the nervous shock was severe and was one of the causes, it was said, of her retirement from the stage after a season in London the following summer.

She settled in Paris in the autumn of 1857, and spent the first summer of her retirement quietly at Spa. "She plays neither at the theatre nor at roulette," wrote *Le Figaro's* observer, giving the news. "The fact of a dancer with her legs stilled is certainly worth mentioning. Mme Cerrito is travelling incognito, and the better to cloak her charming identity, this is how she registered at her hotel: 'Madame Cerrito, householder, Paris.' That is all very well, but what if it rains? Mme Cerrito will hitch up her dress, and all her precautions will have been in vain, for what Parisian will not recognize her when he sees the tip of her foot?" That winter, her presence was recorded at a banquet given in honour of Marie Taglioni.

Although she lived in Paris, the scene of so many of her triumphs, throughout the fifty and more years that remained to her, she disappeared almost completely from public view. About the only occasion when her presence was noticed at the Opéra was at the first performance of *Néméa* in 1864. She lived in several houses in the sixteenth *arrondissement*: Alphonse Royer, in his history of the Opéra, published in 1875, wrote of her "elegant cage, in the midst of green leaves and flowers" in the Rue de la Faisanderie; two years later, she was living at No. 149 Avenue d'Eylau (now Avenue Victor Hugo); and in 1890, according to Arthur Pougin, the historian of the theatre, she was "living in retirement in a pretty little mansion that she

had built herself"—No. 2 Rue Théry (now Rue de Montevidéo).
At some time she also owned some shop premises at No. 90
Rue du Faubourg-Saint-Honoré, which she sold in 1875 to
Messrs. Cadbury Brothers, and which became the Paris branch
of the famous chocolate manufacturers. It is probable that
Cerrito was in Paris during the Siege of 1870–71, for she sent
out invitations to her husband's funeral, which took place
within the city on September 5th, 1870.

Her happy memories of England never left her. In 1878,
George Augustus Sala, who was in Paris covering the Universal
Exhibition for the *Daily Telegraph*, reported; "As for the
English, they are *un peu partout*. A few mornings since I paid a
visit to Mr. Thomas Cook, in his very pleasant quarters in the
Rue de la Faisanderie, fitted up for boarding and lodging the
shoals of tourists who travel under his wing, and found the
accommodation capital. I went over two or three of the handsome suburban villas temporarily tenanted by the 'Cookists';
and the name of the proprietor of one of these mansions struck
me with a pleasant surprise. It was Mme Saint-Léon, who, as
Mlle Cerrito, was one of the most fascinating dancers that
ever adorned the great era of the Terpsichorean stage. . . .
The delightful Cerrito . . . is still extant, hale, prosperous,
and vivacious. Very blithely did she come to terms with Mr.
Cook. 'You are an Englishman,' she said, 'and I love England
and the English.' It is good to think of these former *Reines de
la danse* enjoying a green old age."

It was a little unchivalrous of Sala to speak of old age, for
Cerrito was only sixty-one and still had more than thirty years'
life before her. She was to survive all three ballerinas who had
danced with her in the memorable *Pas de Quatre* of 1845. All
lived to great ages, but only Cerrito passed her ninetieth
birthday: she was nearly ninety-two when she died, at No. 2
Rue Théry, at ten o'clock in the evening of May 6th, 1909.
Curiously, not a single newspaper commented on the passing of
the survivor of the famous quartet, which had in fact happened
at the very moment when the attention of all lovers of the
dance was directed to the future. For only a few days after the
death of Fanny Cerrito, Diaghilev's first Paris season of Russian
ballet and opera opened at the Théâtre du Châtelet.

· · · · · · ·

Just before the Opéra had ceased to be a private enterprise in 1854, Roqueplan had laid the plans for a new ballet for Rosati—*La Fonti*, with choreography by Mazilier and a score by Labarre, the composer of *Jovita*. It was originally hoped to have this work ready before the end of September, and Roqueplan was authorized by the Minister of State—to whom, after the reorganization, such matters had to be referred—to negotiate with Rosati with a view to her giving up part of her holiday so that the ballet could be rehearsed during August. This optimistic schedule soon had to be abandoned, for Rosati fell ill, and as a result it was not until January 8th, 1855, that *La Fonti* was at last presented to the Emperor and Empress and the public.

The scenario, although attributed to the choreographer, was in fact the work of Deligny. Amalia Fonti (Rosati), a ballerina and the idol of Florence in the year 1750, scorns the noblemen who visit her dressing-room and press her for her favours, but to the charms and attentions of the young Count de Monteleone (L. Petipa) she cannot remain indifferent. To his companions' amusement, he offers to marry her. But his father, the Marquis (Lenfant), who has been hiding in the room, refuses to consent to such a misalliance, and orders his son to return to his seat in the theatre. The Count meekly obeys. Babinella (Berthier), the *maître de ballet*, then arrives to announce that the performance is about to begin. Wounded in her pride by the Count's subservience to his father, Amalia at first thinks of refusing to go on, but the three taps recall her to her duty, and, wiping away her tears, she rouges her cheeks and leaves for the stage.

The scene changes to the theatre. After a short overture, the curtain rises, and a ballet within the ballet, *Flore et Zéphyre*, is danced by Amalia and her partner, Carlino (L. Mérante), who is deeply in love with her himself. The ardour of the young Count, who is among the audience, is rekindled by her artistry, and he writes to propose that they leave for France together. His father, however, has observed him, and hurriedly leaves his seat to intercept the note.

Arriving in her dressing-room, the Marquis succeeds in bribing Amalia's maid (Emarot) to give up the note. When the dancer returns shortly afterwards, he commands her to leave Florence immediately and informs her that his carriage is waiting for her outside. On her refusing, he calls in *sbirri* who carry her away. The faithful Carlino, however, has seen everything, and vows to rescue her or perish in the attempt.

Amalia is thrown into prison on a warrant obtained by the Marquis. The prison governor (Dauty) has long desired her, but she still repulses him. A servant, whom she recognizes as Carlino, enters with a basket of food and a despatch that calls for the governor's attention elsewhere. Alone with Amalia for a few minutes, Carlino unfolds his plan. They are to change clothes, and he will take her place in the prison to give her time to make her escape. While he is putting on one of her dresses, she entertains the governor to supper and when the wine has gone to the old man's head, she makes him dance with her. She and Carlino then change places so skilfully that the governor is unaware that he has a different partner, and seeing Amalia a little later in male attire, takes her for an inquisitive servant and orders her to leave. At last the old man discovers the deception and calls in the gaolers to arrest Carlino, but the latter is too quick for them and, making his escape, locks the door behind him.

Amalia, still in male disguise, takes the post of dancing master to the Princess Carolina Tornasari (Forli), whom the Count is shortly to marry at his father's bidding. Amalia tells the Princess of her *fiancé's* affection for the dancer, and, to prove her story, shows her the Count's love letters. She then declares her own love for the Princess, and threatens to kill herself if the marriage contract is signed. The young Princess is disturbed and cannot bring herself to sign the document. The Count challenges Amalia to a duel, but when he recognizes her, his love for her returns and he begs her forgiveness. But Amalia tells him that it is now too late, since he has broken faith by signing a marriage contract with another. He tries to hold her, but she eludes his grasp and escapes from the room.

The final scene takes place on the Corso in Rome. It is the Carnival season. Amalia is suddenly seen threading her way through a merry crowd of revellers. She seems bewildered and distraught. The effort to conquer her love has broken her. A shudder of horror passes through the crowd as they recognize her as the ballerina whom they were applauding only a few months before. Seeing that all eyes are upon her, Amalia begins to dance. Her movements are confused and wild. One moment her reason seems to be returning, then her strength fails her and she falls to the ground, lifeless.

"The ballet belongs to the type known as *ballets d'action*," wrote Gautier, "and represents a drama interpreted by gestures rather than a sequence of choreographic poses. It has been translated with talent by M. Mazilier, one of our best producers of mimed action, and well rendered by La Rosati, but we nevertheless continue to hold that the *ballet d'action* does not satisfy the conditions of true dancing. Every art corresponds to a certain order of subjects which it can alone render. Sculpture expresses form; painting, form and colour; poetry, form, colour, sound and thought; music, number, tone, the infinite and the indefinite, the presentiment of what is not and the memory of what has never been; dancing, *plastique* and rhythm of movement, and—why not say it?—physical delight and feminine beauty. Ballet must be a kind of painted bas-relief or sculptured painting; it is not in stories or novels that it should seek its themes, but in the graceful bacchanals, processions and *panathenæa* which encircle antique vases. Mythologies of every age and every country—of India, Egypt, Greece, Scandinavia—legends, fairy-tales, dreams inspired by hashish and opium, all the fancies that are beyond the bounds of the possible—this is the true domain of ballet. Otherwise, it is inferior to every form of art, for it can specify nothing, develop nothing. The past and the future are denied it; the action must always be conjugated in the present tense.

"A few very limited gestures, some taken from nature, others from convention, are the only resources with which to paint human passions. Thus a *ballet d'action* has the appearance of a drama played by a troupe of deaf-mutes, especially as French dancers do not follow the music in their miming. But managers, deprived of their sense by theatrical custom, are very fond of the *ballet d'action*, for it represents to them a fable, a story, a massive, straightforward theme.

"If ever we have the honour of being Director of the Opéra, we will have ballets invented by painters, not by playwrights— by Decamps, Camille Roqueplan, Diaz, Gérome, Picou, Chasseriau, or Gendron, whose delightful picture of the Wilis shows what artists could do in this style."

Other critics, with less individualistic opinions than Gautier, acclaimed *La Fonti* as the greatest success since *Giselle, La Péri* and *Le Diable à quatre*. They praised Mazilier's choreography as being pleasing and elegant, particularly in the *divertissement* of *Flore et Zéphyre*; but they noticed an occasional lack of inspiration and invention, and detected reminiscences of earlier works, of a *pas* danced by the Viennese Children at the Opéra in the forties, and the *défilé* from *La Jolie fille de Gand*. Labarre's score, according to Gautier, was "remarkable" and "not inferior to that of *Jovita*;" "it is a real opera," added Fiorentino, "lacking only the words."

The ballet was a perfect vehicle for Rosati, whose triumph was undisputed. "Her dancing," wrote Gautier, "although somewhat lacking in elevation, is especially brilliant in *tacqueté*, being precise and quick, and having a flavour of Montessu and Noblet." Fiorentino described some of her *pas* in the *divertissement*. Her first *variation* contained *cabrioles* and finished with *petits jetés*; there was an *adage* remarkable for "one very inclined pose in which the dancer, with her leg *à la seconde*, turns back her head quickly to look at her partner;" then followed a *pas de basque* in waltz-time, danced with great speed and lightness and including brilliantly executed *cabrioles à côté*; and finally, producing the greatest effect of all, there was a *variation* which required an almost superhuman balance, with *temps ballottés* and *posés en arabesque sur l'orteil* in the gentle manner of Taglioni, and which ended with a dazzling sequence of *ronds de jambe en dedans*.

However brilliant her dancing, it was Rosati's powerful miming that created the greatest impression. When, in the last scene but one, she bade farewell to her lover, many people in the audience were moved to tears. Greater efforts were to follow in the last scene, which had in fact been added only as an afterthought to give Rosati an opportunity of expressing tragedy. "It is incontestable," wrote Fiorentino of this final passage, "that neither Fanny Elssler, who is often cited when Rosati is discussed, nor any other mime or dancer among all those we have seen at the Opéra, ever approached such perfection." "She appears," he described, "with dishevelled hair, wild eyes and livid cheeks. She is surrounded by the crowd, gazing curiously at her and mockingly applauding. The poor girl believes she is on the stage, amid an enthusiastic audience of her former admirers. The *moccoletti* that the people are shaking about her in the fury of their grotesque saturnalia recall to her mind the dazzling flames of the footlights. She begins to dance, then stops suddenly, dejected, bewildered. Her pupils dilate. Stupefied, she casts her eye round that enormous circle of grimacing masks, that wheel of flickering lights. She grips her poor head between her hands, as though to tear out some memory. Then the frenzy takes possession of her, and she dances, dances, turns, turns, feverishly beating time in a crazy *tarantella*, until she tires, weakens, then, stiffening, falls to the ground dead."

She had plumbed the uttermost depths of tragedy in her portrayal of what was certainly the greatest rôle of her career. Her teacher, Blasis, was amazed at her perfection. "I have seen La Rosati in the ballet, *La Fonti*," he wrote. "She is all that the accomplished dancer, the model artiste, should be, because she is both dancer and mime at the same time. There is no separation of her choreographic and dramatic skill; her verve and her taste are quite superior. To the personal charms that Nature has bestowed upon her, La Rosati adds all the perfections that result from study. Her soul responds to every impression, which she can translate into the most eloquent and precise gestures. This is how a dancer, who wishes to attain the heights of the painter, the sculptor and the orator all at the same time, should display herself on the stage. Rosati's *pas* are genuine songs in choreography; they glisten like precious stones. Above all, La Rosati instils a seductive quality into her poses, the voluptuousness of which, like Apollo's, is always subtly concealed. This is the sign of an artistic intelligence stretched to its utmost limits."

In the rôle of Carlino, Mérante added to the impression that he had created when playing the sinister figure of Santa Croce in *Gemma* a few months earlier. He now gave proof of a most versatile talent. In the *divertissement* of *Flore et Zéphyre*, he "imitated with infinite spirit and wit the rococo style of dancing of the eighteenth century;" and in the prison scene, he showed himself an excellent comedian when, clad in woman's clothes, he imitated the mincing graces and the technique of a ballerina. He was loudly applauded by the whole house, an almost unprecedented experience for a male dancer in those days. "Mérante," declared Fiorentino, "has rehabilitated the male dancer."

. . . .

Crosnier assumed the management of the Opéra at a time when the services of Rosati alone among the great ballerinas could be counted on for some time to come. To remedy this deficiency, he engaged a sixteen-year-old Italian prodigy, Caterina Beretta, the daughter of a well-known mime and a pupil of Augusto Hus, for a term of three years, at a salary ranging from 18,000 francs for the first year, to 24,000 francs for the second and 36,000 francs for the third. It was originally agreed that she should make her début at the Opéra in a new ballet, but Crosnier was anxious to put her to the test as soon as possible and decided to revive *Le Diable à quatre* for her, before resolving whether to include her in the cast of *Le Corsaire*, which was then in its early stages of production.

Beretta was at a great disadvantage in making her first appearance in the rôle of Mazourka. Unfavourable comparisons with Carlotta Grisi were inevitable; her lack of experience was obvious in her miming, and the haste with which the revival had been produced was betrayed by the dilapidated state of the sets.

"Mlle Beretta," described Gautier, after witnessing her début on February 21st, 1855, "is small, and, with a body developed by the violent gymnastics of dancing exercises, possesses perhaps more strength than grace. Her legs, set in a network of powerful muscles, express vigour rather than elegance by their shape. Her figure is more that of a healthy daughter of the earth than that of a vaporous sylphide with shimmering, variegated wings. Later, perhaps, maturity will lengthen those lines which are at present somewhat short, and add the slenderness that is now lacking. Her features are lively, arch, childlike, lit by beautiful southern eyes. So much for the physical aspect, which we have spoken about in detail, because it is important for a dancer and forms part, so to speak, of her necessarily plastic and silent talent.

"Her technical qualities are remarkable. . . . Mlle Beretta has been trained and broken in early in the hard school of dancing. She is completely versed in the principles and the mechanics of her art, the difficulties of which no longer exist for her. Everything she does is neat, precise and firm. She does not blur a single movement of her *jetés battus*; she rises energetically, if not to a great height; she covers the stage with speed and agility; and in *poses renversées*, she ventures positions so off-balance as would break the back of any dancer attempting them without that suppleness and clownlike elasticity which are characteristics of Mlle Beretta. Her *double tour sur la pointe de la jambe gauche*, executed with a dazzling rapidity, was loudly applauded."

Fiorentino, too, was astounded by Beretta's suppleness and strength, her balance in *adage*, and her complete mastery of technique. "In her first *variation*," he wrote, "after starting with *ronds de jambe* and *doubles cabrioles*, she followed with thirty bars of *ballon* and finished with twenty bars of sheer vigour that brought forth thunders of applause."

In June, Beretta was given the rôle of Autumn to create in Lucien Petipa's *divertissement* in the opera, *Les Vêpres siciliennes*, and learned that technique alone does not ensure success. To Saint-Victor she appeared as "a little female clown turning on an athletic limb," and Jouvin was reminded of a "goose girl who has learnt to dance." She was coldly received, and in consequence the Opéra broke off her engagement at the end of the first year. She sued the management for breach of contract and, judgment being given in her favour, continued to appear at the Opéra until January 1857, when her engagement was terminated at her own request for personal reasons. Afterwards she danced at the Scala, Milan, and taught at the dancing school there for some years early in the present century. Tamara Karsavina, in her memoirs, described a visit to Caterina Beretta in her old age, whom she found very poor and very stout, "a ludicrous little figure," but nevertheless very imposing, "like an old queen." Beretta died in Milan in January 1911.

Making her début in the same *divertissement* was another young Italian dancer, Claudina Cucchi, a pupil of Blasis. She was blonde, with pretty, delicate features, and long legs with rather short thighs. Her freshness was ideally suited to the rôle of Spring, and brought forth the exclamation from Saint-Victor, "*O Gioventù, primavera della vita.*" The other two seasons, Summer and Winter, were portrayed by Adèle Nathan, a pretty Jewess, and Victorine Legrain.

. . . .

That summer, the war in the Crimea, in which the French armies, fighting alongside the British and the Sardinians, had been engaged for more than a year, was drawing to its close.

Sevastopol had been invested for several months, and its fall was imminent. The military alliance between France and England had been cemented in April by a State Visit to England by the Emperor and Empress, and in August, Queen Victoria and Prince Albert, with the young Princess Royal and Prince of Wales, were given a warm welcome in Paris. The full programme arranged for the royal visitors included a Gala Performance at the Opéra on Tuesday, August 21st. For the occasion, the six centre boxes on the first tier had been combined to form the State Box, which was decorated with heavy velvet hangings and Imperial coats of arms crowned with Napoleonic eagles. Other parts of the house were reserved for the Court and the *corps diplomatique*. Garlands of flowers were arranged in profusion about the building, Gobelin carpets laid on the floors, and gas-light illuminations erected on the façade of the theatre. In the street outside stood a triumphal arch, from which hung an enormous chandelier, made, it was reported, of some five thousand pieces of coloured glass.

Although the prices of admission had not been raised, seats changed hands privately for fabulous sums, one Englishman being reputed to have given 1,000 francs for the privilege of a place in a third-tier box. Seldom, if ever, before had a more brilliant audience been gathered within the theatre. The occasion was long to be remembered as the *soirée aux diamants*. Before the State Box, and on either side of the stage, were the tall, still figures of the Cent Gardes, in their tight-fitting sky-blue tunics, white buckskin breeches and shining black top-boots, their steel casques and breastplates glittering with the reflections of the lights.

A burst of applause swept through the house as the Emperor led Queen Victoria into the State Box, followed by the Empress with Prince Albert. When the cheering at last subsided, the performance began. There were excerpts from various operas, a shortened version of *La Fonti*, and finally *God Save the Queen*, sung by Cruvelli and Alboni before a dropcloth representing Napoleon III and Eugénie arriving at Windsor Castle, and adorned by some of the youngest and prettiest members of the *corps de ballet* suspended from the flies. The Queen was not very impressed by *La Fonti*, which she dismissed in her Journal as "a long, too long ballet, in three acts, with Rosati as the principal dancer."

In the audience that evening was George Augustus Sala, the journalist. "By great good fortune," he wrote, "I gained admission to the *coulisses* on that memorable night, and I remember the fun which the juvenile members of the *corps de ballet* made between the acts of the two towering Cent Gardes who, motionless as statues, stood sentry on either side of the proscenium. So soon as the curtain was down, an impudent little minx of a *rat d'opéra* ran across to one of these mailed giants; examined him from crested helm to spurred jack-boot; tapped with one little rosy finger-nail the steel of his cuirass, and cried to one of her companions in the *cantonade*, '*Tiens! c'est vivant!*'"

.   .   .   .

While Paris was rejoicing at the good news coming from the East, the Russian dancer, Nadezhda Bogdanova, found herself in a very embarrassing position. She had been out of Paris when war had broken out. In the days immediately preceding the declaration, when the whole city, and in particular the brokers who did business in the Passage de l'Opéra, were anxiously awaiting news of the Government's decision, the rumour spread that her engagement had been terminated. The funds dropped nearly as rapidly as if the Russian Ambassador had been handed his passports, before the news was found to be false. "Had M. Nestor Roqueplan speculated on a fall the evening before?" queried the *Almanach de la Bourse*. "This serious move in political choreography could have been launched as a very profitable speculation."

Bogdanova returned to Paris and reappeared at the Opéra early in August 1854. Her admirer, Jules Janin, was amazed at her audacity. "This week," he wrote, "(Oh! the vanity of the Eastern Question!) picture this insolent little Bogdanova, with her rosy cheeks and her name ending in 'ova,' a child of Russia, a Russian, daring, having actually dared, to return to us!" She dared even more, for the following month, shortly after French troops had begun to embark for the invasion of the Crimea, she signed a new contract to appear at the Opéra for a further year.

She must have suffered much during the war on account of her nationality. According to Janin, she was the last dancer to have appeared in Sevastopol's theatre before the town was besieged. Her comrades, considering her no doubt as an enemy, lost no opportunity of complaining that whenever she appeared with them in a *pas de trois* or a *pas de quatre*, she intentionally outshone them. Her position at last became untenable. When Sevastopol fell early in September 1855, her contract had only three more weeks to run. It was not renewed, and as soon as she could, she left Paris and returned to Russia. "She loves France as her foster-country," wrote her champion, Janin, shortly after her departure, "and yet she no longer wishes to dance for France. She will wait for better days, days of peace, when the world will be but one and the same nation, and dancing will once again be the universal language of the countries who have eyes to see everything and to see well."

Another explanation of Bogdanova's departure, which reached the ears of the English journalist, George Augustus Sala, was that certain of the critics had plotted against her. "Two *feuilletonistes* of the highest celebrity and social position had declared publicly that they would decline and return the retaining fee, sent by *débutantes* and accepted by *feuilletonistes* as a matter of course in such cases."

Arriving in St. Petersburg, still smarting under the humiliations she had suffered, Bogdanova posed as a victim of her nationality. She complained that she had been persecuted in Paris, and that the Opéra had attempted to make her dance at the special performance in celebration of the taking of Sevastopol. Her story had the effect of gaining her much sympathy among her countrymen, for she took thirty curtain calls after her début at St. Petersburg in *Giselle* early in 1856. She became almost a national heroine. The tremendous enthusiasm of the Russian audiences inspired her to an artistry that she might never have attained had she remained in Paris. She was applauded vigorously on her travels, which at last, in the summer of 1857, brought her back to Paris, with her brother Nicolai, to make a single appearance in a *pas de deux* at the Théâtre Italien.

"If only she would revive *La Sylphide* for us," sighed Janin hopefully but in vain, as he watched her.

.   .   .   .

After the first performance of *Le Corsaire* on the evening of January 23rd, 1856, Crosnier was summoned to the Imperial

Le Corsaire, Act II

Design by Despléchin for *Le Corsaire*,
Act III, Scene I

Le Corsaire, Act III, Scene II
The Orgy on Board

Le Corsaire, Act III, Scene II
The Shipwreck
From a drawing by Gustave Doré

Box to receive the compliments of the Emperor and Empress. The latter was particularly enthusiastic. "In all my life I have never seen, and probably never shall see, anything so beautiful or so moving," she told him. Her satisfaction was all the more gratifying to Crosnier, since, although the fact could not be announced publicly, she had interested herself in the work at an early stage and had made several suggestions that Saint-Georges, the scenarist, had adopted. Some said that her share in the ballet was even greater.

The Empress Eugénie's interest in ballet was no passing fancy, for a first night seldom passed that she did not attend. After the success of *Le Corsaire*, there were rumours that she had suggested an idea for a ballet based on Byron's *Manfred*, and it was also said that Saint-Georges hoped for further assistance in a work founded on one of Molière's plays. She even approached Gounod, who was dumbfounded and not a little flattered by her proposal of collaboration in a ballet, made in all seriousness one evening at Compiègne in the winter of 1861. Her increasing preoccupation with affairs of State, however, unfortunately prevented these projects from reaching fruition, and *Le Corsaire* was to remain unique as the only ballet to which an Empress of the French made a contribution.

During the twelve months that separated *La Fonti* and *Le Corsaire*, Carolina Rosati appeared in only one new work, the opera, *Sainte-Claire*, condescending to do so only at the special request of the composer, Ernst II, Duke of Saxe-Coburg-Gotha. What success the ducal work obtained was. said to be due principally to her participation.

As the winter drew on and the first night of *Le Corsaire* approached, Rosati practised assiduously to perfect her art, working not only in the classroom, but also in the seclusion of her own apartment. The thick carpets which she had had laid on her floors were not enough to prevent all the sound from penetrating to the rooms below, and her neighbour, an Englishman with a regrettable lack of gallantry, complained.

"You cannot possibly hear me," Rosati replied angrily.

The Englishman was obdurate.

"If you can hear me," she retorted, "then I cannot dance, and I shall retire from the stage!"

This threat had no effect on the unfeeling Englishman, and they finally had to appeal to their landlord. Two gentlemen whose sense of hearing was very acute were then selected as arbitrators and placed in the lower apartment, while Rosati danced above them. Alas! the complaint proved to be only too well founded, and for some days the dancer was inconsolable. Fortunately, she was eventually persuaded to lay the blame on the structure of the building, and the ballet of *Le Corsaire* proceeded smoothly from the final rehearsals to its first performance.

Its scenario was very lightly based on Byron's poem, *The Corsair*. The story opens in the slave market of Adrianople. Seyd (Dauty), a rich and elderly pasha, arrives to seek an addition to his harem, and selects Médora (Rosati), the ward of Isaac (Berthier) the bazaar-master. Before he can remove his purchase, the girl's lover, Conrad (Segarelli), a pirate chief, gives a sign to his men, who seize Médora and the other slave-girls and carry them away to a vast subterranean palace. There Conrad orders the girls to be freed, but his henchman, Birbanto (Fuchs), feeling cheated of his rightful booty, secretly agrees to sell Médora back to Isaac. He drugs Conrad with a bouquet of lotus flowers, and his followers bear Médora away.

Isaac takes Médora to the pasha's palace on the island of Cos, where she is introduced into the harem and soon befriended by the irrepressible Gulnare (Cucchi), one of the concubines. Later, Conrad and his men arrive, disguised as pilgrims, but their plan to rescue Médora is foiled by the treachery of Birbanto. Conrad is captured by the pasha's men, and not even the prayers of Gulnare can move Seyd from his resolution that his prisoner shall die.

The third act opens in a kiosk in the grounds of the pasha's palace, overlooking the sea. Seyd tells Médora that he will set Conrad free on condition that she consents to become his wife. She is about to refuse indignantly, when Gulnare appears and tells her to accept the proposal. Gulnare's plan unfolds smoothly. Unknown to the pasha, she takes Médora's place at the wedding, but it is Médora again with whom the pasha returns to the kiosk. Médora playfully makes him give up his pistols and dagger, leaving him unarmed at the moment when Conrad appears suddenly at the window. After the lovers have escaped, Gulnare approaches and reveals that it is she whom Seyd has married. Meanwhile, Conrad and Médora sail away, rejoicing.

But the sky soon darkens, and a storm breaks overhead. Their ship founders and sinks, but as the sea calms again, the lovers are seen to reach the safety of a rock and kneel in prayer and thanksgiving for their miraculous escape.

Rosati's performance in the rôle of Médora roused the enthusiasm of audience and critics alike to a greater frenzy than ever before. Jouvin hailed her as "the first ballerina in the world," and went on, "The latest comer among the *danseuses* of 'style'—Carlotta Grisi, Cerrito, Fuoco—La Rosati possesses

CAROLINA ROSATI AND DOMENICO SEGARELLI IN "LE CORSAIRE"
Caricature by Marcelin

more stamina than the first, a more distinguished grace than the second, and quite as much intrepidity as the third, and in addition has an originality more marked than that of all three put together." Janin, who had been so critical at her début, went still further. "Carlotta, who was so enchanting, had not greater charm; Fanny Elssler was never more enticing. [Rosati] is light-footed in the manner of Mlle Taglioni herself." Others expressed their admiration in more material form. One gentleman sent an enormous bouquet that aroused great interest when it was exposed for some time in the window of Barjon's, the florists; and on her reappearance the following winter,

Rosati was to receive a bouquet wrapped up in six metres of the very finest Point d'Alençon. *Le Figaro* bestowed upon her an honour of a different kind, announcing that its composite Venus, which possessed the qualities of the most beautiful women in Paris, would be graced with Rosati's legs.

Although Mérante, on his showing in *Gemma* and *La Fonti*, might have seemed the obvious choice for the rôle of Conrad,

CAROLINA ROSATI AND DOMENICO SEGARELLI IN THE FINAL GROUP
OF "LE CORSAIRE"
Caricature by Marcelin

the Opéra had engaged specially for the part a famous Italian mime, Domenico Segarelli, at an annual salary of 9,600 francs. A man of wild aspect and uncertain temperament, Segarelli was indeed admirably suited to the rôle, with the "dark" and "terrible, menacing looks" required by the scenario, although, by French standards, his essentially Italian style of miming seemed exaggerated.

The ballet was uncompromisingly a *ballet d'action*, depending largely on mime passages, and, for its length, containing relatively little dancing. Though there were no dull moments, Mazilier's choreography was considered to be somewhat lacking in originality. A *pas des éventails* by Rosati and sixteen *danseuses* in the second scene of Act I was remarkable more for the blending of the colours of their fans than the steps they danced; Rosati had a *pas seul* in the second act, and danced again on the deck of the ship in the third act. There was also a *divertissement* in the first scene, in which five *sujets*, as slaves from different countries—Moldavia, Italy, France, England (so said the scenario, although Victorine Legrain wore Scottish costume) and Spain—each danced a national *pas*.

The key to the ballet's success lay in the great spectacle of the last scene. "Crosnier has saved the Opéra by a shipwreck," it was said, although the credit in fact belonged to Sacré, the chief machinist. "It is the spectacle of a vessel surprised by a terrible tempest and sinking in the open sea," described Jouvin. "The sky, the waves, the horizon pass, by degrees that are admirably arranged, through every meteorological phenomenon. A splendid sunset in the Black Sea—a ship that seems to fall asleep to the murmur of the waves, like a child soothed by its nurse's lullaby—the dancing and the orgy on board. Then, suddenly, a black speck on the horizon—the whistling of the rising wind—darkness falling—the sky here and there fringed with a sinister red glow—heavy peals of thunder in the distance. Finally, the storm—nightfall—the furious sea—the silhouette of the vessel, rocking with increasing force and then foundering with a dreadful noise. All these incidents of a shipwreck were rendered with a complete illusion by the scene-painter and the machinist. The Opéra stage seemed to have taken on suddenly the vast proportions of the open sea. It was better than the mirage produced by the Diorama; it was reality in all its grandiose horror."

Much of the beauty of the ballet was to be found in Adolphe Adam's score, and in particular to a symphonic interlude between the last two acts, in which, on the first night, the tones of saxophones were to be heard. It was Adam's last work. On the evening of May 2nd, 1856, he visited the Opéra to see *La Reine de Chypre*, and that very night he died in his sleep, so peacefully that his pet dog, who lay on his bed, was unaware of what had happened. Large crowds gathered a few days later about the church of Notre-Dame de Lorette, where the funeral service was held, and some three thousand persons followed his coffin to the cemetery. The Opéra could not be closed that evening, for Napoleon III was to take the King of Württemberg to see *Le Corsaire*, but on the following day the Emperor gave orders that the receipts, amounting to nearly 10,000 francs, were to be given to the composer's widow.

Adam was only fifty-two when he died. Of his thirteen ballet scores, nine had been first heard at the Opéra: *La Fille du Danube, Les Mohicans, Giselle, La Jolie fille de Gand, Le Diable à quatre, Griseldis, La Filleule des fées, Orfa* and *Le Corsaire*.[1] In his last years, he had been greatly disturbed by the new trends in music and by the thought of approaching old age. "I see that I shall be completely worn out by this musical hysteria which forces me to create without cease," he wrote to Jouvin on May 20th, 1855. "And as I neither know nor want to know how to play whist, *God knows what old age has in store for me* when my music is no longer wanted. Perhaps that time is not far off. I can only compose soothing music, and the public is now feverish. It is beginning to want to be scratched; soon it will want to be grazed and scoured, and then I shall give up."

---

[1] *L'Entr'acte* of May 24th and 30th, 1855, gave news of a forthcoming ballet, entitled *Lucinde*, which was to have a score by Adolphe Adam and Giunti Bellini, and a scenario by Gérard de Nerval (who had committed suicide in the January of that year) and Albert Asseline. The scenario, which was no doubt based on Asseline's *Les Noces de Lucinde* (published in 1845), had been submitted in December 1854 and was said to be written entirely in the hand of Gérard de Nerval. Presumably, this ballet was identical with *Les Gaîtés champêtres*, which Jules Janin, in the *Journal des Débats* of May 7th, announced was being prepared "so mysteriously" for Marie Guy-Stéphan. The work was never performed, probably on account of the quarrel between Guy-Stéphan and Crosnier which led to her departure from the Opéra later that summer.

V

ROSATI AND FERRARIS

The year 1856, which brought both peace after the Crimean War and an heir to the Imperial throne of France, saw also another change in the management of the Paris Opéra and the appearance of yet another distinguished Italian ballerina on its stage. Alphonse Royer succeeded Crosnier as Director on July 1st. A journalist and novelist who had had a hand in translating the libretti of several Italian operas, Royer had proved his worth as a theatre manager at the Théâtre de l'Odéon since 1853. His management of the Opéra was to endure for more than six years, and to be marked by three tragedies: the death, on duty, of the conductor, Narcisse Girard; the hunting accident which robbed Roger of his right arm and the Opéra of its greatest tenor; and, most terrible of all, the fatal burning of Emma Livry.

For some months before Royer's succession, Carolina Rosati had been constantly expressing a desire to visit America, where fifteen years previously Fanny Elssler had crowned her career with such an unforgettable triumph. Fearing that he might be unable to retain her services after November 1856, when her current contract ended, Crosnier had taken the precaution of engaging Amalia Ferraris for one year from June 5th, 1856, at a salary of 3,600 francs a month; and it was her début that first engaged Royer's attention after he had taken up his new functions.

Amalia Ferraris was born at Voghera, in Lombardy, in 1830. After studying first with Chouchoux, and later with Blasis, she made her début at the Scala, Milan, in the autumn of 1844. Her unusual lightness and vigorous *pointe* work rapidly gained her many admirers throughout Italy; the sculptor Gajazzi modelled a statuette of her, and at Rome she was presented with a golden garland bearing the words, "From the Romans to the most celebrated of dancers, the rival of Elssler." She also achieved success in London and Vienna.

She was a very conscientious artiste, and Enrico Cecchetti, in his old age, would recall how she used to place a stage hand in the stalls during a rehearsal to obtain a layman's reaction to her dancing, afterwards rewarding him with a glass of beer. Away from the theatre, she assumed the modest guise of a housewife. "In town, in her small apartment in the Rue de Provence," wrote Paul Mahalin, "it was difficult to drag her away from her *polenta*, her *rizotto*, her *ravioli*—and her husband," a learned gentleman named Giuseppe Torre.

Amalia Ferraris made her first appearance at the Opéra in a new ballet, *Les Elfes*, on August 11th, 1856, when the temperature during the day had approached 100° Fahrenheit. It was the time of year when fashionable society was out of Paris, but many returned to the capital specially to attend her début.

Saint-Georges' scenario for *Les Elfes* [1] was carefully constructed, erring perhaps by its intricacy which required a deal of explanatory miming. While out hunting with Prince Albert of Hungary (L. Petipa), Count Frederick (Segarelli) discovers a temple containing a beautiful statue of Sylvia (Ferraris). The Prince decides to take it to his palace, and orders it to be covered with a purple veil as a sign of his ownership. The hunt continues, but the Count remains behind and falls asleep. He wakes to find himself surrounded by elves. Their Queen (Legrain) perceives his passion for the statue and commands the spirit of one of her elves (Nathan) to enter into it so that by day it will become a woman. When the Prince returns, daylight is fading and, to the Count's relief, Sylvia has turned back into stone. Back at the palace, preparations are being made for the marriage of Prince Albert to the Princess Bathilde (L. Marquet). When the Prince goes to show the statue to his guests, the pedestal is empty. Later, a lovely girl, whom the Prince tries in vain to recognize, is found among the company. In the palace garden, the Queen of the Elves appears to the Count and gives him three roses, which will confer reason, grace and the power to love on Sylvia, warning him that with each gift he will age by ten years. Heedless, the Count bestows all three, becoming himself a wizened old man. He then approaches Sylvia hopefully, only to find that the object of

---

[1] It bore a certain resemblance to the same author's scenario for *The Marble Maiden* (choreography by Albert), produced at the Theatre Royal, Drury Lane, London, on September 27th, 1845.

Amalia Ferraris in *Les Elfes*

Marco Spada, Act III, Scene III

Sacountala, Act I

Sacountala, Act II

Louis Mérante and Emma Livry
in *La Sylphide*

Emma Livry in *Herculanum*

Emma Livry and Louis Mérante
in *Le Papillon*, Act I, Scene I

Emma Livry in *Le Papillon*
Act I, Scene II

her new-found emotion is the Prince. Almost reluctantly, the Prince leads his betrothed to the wedding ceremony. Before Sylvia can make a last appeal, darkness spreads over the scene and she becomes a statue again. The Count takes the statue to a grotto, where he is found by the Prince, who accuses him of having stolen it. The two men draw their swords. As they fight, dawn breaks and Sylvia comes to life. The Prince drops his sword in amazement, but Sylvia places herself between the duellists to protect him from his opponent's attack. Finally, the Count is disarmed and taken away under arrest. Though grateful to her, the Prince does not return Sylvia's love, and slowly she hardens into stone. The Count, having escaped from his guards, reappears, and, in a fit of madness, smashes the statue. As he does so, a tiny flame is seen to rise from one of the fragments and settle on the tomb of the sacrificed elf, who springs to life again and is joyfully welcomed back by the Queen and her companions.

The ballet was long, Gabrielli's score being colourless and Mazilier's choreography at times lacking in originality. Lucien Petipa, who had to dance a fiery mazurka, clad in furs, despite the sultry August heat, was criticized for his lack of buoyancy; Segarelli was blamed for showing excessive zeal in his miming, and in particular for rolling his eyes furiously when others held the centre of the stage; while Victorine Legrain, as the ethereal Queen of the Elves, seemed all too obviously miscast.

But these shortcomings were almost forgotten in the light of Ferraris' personal triumph. The Emperor and Empress were in their box when the curtain rose after the short overture. A few minutes later, the purple covering that had been thrown over the statue fell to the ground to reveal the new dancer for the first time. All eyes were upon her as she darted forward. "She flew rather than stepped on this large stage," wrote Fiorentino. "Her first *pas* was composed only of one *variation*, but what a *variation*! Nothing more exquisite or more perfect has ever been seen. There are *tours de jambe relevés d'aplomb sur la pointe* of magistral grace, precision and neatness, all being crowned by *gargouillades* . . . so rapid and so brilliant that the whole house was, so to speak, dazzled. The Emperor gave the signal for the applause, and the public replied with tremendous cheering.

"In the *adage* of the first *pas de trois*, which she dances in the second act, she displays attitudes and poses of rare elegance and marvellous suppleness; her body undulates like a scarf on the arm of her partner with such grace and ease that her positions might be the most familiar and the most natural. . . . The second *écot* of this *pas de trois* shows how firm and precise is Mme Ferraris' style. Her *cabrioles*, her *jetés battus* are beaten as cleanly as they are vigorously. The *coda*, composed of *pirouettes cambrées*, throws into particular relief the lightness, elasticity and *parcours* which Mme Ferraris possesses to a supreme degree.

"The last *pas* in the *ballabile* of *Les Elfes* is a marvel of execution which no dancer until now has attempted. Generally, whenever a *pas* requires *temps d'élévation*, the composer is careful to employ every instrument in the orchestra to cover the sound made by the dancer on alighting. But Mme Ferraris wished to dance the *pas* in which she reaches the highest elevation to a simple harp accompaniment. There was a great silence in the theatre. The harp murmured so softly that the imperceptible sound of a leaf falling could have been heard. Yet the dancer rose to a prodigious height with her *entrechats huit*, and alighted on the boards so gently that it seemed she had not touched them. . . ."

According to *Le Théâtre*, Ferraris excelled in *poses renversées avec battements de jambes*, and her *entrechats huit* were more perfect than any that had been seen before. The critic of *L'Illustration* described how she crossed the stage "on the toe of one foot alone, without the other once touching the floor."

The rôle of Sylvia was exacting, for Ferraris was on the stage almost continuously. It afforded her few opportunities of miming, and it was therefore principally as a dancer that she was judged. She belonged, said Saint-Victor, to the "platonic school of Taglioni." Her movements were ample, her gestures gentle and flowing, her poise superb; better elevation and *ballon* had seldom been seen; and the strength of her *pointes* left nothing to be desired. She possessed more ardour and better breath control than Rosati, and her attack recalled memories of the remarkable Fuoco. Though not beautiful, her features were pleasing and regular, and her expression piquant.

At the end of the ballet, she was nearly smothered by the shower of bouquets. Rather than to add yet more flowers to those she had already received, Saint-Georges preferred to express his own pleasure and admiration in words, and sent her the following verse:—

> *Quand à vous applaudir tout Paris s'évertue,*
> *Moi seul, je blâme fort ce ' galant carillon ' ;*
> *J'ai fait pour vous une statue,*
> *Vous en faites un papillon.*

.   .   .   .

The following year, 1857, marked the departure of four dancers from the Opéra. The first to leave were Louise Taglioni, who danced in Paris for the last time at the end of February, and her husband, Alexandre Fuchs; and the last, Victorine Legrain, who departed at the end of December, dismayed partly by the failure of the Opéra to take notice of her recent triumph in Vienna, and partly by being passed over, on the ground that she was not voluptuous enough, when a replacement was being sought for Ferraris in *Le Cheval de bronze.* The greatest loss was that of Adeline Plunkett, who went in the summer; she was then thirty-three, and earning 24,000 francs a year. After leaving the Opéra, she danced for some years in Rome. She became the wife of Paul Dalloz, who at one time was the proprietor of *Le Moniteur,* and survived him by twenty-three years, dying in Paris on November 8th, 1910, at the age of eighty-six.

In their place came Zinaida Iosefovna Richard, from St. Petersburg, a *protégée,* it was said, of Jules Perrot. Though she had been born in Russia, in 1832, her father, the *maître de ballet,* Joseph Richard, was a Frenchman and had in fact once been engaged at the Opéra; her mother, Daria Lapukina, had also been a dancer. Zina Richard had left Russia with a maintenance allowance from the St. Petersburg Conservatoire and her travelling expenses paid out of the Tsar's Civil List, with the object of gaining further experience in France and England. Her Paris début, in *Le Trouvère* on January 12th, 1857, was a memorable occasion.

Some weeks afterwards, a gentleman sitting in the orchestra stalls failed to recognize her when she made her entrance, and enquired who she was.

"It is Mlle Zina," his neighbour told him, "whose tights came undone on the evening of her début."

"A remarkable accident," observed Auber, who was close by. "It was one of those rare occasions when an undoing is turned into a success."

She followed her début by taking over Ferraris' rôle in *Le Cheval de bronze* for a few weeks in the autumn, and the following spring appeared in Halévy's opera, *La Magicienne*, which contained a *divertissement* by Mazilier, based on a game of chess, with six moves, culminating in the taking of the King.

An attractive newcomer to the Foyer de la Danse, Zina Richard soon found herself assailed with proposals from the wealthy *abonnés*. Early in 1858, it was reported that "Mlle Zina, the Russian dancer lately arrived, whose success as a dancer, however doubtful, left her *succès de nu* quite undisputed, is about to retire from publicity, by the acceptance of the left hand of Prince Ga—— in marriage."

Some years later, on July 20th, 1861, she married Louis Mérante at the church of Notre-Dame de Lorette. The wedding was quite an event in the dancing world of Paris. Perrot, Lucien Petipa, Mazilier and Berthier acted as witnesses; Marius and Marie Petipa were present; and Emma Livry was the maid of honour. Zina Mérante danced at the Opéra for the last time in 1864, and shortly afterwards temporarily abandoned her career to become a mother. In 1871, after the Franco-German War, she returned to the Opéra as a teacher, eventually, in 1879, succeeding Mme Dominique as *professeur de la classe de perfectionnement*, a post which she held until May 31st, 1890; she was a very conscientious and often severe teacher, and was much loved by her pupils, the most famous of whom was Julia Subra. Zina Mérante died in the Villa Zina, at Courbevoie, in September 1890, little more than three years after her husband.

.   .   .   .

Feeling rich in the possession of two great dancers, Royer decided on the dangerous hazard of casting them both in the same ballet. The tale of Marco Spada, which Auber had already used, in 1852, for a comic opera, and which contained two major feminine rôles of equal importance, was chosen, and Mazilier entrusted with the choreography. Rosati was fortunately an "exceptionally good comrade" and raised no objection to appearing beside Ferraris. The two dancers were in fact on very amicable terms. Both, however, dreaded the test that had been placed before them: Ferraris became prone to bouts of weeping and Rosati would fly into a temper at the slightest provocation. Afterwards, Rosati confessed to Royer that she nearly fled to England on the very morning of the first performance.

The plot of the ballet was similar to that of the comic opera. The Marchesa Sampietri (Ferraris), niece of the Governor of Rome (Lenfant), is betrothed to her cousin, Count Frederici (L. Petipa), and loved by a Captain of Dragoons, Pepinelli (L. Mérante). The Governor, the Marchesa and Pepinelli seek shelter from a storm in a house, unaware that it is the home of the bandit chief Marco Spada (Segarelli), with whose daughter Angela (Rosati) Frederici has fallen in love. Spada's lieutenant, Genario (E. Coralli), counsels his chief to kill the Governor, but Spada stays his hand and offers hospitality to his visitors. The Governor then invites Spada, of whose identity he is unaware, to attend the ball he is giving the next day. At the ball, Frederici asks Angela to marry him, but she refuses, preferring to share her father's danger. In his annoyance, Frederici decides to marry the Marchesa without further delay. As she is trying on her wedding-dress, Pepinelli enters her boudoir to declare his love for her, but no sooner has he thrown himself at her feet than Spada's men arrive and carry her off, with all her finery and jewellery, together with a large basket in which Pepinelli has hidden. The prisoners are taken to the bandits' cavern, where Spada, discovering the reason for Angela's sadness, orders the Marchesa and Pepinelli to be married. Spada then leads his men into battle with the dragoons, who are searching the forest above. The bandits are defeated. Spada, mortally wounded, is carried into the cavern, but before he dies he declares that Angela is not his daughter, thus ensuring her happiness by enabling Frederici to marry her.

A sure sign of the success of any new work at the Opéra was to be sought, it was said, in the appetite of M. David, the leader of the *claque* and a man of very regular habits. He never dined before a first night, so as to conserve his *sang froid*, and a failure would leave him so exhausted that he could eat no supper. After the first performance of *Marco Spada*, however, on April 1st, 1857, he consumed a hearty meal.

The success of the ballet depended mainly on the choreographic duel between Rosati and Ferraris, and a spectacular
example of the machinist's art in the last act—the raising of the
whole stage, as far back as the eighth groove, with some thirty
people upon it, to show another scene, the underground cavern,
beneath it. The ballet itself was not otherwise remarkable. The
plot of the comic opera had been transposed without sufficient
simplification, with the result that the development of the plot
demanded tedious passages of mime, which the cuts made after
the first performance did not entirely succeed in eliminating.

The appearance of Rosati and Ferraris side by side in the
same work of course invited comparisons. Most critics were
scrupulously impartial, allotting to each dancer an equal share
of praise and venturing no opinion as to which was the better.
There were, however, exceptions, such as Saint-Victor, who
roundly declared that Ferraris had carried the day. "It was,"
he wrote, "a struggle between the wing and the foot, between
the spirit and the flesh, between the imponderable elf . . . and
the robust bacchante."

Fiorentino, who was no less an admirer of Ferraris than
Saint-Victor, refused to judge between the two dancers, merely
observing that Mazilier had been so concerned with preserving
the balance, that much of the effect of the *pas de leçon* which they
danced together was lost. This *pas* occurred in the scene in
Marco Spada's house, after the Governor has invited Spada to
his ball and Angela has confessed to the Marchesa that she
cannot dance a step. Describing the dancing lesson that
followed, Fiorentino wrote: "La Rosati, miming wonderfully,
was adorably clumsy in her feigned ignorance, and La Ferraris
performed prodigious leaps which sent the audience into
raptures."

Of Ferraris, he wrote that no other dancer since Marie
Taglioni had possessed such elevation, *ballon* and *parcours*. The
adage of her *grand pas* in the ball scene contained *attitudes* and
développements of an unbelievable daring, and ended by her
twice circling the stage on her *pointes* with astonishing rapidity
and precision and not the slightest sign of fatigue. The first
variation was composed of *temps de ballon*; the second included a
neat sequence of *ronds de jambe en tournant*; and the *allegro* ended
with *cabrioles à mains jointes* "of diabolical difficulty." Her last
pas, in the boudoir scene, contained *attitudes sur les pointes* "so

perfectly executed," said Fiorentino, "that they alone would suffice to prove that Mme Ferraris has no rival as a dancer."

The contrast between her style and Rosati's was similar to that which had divided the Opéra audiences into two factions in the days of Taglioni and Elssler. Rosati's style, like Elssler's, could be defined as *terre à terre*. She lacked the elevation and *ballon* of her rival, and after an intrepid passage was often visibly a little out of breath. In the *pas de masque*, she triumphed by a sequence of *ronds de jambe en retour*, "so light, so exquisitely

DOMENICO SEGARELLI, AMALIA FERRARIS, LOUIS MÉRANTE, AND
CAROLINA ROSATI IN "MARCO SPADA"
Caricature by Marcelin

neat, so unexpected, spontaneous, lively and dazzling," wrote Fiorentino, "as to defy description." Her outstanding quality was her dramatic power. She lived the character of Angela. "When La Rosati no longer has legs," wrote Jouvin, "she will dance with a smile or a lock of her hair."

The ballet, though financially very successful, was dogged by ill luck. During one of the first few performances, a gentleman rumoured to possess the "evil eye" was talking to Constance Quéniaux in the wings, when a heavy piece of scenery fell at their feet, sending the terrified dancer running to the Foyer. Later, when Sacré gave the order for the stage to rise to show the cavern, nothing happened. The audience began to laugh at the unfortunate men representing dragoons, who had to while away several minutes with improvised miming until the set was raised manually. At the end, a super, blinded by the smoke from a Bengal light, fell head first from the upper part of the scene to the lower, a distance of some fifteen feet, and was unconscious for two hours. Nor was this all. The sinister gentleman then complimented Rosati, who immediately developed a sore throat and was unable to dance for a week. The *corps de ballet* was greatly impressed by this series of mishaps, and soon everyone was carrying charms to ward off any further evil influence.

Segarelli, who had been criticized for his overdrawn characterization of the rôle of Spada, left the Opéra in May 1858 under somewhat mysterious circumstances. Nearly five years later, *The Court Journal* gave a highly coloured and perhaps fanciful account of the incident that was supposed to have led to his retirement.

"One of [Mérante's] fellow artistes," the story ran, "was desperately in love with a young dancer then making her début. It was in vain to tell the poor artiste that the great beauty of the young lady was ensuring her the homage of the richest and most noble of all the frequenters of the Opéra; the unhappy artiste still went on displaying light heels and heavy heart, bent upon bringing his passion to a close, either by success with the fair one or a catastrophe in which both should be involved. One night the ballet was *Marco Spada*. The hero of our tale was dancing the principal rôle, when, on leaving the stage after the first scene, he rushed into Mérante's dressing-room with the look and gesture of one desperate.

"'I have seen her! She is with him! She does not dance to-night! She sent in a plea of indisposition, but I see her wrapped in his cloak, seated at the back of his box, while he lolls forward for no other purpose than to gaze with insolence at me. But keep near me, Mérante, there will be some fatal blow to-night! *Attendez*, and you will see.'

"At that moment they were called upon the stage, and so well had the poor player learned to disguise his feelings that he went bounding on the stage with the same unmeaning smile with which in general he greeted the spectators, and was received with the same loud burst of applause in consequence. The short carbine with which Marco Spada is armed had been placed meanwhile against one of the 'flats'; Mérante caught the glance with which the dancer turned once to see if it were still there safe—the look was a revelation. He crept close to the

Le Papillon, Act I, Scene II

Le Papillon, Act I, Scene II: Valse des rayons

Le Papillon, Act II, Scene II

Le Papillon, Act II, Scene II: The apotheosis

'flat,' and while the *premier sujet* was whirling round and round in one of his most terrible *pirouettes*, he exchanged the one he bore for that which his comrade had deposited there, slinging that which had belonged to Marco Spada across his own shoulders.

"The ballet proceeded. Presently, and in the midst of one of the most fiery of the brigand's *pas*, the dragoons appear. All is confusion on the stage. Marco Spada fights desperately, and, in the excitement and confusion, fires right across the pit straight at the very heart of Prince ——, who, forgetful of propriety, had just then dragged his hidden companion forward to see the magnificent effect. Such a thing might have passed unperceived, had it not been for the wild exclamation by which the act was accompanied, and by the immediate catastrophe which followed, for the poor dancer, imagining he had done the deed, drew from his belt the jewelled dagger he wore in his costume and plunged it at once in his side. The curtain fell on the instant, and all was uproar. The poor victim, an Italian by birth, did not die actually there upon the stage, but expired at his own lodgings before the morning.[1] Mérante's disclosure of the means he had adopted of averting the vengeance intended for Prince —— was fully borne out by the ball which was found in the carbine for which he had exchanged his own. Prince ——'s gratitude was displayed in princely fashion, and Mérante's comrades whisper that he might long ago have retired from the stage, had he preferred inglorious ease to toilsome triumph."

.   .   .   .

The salaries of the two principal dancers of the Opéra now formed a very large item in the theatre's budget. Rosati was under contract until the end of November 1858 at 6,000 francs a month, while, in the summer of 1857, Ferraris' contract was renewed for a further year at an annual salary of 40,000 francs, which a year later was increased to 42,000 francs. The management, therefore, could certainly not afford to have either of them idle, and planned a series of revivals to bridge the interval before the next new ballet.

The first of these revivals was *Orfa*, which was given in July 1857, with Ferraris in the title-rôle. Her rendering of the part

---

[1] Actually, Segarelli died in Turin in 1860.

was very different to Cerrito's. The warmth and the unexpected little improvisations that had been the charm of Cerrito's interpretation were replaced by Ferraris' superior technique and perfect precision.

Two months later, Ferraris appeared in Auber's opera-ballet, *Le Cheval de bronze*, waiving the condition in her contract that she was not to dance in opera *divertissements*, as a token of gratitude to the composer for her rôle in *Marco Spada*. As a faery

AMALIA FERRARIS IN ''ORFA''
Caricature by Marcelin

opera in three acts, *Le Cheval de bronze* had first been produced at the Opéra-Comique in 1835; now another act had been added, containing a *divertissement* by Lucien Petipa, for which Auber had composed new music. The success that had formerly attended the work at the Opéra-Comique was not, however, repeated, and failure was only averted by the irreproachable technique of Ferraris. Her style, it was said, only just lacked the final touch of grace.

Rosati's turn was to come in the winter. For her, the thirty-year-old ballet, *La Somnambule*, with choreography by Aumer and music by Hérold, was revived, the first performance on November 21st, 1857, being given for her benefit. At the dress rehearsal a few days before, while practising the scene in which the heroine sleepwalks along the roof of the old mill, Rosati slipped and badly grazed her leg. To avoid a recurrence of this disaster on the first night, it was arranged that a super should undertake the dangerous journey from the roof of the mill to the ground, after which Rosati would take her place by gliding out from behind a large rock. Unfortunately, the super did not withdraw quickly enough, and for a few moments there were two somnambulists visible on the stage at the same time. Above

CAROLINA ROSATI IN "LA SOMNAMBULE"
Caricature by Marcelin

the laughter that arose could be heard "strong marks of dis-approval" from certain parts of the house. The incident was typical of the negligent production of this revival. Little attempt had been made to adapt the ballet to more modern tastes, about the only change being the addition of a *pas de deux* to music by a M. Gondois. The scenario was adjudged puerile. The scenery, the same as had been used in the 1827 production, was found insipid and lacking in conception and colour; and the mill scene of the third act, which had caused a sensation thirty years before, now appeared almost ludicrously artificial.

Rosati's artistry went far towards compensating for these shortcomings. Her interpretation of the rôle of Thérèse was beyond all criticism, while, as a dancer, "skimming over the ground, she displayed all the trills and the demisemiquavers of the *tacqueté*."

Scribe, the scenarist, would not take the royalties that were due to him out of the receipts of Rosati's benefit. "My charming neighbour," he wrote to her the day before. "You must have been told at the Opéra that Box No. 26 on the second tier belongs to me for every performance. This is laid down by my contract, but this contract does not exist so far as you are concerned, so please dispose of my box as you wish. I also beg you to accept my royalties, whatever they might be, for this performance. You have revived my old *Somnambule*, which has been asleep these thirty years in the archives of the Opéra, and you have made it a masterpiece of freshness and youth. No songs, not even those of Bellini [1] . . . ever had the conviction and eloquence of your miming. In gratitude and admiration, Scribe."

Four days later, Napoleon III attended the second performance with the Empress, and afterwards sent Rosati a magnificent bracelet in diamonds, rubies and emeralds.

. . . .

Joseph Mazilier, the *premier maître de ballet*, had now turned sixty and felt that his failing strength could no longer endure the preparation of another full-length ballet. Although he did not formally retire until he had completed thirty years of service at the end of 1859, it was Lucien Petipa, the *second maître de ballet*, who, in 1858, was chosen to produce Ferraris' third ballet. A composer new to the Opéra, Ernest Reyer, was commissioned to write the music, and, as though to make up for the lack of experience in his colleagues, Théophile Gautier was asked to provide a scenario.

Gautier entitled the ballet *Sacountala*, founding the plot on the drama of the same name by the fourth-century Sanskrit poet, Kalidasa. The first act takes place near a small temple in one of India's sacred forests. The tranquillity of the scene is disturbed by the arrival of a hunt, led by the King, Douchmata (L. Petipa). Realizing where he is, the King dismisses his retinue and prays at the altar. The sound of women's voices is heard, and he hides in the thick foliage. Some girls come to fill their pitchers at the sacred well. One of them, Sacountala (Ferraris), starts to water the flowers. A bee, mistaking her

[1] The composer of the opera, *La Sonnambula*, first produced at the Teatro Carcano, Milan, on March 6th, 1831.

for a flower, flies after her, until the King comes out of hiding and chases the insect away. The King then declares his love for Sacountala and gives her a ring as a token of betrothal. The fakir Durwasas (E. Coralli), shocked at the sight of the lovers embracing in the hallowed spot, snatches the ring from Sacountala's finger and throws it into the sacred stream. Despite the loss of her ring, Sacountala departs for the King's palace, where the second act takes place. The fakir, however, has cast a spell over the King, who does not recognize Sacountala when she arrives. His favourite, Hamsati (L. Marquet), commands her to be burnt. At that moment, a fisherman is admitted to the palace, bringing the King's ring, which he has found inside a fish. The King recovers his memory, and places the ring again on Sacountala's finger.

The Empress had driven into Paris from Saint-Cloud specially to see the first performance on July 14th, 1858. It was nearly as hot an evening as on the first night of *Les Elfes*, and many ladies were reported to have come suitably *décolletées*. One curious miscalculation had happily been rectified after the general rehearsal. Someone had ingeniously proposed that the hoofs of the horses taking part in the hunt in the first act should be muffled to deaden the sound of their shoes on the wooden boards, but the unfortunate animals found the absence of noise when they walked so strange, that at the rehearsal they had lain down on the stage in bewilderment.

Commenting on the scenario, one journal remarked that "the *gamins* who try to read the playbills of the Opéra are awe-struck at its appearance, covered as it is with the most repulsive and extraordinary-looking words." Gautier's display of erudition was followed a month later, on August 15th—the anniversary of Napoleon's birth, and France's national holiday during the Second Empire—by the announcement that he had been made an Officer of the Legion of Honour.

Gautier and Petipa had not always been in agreement on the subject of the ballet's action. After the dress rehearsal, when a friend had expressed his opinion that the ballet contained dull passages, Gautier discovered that, unknown to him, additions had been made at the instance both of the choreographer and of the management. However, the poet bore no ill feelings for this interference, and in his notice of *Sacountala* in *Le Moniteur*, warmly praised Petipa's choreography as original and distinguished by the *plastique* of the groups and the able handling of the crowd scenes.

Gautier also praised the composer, who, to his mind, had displayed a deep understanding of oriental melody in a score that was "as local, as Indian as possible" without being a comic imitation of Eastern music. He voiced too his admiration for the sets: the forest scene by Martin, who had lived in India for many years, and the palace scene by Nolau and Rubé, which he considered one of the most beautiful that had been seen at the Opéra for a long time, and which reminded him of "one of the prodigious architectures of John Martin, reaching up to the heavens until it is lost in infinite perspective." Jules Janin disagreed. "The scenery has been praised, over-praised," he thought. "The three artists have lavished grand monumental stairways, marble steps, palaces, masses of exotic flowers, heavy-leafed plants, flowers with enormous blooms . . . but they have provided much too much to please simple folk. Away with these white metal roses and rubber tulips!"

After their joint triumph in *Marco Spada*, it was perhaps inevitable that Ferraris and Rosati should be considered as rivals contesting for supremacy. "One could not wish for higher elevation, more novelty or more originality in her style," wrote Jouvin, after seeing Ferraris in *Sacountala*, "but at times one begins to regret that she has not more flow as a dancer. The upper part of Ferraris' body is a little stiff and lacking in grace, as though it were in protest against the trilling of her legs; and her arms, restrained by a visible effort, walk when her feet are flying. It is otherwise with her rival. La Rosati dances with her arms, with her body, with her features, with her intellect—in fact, with her all . . . except her legs. La Rosati is a *danseuse d'expression*; La Ferraris a *danseuse à roulades*."

"A feather, a wisp of swan's down fluttering in the air, a dream, a vision—such is this incomparable dancer," wrote Fiorentino of Ferraris. "It seems as though she is not made of the same opaque, heavy clay of which we are fashioned . . . or as though she is gifted with being able to suspend at will the natural laws that attract bodies towards the earth. She no longer dances, she hovers, glides, floats in space. . . .

"La Ferraris must be seen in the marvellous *adage* of her first *pas de deux* [with Petipa in the forest scene]. Straight and firm on *pointes* that are as sharp as arrows and as precise as the two arms of a compass, she circles the stage, brushing and running through the bushes by which her companions are grouped. Then, in an impetuous and brilliant *variation*, she lavishes, with a superb ease, *jetés sautés en tournant* . . . which no dancer has ever attempted since Mlle Taglioni. You think the wonders are at an end, but this is only a beginning. There follows a *variation* completely novel, bold, charming, that belongs to La Ferraris alone. Accompanied by a clarinet solo, a murmur, a purring from the orchestra, she pirouettes on the *pointe* . . . with unbelievable speed and lightness. The instrument, put on its

LUCIEN PETIPA AND AMALIA FERRARIS IN "SACOUNTALA"
Caricature by Marcelin

mettle, multiplies its notes and its shades, but the dancer will not let it outstrip her, and the more hurried the tempo becomes, the more precisely does she mark her steps, which are as numerous, as delicate, as rapid as a shower of sparks.

"I do not intend to describe all the pretty details, the magistral attitudes, the elegance and grace of movement, expression and gesture that she displays in these two acts, for I should never finish. I come to the final *pas de deux* with Mérante, and I declare that nothing could be more astonishing. Let your eyes follow those *doubles tours sur la pointe*, admire the suppleness, the softness, the supreme distinction of those delightful poses, see her literally cleave the air and come down the stage describing a horizontal line with her two legs coiling beneath her and her small feet not touching the ground. Then, like a heedless bird lazily brushing its wing on the surface of a lake, Mme Ferraris, with a twirl of a wounded nightingale, lightly grazes the ground and alights to make her bow, blushing and confused, beneath a rain of bouquets."

.   .   .   .   .   .

In fairness to Rosati, the Opéra decided to bring to Paris the famous Italian choreographer, Giuseppe Rota, to produce her next ballet. Rota began work in the winter of 1858, and Rosati had agreed, for a consideration, to forgo her three months' holiday in 1859 to maintain the continuity of the rehearsals.

There were many conjectures as to the subject that Rota had chosen. One report had it that he was to produce two tragedy ballets, first *Artaxerxes*, and later *Le Faux Smerdis* to a score by Gabrielli; another hinted at a revival of his *I Bianchi ed i Negri*, with the two title-rôles taken by Ferraris and Rosati; and later, there was talk of a ballet based on Byron's *Don Juan*, Gabrielli again being mentioned as the composer. But these were only conjectures, although they may have indicated Rota's plans for the future. His immediate task was the production of a ballet entitled *La Comtesse d'Egmont*.

Paris was destined never to see this work, for early in the summer of 1859, Rosati, resenting what she considered to be preferential treatment given to Ferraris, severed her connection with the Opéra. The year before, the management had granted Ferraris additional leave only two months after the first night of *Sacountala*, to enable her to accept an engagement in St. Petersburg, and Rosati, who had been approached with an offer from the same quarter for the autumn of 1859, expected a similar concession to be made to her. Royer, however, presumably anticipating an unprecedented success for the approaching Rota ballet, refused to grant her request, leaving her to decide whether to rescind her contract with the Opéra or lose the opportunity of a Russian triumph. At the end of May 1859, she informed Royer that she had elected to go to Russia and asked that her contract should be terminated as from September 1st.

Royer wished Rota to continue his rehearsals with Ferraris, but the choreographer adamantly refused. He had devised the rôle for Rosati, he said, and she alone was suitable. Relations between Rota and the Opéra became very strained.

Towards the end of the year, *The Court Journal's* Paris

correspondent reported: "The *coulisses* have been actively engaged in canvassing the merits of the different *danseuses* of the Opéra, who have been convoked to a species of competition for the part in the new ballet, by the departure of Rosati. The new work by Rota has been keeping us alive for some time past. The author, who declares with the greatest naïvety that whatever merit the composition may possess is entirely owing to the inspiration produced in his brain by the contemplation of the well-turned ankles of Mlle Rosati, brings a lawsuit against the management of the Opéra, who had accepted his work with the engagement that no other ankles were to twinkle through the principal part. Meanwhile, the fair ballerina, making better use of the admired ankles than by standing motionless upon them, waiting the manager's good pleasure to get up the ballet, trips off to St. Petersburg, leaving the poor author miserable and disconsolate, to replace his aerial fancies with ankles of ordinary growth and doubtful elasticity. Other dancers are offered in Rosati's place—the very first, the very best. No; none will do. There is a situation in the piece wherein first-rate ankles are a strict necessity; and the judges, seeing at once the urgency of the case and the wrong done to the author, give the full extent of damages to the injured Rota. He is, however, of *bonne pâte* enough to consent to a choice of ankles in the *corps de ballet* for the performance of the one scene in question, and, should he succeed in finding a pair to suit him, will forgo the penalty and recommence his labours; but, up to the present hour, none have been found sufficiently neat and sound to answer his expectations, and they say he has serious thoughts of offering an indemnity to Mlle Rosati to induce her to return to Paris, in order to prove to the world how right he was to insist upon 'Rosati's ankles' or none. The cause has become so popular, that, all round the Opéra, bonbon sellers are making money by the sale of bonbons tied up in pink and blue paper and labelled in gold letters, 'Rosati's ankles.'"

Rota's suspicions were confirmed. Rosati's ankles were inimitable. Disappointed, he returned to Italy, where later he mounted his ballet with considerable success, but without Rosati, both in Rome and Milan. Rosati meanwhile made her début in St. Petersburg in *Jovita*, and remained in Russia for more than two years. In 1862, there were rumours that she was about to reappear in Paris, at the Théâtre de la

Porte-Saint-Martin, but these were unfounded. She had danced in public for the last time.

Like many another dancer who lived to a great age, she retired into a seclusion which was seldom troubled. Some twenty years afterwards, Gaston Jollivet, an old *abonné* of the Opéra, happened to visit the South of France and noticed some wonderful tangerines growing in a garden overlooking the road leading from Cannes to Antibes. Tempted, he went up to the house and rang the bell. The door was opened by a middle-aged woman whom he took for a peasant. To his enquiry whether the oranges were for sale, she replied, "Certainly, *monsieur*," and coming out into the garden, began picking the fruit. Then suddenly she turned to him. "You have not recognized me, *monsieur*," she said, laughing, "although you have applauded me many times at the Opéra." It was Carolina Rosati in her chosen retreat, where she was still to live undisturbed for many years before she died there in May 1905.

VI

THE TRAGEDY OF EMMA LIVRY

THE career of Emma Livry, for its brevity and brilliance, resembled the passing of a shooting star. She appeared suddenly, almost without warning, so bewildering those who saw her that, when she was gone, she seemed some ideal once seen in a dream. It was her début in the autumn of 1858 that interrupted the line of Italian ballerinas who had reigned for so long in undisputed succession at the Opéra, a line that was to resume its unchallenged sway only four years later, when her brief career was brought to its terrible close. Emma Livry made her début at the age of sixteen, and her twentieth birthday was not three months past when she danced for the last time; she never reached the age of Taglioni at the time of *La Sylphide*, of Carlotta Grisi at the time of *Giselle*, or of Cerrito at the time of *Alma*. Had her career been permitted to continue for its expected span, the history of French ballet might well have taken a different course, and a name to commemorate among the most illustrious been inscribed in the annals of the dance. For in the four years that were allotted to her, almost before she grew into full womanhood, Emma Livry achieved such distinction as to be chosen, with Marie Taglioni and Carlotta Grisi, as one of the three representative *danseuses* of the Romantic Ballet whose portrait busts were commissioned to be placed in the Foyer des Abonnés of the new Paris Opéra, where they proudly stand to this day.

. . . . . .

It was with a note of surprise that Jules Janin recorded, at the time of her début, that Emma Livry was "quite absurdly a Frenchwoman and a Parisienne". The Emarot family, from which she came, in fact originated in Dijon, where her grandmother had been employed in the linen trade before coming to Paris in about 1834 to seek better fortune. Some two or three years later, through the influence of friends, her daughter, Marguerite Adélaïde, was admitted into the Opéra dancing school, adopting the name Célestine. Being alert and eager to learn, the girl made steady enough progress, but without showing any unusual promise. So, when the opportunity offered, she became the mistress of the Baron Charles de Chassiron, a member of the Jockey Club who spent much of his time in the Foyer de la Danse. In time, Célestine gave birth to a daughter at her apartment in No. 48 Rue Laffitte.[1] The child was baptized more than a year later, on December 14th, 1843, at the church of Notre-Dame de Lorette, and was given the names Emma Marie.

Célestine Emarot made her début as a *sujet* on August 11th, 1845, by creating the rôle of Yelva in *Le Diable à quatre*. She was manifestly painstaking, but all her toil was unrewarded, for her talent was mediocre and few found her dancing pleasing. She filled secondary rôles adequately enough, but failed pathetically when called upon to take an important part, such as the Abbess in *Robert le Diable*: many gentlemen whose memories of Taglioni were still vivid could not bear to watch her in this rôle and retired to the Foyer, while laughter was heard from the pit. One critic described her as "*une grosse inutilité*".

The Baron de Chassiron soon tired of his mistress and his little daughter, and in 1850 married the Princesse Caroline Murat, a cousin of the Emperor, whom he abandoned in turn after a few years to embark on a long voyage through Asia. Despite the passing nature of his liaison with Célestine Emarot, however, not a few were aware of the secret of Emma's birth. Paul Mahalin, for instance, wrote that "not every dancer has the privilege, like Emma Livry, of being born of the love of a rose of the Opéra and a butterfly of the Jockey Club"; and the identity of the member in question was obvious to all who heard the quip that was going the rounds at the time of Emma's début:—

> "*Se peut-il qu'un 'rat' si maigre*
> *Soit la fille d'un 'chat si rond'?*"

---

[1] There is some confusion as to the date of Emma Livry's birth, which is given in the entry of her baptism in the parish register as September 24th, 1841. This is undoubtedly an error, for Célestine Emarot was dancing at Her Majesty's Theatre, London, in the summer of that year. Most probably, Emma Livry was born in 1842. She was referred to almost without exception at the time of her début, in October 1858, as being sixteen; a note by Royer, in the Archives of the Opéra, concerning her re-engagement and dated September 4th, 1861, gives her age as nineteen; and the inscription on her tomb gives her age when she died, in July 1863, as twenty. On the other hand, her death certificate states that she died at the age of twenty-two.

Célestine Emarot's earnings as a dancer never exceeded six thousand francs a year, but she probably received an allowance from Chassiron or some other protector, for she was able to give her daughter a good education, sending her to a respectable girls' school in the Rue du Faubourg-Poissonnière, where the little girl quickly made many friends.

Célestine Emarot first became aware of her daughter's destiny when she entered the dining-room one day and found Emma, then a child of six, in the act of reaching for a jar of sweets on the sideboard, balanced precariously on the very tips of her toes, her legs as straight and firm as a pair of compasses.

"What are you doing, Emma?" she asked.

"*Maman*", replied the little girl, losing neither her balance nor her presence of mind, "I am learning my geography."

"What diplomacy and what *pointes*!" thought Mme Emarot. "My daughter will make a dancer!"

Soon afterwards Emma began attending the dancing classes of Mme Dominique, who had danced many times beside Mme Emarot, and who, as well as being a strict disciplinarian, was an excellent wife and mother. It was this latter merit particularly that recommended her to Mme Emarot, who, presumably wiser from her own experience, confided her child to Mme Dominique's care only on condition that she should form no associations which might be harmful to her.

The fickle Chassiron seemed long to have forgotten the existence of his daughter, but his place in Mme Emarot's affections was apparently soon filled by another nobleman, the Vicomte Ferdinand de Montguyon. Montguyon was one of the original members of the Jockey Club, and his ugly, painted face was a familiar sight backstage at the Opéra. He was a bizarre character. "This hardened gambler, this incorrigible spendthrift, this bedroom rover, indefatigable till his ripe old age", as the Comte de Maugny described him, "was an interesting mixture of great lord and bohemian, with a caustic and impertinent wit, and manners that were both superlatively elegant, and sometimes astonishingly trivial; a man by turns affable and insinuating, and brusque and morose. He always had a serious and open liaison with a *sujet* or *demi-sujet* of the *corps de ballet*—one of these made a great stir—and spent the rest of his time at his club, playing cards. . . . He knew all the scandals, all the intrigues, all the storms in teacups which bubbled incessantly in this little closed world, and did not scorn an occasion to meddle himself, to take sides, even to exert pressure to weight the scales in favour of his preferences and especially his preferred ones." He was the very type of old *beau*, upon whose exaggerated nonchalance, negligent manner of speech, and studied forgetfulness in remembering people's names, Alphonse Daudet based the character of the Marquis de Monpavon in his novel, *Le Nabab*. Beneath Montguyon's eccentric exterior, however, lay many worthy qualities: a steadfast and warm-hearted loyalty, great persistence, and strong and sincere religious beliefs which he saw were instilled into his ward from a very early age. Emma responded willingly to his guidance; the Abbé Mailly, from whose hands she received her first Communion at the church of Saint-Vincent de Paul in 1853, and who remained her confessor till the end, long remembered her piety.

Being on intimate terms with the Comte de Morny, the Emperor's half-brother and one of the most powerful men in France, Montguyon was a man to be reckoned with. Emma could not have had a better champion. His representations on her behalf to the Director of the Opéra, added no doubt to Mme Dominique's reports and perhaps a few words from Morny himself, resulted in the decision, made when Emma was still a child, that she should make her début only when able to bear the responsibility of a principal rôle. By 1858, before she had reached her sixteenth birthday, she had already acquired sufficient command of technique for negotiations to be opened. The choice of *La Sylphide* as the ballet in which she should first appear satisfied Montguyon's requirement of what he called "*une estampille dorée*", a golden trade mark, and he then saw to it that word was sent to Marie Taglioni, in her retirement by Lake Como, to arouse her interest in the miraculous young dancer.

The terms of Emma's first contract were drawn up by Montguyon and Royer. "Mlle Emma Emarot is engaged for one year from July 1st, 1858", ran the memorandum. "She is to make her début in *La Sylphide* when Mme Ferraris is on holiday, and is to take part in *Le Dieu et la Bayadère*, subject to the approval of the management, after *La Sylphide*. Mlle Emma Emarot is engaged as *première danseuse* and is only to dance in *pas de deux* or *pas seuls*, or *pas de deux* with a *corps de ballet.* If the management thinks fit, it may give her *pas* in operas. Mlle Emma Emarot will not be called upon to double any rôle or *pas* whatsoever without her consent. The Director of the Opéra will himself fix the amount of Mlle Emma Emarot's salary after the third performance of *La Sylphide.* She is to accept without demur the figure fixed by the Director, and will not receive the salary for the first three months until after the third performance of *La Sylphide.*"

The choice of *La Sylphide* for Emma's début was both brave and hazardous, for no other rôle was stamped more indelibly with the memory of its creator, and the failures of Priora in *La Sylphide* and Forli in *Giselle* in 1852, and of Besson in *La Fille mal gardée* in 1853, might well have deterred the young dancer from so bold an attempt.

In the summer of 1858, while Emma was preparing for her approaching début, Katrine Friedberg, a dancer who had achieved considerable success in Russia and England, arrived in Paris with a recommendation from the Minister of the Tsar's Household. On an introduction of Dr. Véron, she was at once received by the Minister of State, Achille Fould, to whom she expressed her desire to dance at the Opéra. As a result of this interview, Fould wrote to Royer on July 20th, suggesting that she should take over the rôle of Médora in *Le Corsaire* while Rosati was on holiday, and that her début should be arranged to take place with the least possible delay.

This was disquieting news to Montguyon, who immediately protested to the Director. "My dear Royer", he wrote on August 1st, " I am told that a ballet is about to be rehearsed for the début of Mlle Katrine . . . and that the rehearsals of *La Sylphide* will consequently have to be interrupted. . . . This will necessarily delay the début of Mlle Emma Emarot. Apart from it being important to her that she makes her début at the time you have fixed, *i.e.* the end of September or the beginning of October, a still more pressing reason is, that in order to be able to work in a place of reasonable size, she has had to be at the Foyer de la Danse at six o'clock in the morning for the past six months. If her début is postponed, she will have to give up going to the Foyer in October, because it will not be light at that hour and it is occupied for the rest of the day, and she will have to continue her practising in a place too small for her at the very moment of her début; she will have been needlessly inconvenienced for six months. If it is you who are behind the début of Mlle Katrine, be so good as to see if there is not some means of arranging matters with Mazilier so that there will be no interruption of the rehearsals of *La Sylphide*. If it is by an order of the Minister, please oblige me by submitting my complaint to him. I think he will show interest in my *protégée*, and even if he should not, at least I want him to be aware of it, especially as Mlle Katrine has other engagements and would be able to make her début later without inconvenience to herself. I know, my dear Royer, your sense of justice, and if you are convinced, as I hope you are, of the inconvenience to Mlle Emarot of having the rehearsals of *La Sylphide* interrupted, I have no doubt that you will remove it."

A few days later Montguyon wrote again. "[The Minister] may, if he chooses, take no notice, but I do not want him to say to me, 'Why did you not complain?' I consider the delay that will *necessarily* be caused to Mlle Emarot's début to be very prejudicial to her, and I want the Minister to act in knowledge of the matter."

Katrine Friedberg made a single appearance as Thérèse in *La Somnambule* on August 27th, and shortly afterwards Emma's début was fixed to take place on October 20th. Whether because the names Emma Emarot were not very euphonious, or because that of Emarot might prove a hindrance, it was decided that she should adopt the *nom de théâtre* of Emma Livry. The Marquis Charles de Livry, a playwright, was incensed when he learnt that his noble name had been taken without his consent, and was only with difficulty persuaded not to institute legal proceedings!

The publicity for the approaching début was well handled, thanks in part to the diligence of Montguyon. "I called at the Opéra yesterday to see you, my dear Royer", he wrote a few days before. "In your absence, I saw Vaëz [the Secretary-General] and we agreed that the puffs for Mlle Emma Livry's début should be sent to the papers to-day. As Vaëz told me that he was taking a week's holiday, I am afraid he may forget to speak to you about this before his departure. Please attend to this little affair, and in the puff try to give the greatest possible importance to the début of my *protégée*. I believe it is the best way of being of service to her."

The Burning of Emma Livry during a rehearsal of *La Muette de Portici*

Célestine Emarot, mother of
Emma Livry

Augustine Malot in *La Muette de
Portici*

Louise Fiocre, Louis Mérante, Amalia Ferraris and Eugène Coralli in *Pierre de Médicis*

Amalia Ferraris in *Graziosa*

Louise Marquet in *Graziosa*

Marie S. Petipa in *Le Marché des Innocents*

Montguyon must have been satisfied with the result, for on October 3rd *Le Figaro* had announced: "If the auguries of choreography are to be believed, in two months' time [Emma Livry] will be known as Taglioni II." And four days later, in the same paper, Jouvin wrote: "There is talk of a new dancer who will leap to the heights of the Opéra's two prima ballerinas with her first *jeté battu*. For that there are two small difficulties: the great artiste in question is only sixteen years old, and she is a Frenchwoman. The 'sixteen springs that make up the age' of the *débutante* are no doubt all that is necessary to embellish the *Rose d'amour* of the late Théaulon, but they will not suffice to make a Rosati or a Ferraris. And then the *débutante* is a Frenchwoman. But perhaps you believe in French *danseuses*?"

Preluded by such a fanfare of publicity, the début could not have been more successful. Emma went far to fulfil the expectations held of her, and owed her success entirely to her grace of movement, for she could lay little claim to beauty. "Picture a child of fifteen or sixteen at most", wrote Jules Janin, " in the chaste slenderness—the Romans had a delightful word for it: *gracilis*—of her fifteenth year. She is formed in the fashion of a sculptured marble, designed and embellished by Clodion. Two long arms, like the arms of Mlle Taglioni herself, add to her agile lightness. Two beautiful eyes, filled with fire and gentleness, light up that small ethereal face. Add to these beauties, untouched by rough graces, the tendons of a swan and the wings of a frail bird, rising and hovering in the air."

It was, wrote Fiorentino, "not only a success, but an adoption. . . . At each entrance, at each *variation*, there were bravos without number and without end; after every *pas*, there were loud acclamations and calls. So much had been said beforehand about this young dancer, that for her to have succeeded as she has done means that she must indeed have great talent.

"The words of Shakespeare—'Then there was a star danced, and under that I was born'—come to mind. I am not interested in knowing to what school Mlle Livry belongs, nor who had the honour of guiding her first steps. Nature has given her marvellous qualities: she has unusual lightness, fluidity, elasticity; she has . . . *ballon* to such a degree that few dancers—and I speak of the most illustrious and the most applauded—equal her in this quality. It seems that she cannot touch the stage with the tip of her toe without being repelled and at the same time forced to rebound like a shuttlecock returned with a vigorous stroke of the racquet. She rises without effort and alights softly and gracefully. . . .

"*La Sylphide* and Marie Taglioni have remained synonymous. Only at rare intervals has anyone dared to touch this charming ballet, which the first dancer in the world had made her masterpiece. Mlle Adèle Dumilâtre, a pale reflection of a dazzling star, attempted it not without some success. After her, if I am not mistaken, one or two obscure *débutantes*, having nothing to lose by risking all, have given us sad parodies, but no trace remains either of them or of their indiscretions. To-day that great memory of Mlle Taglioni is evoked afresh, but it must be said at once, to avoid any misunderstanding, that there is no question of making impossible comparisons. Mlle Livry is barely sixteen; she is of a perfect modesty, and it would pain her beyond measure if she were supposed to have pretensions to which she has never aspired. Burdened with an overwhelming rôle, before which the most celebrated dancers have recoiled, she acquitted herself with the happy ingenuity and naïve confidence of youth; she followed the tradition as far as she was able to assimilate it, and in the *écots, variations* and passages that have been faithfully preserved, she is, of all the artistes we have seen up to now, the one who has best recalled to us her incomparable model. In the new *pas*, she was charming, and it is still in them that. we ourself like her best.

"Nothing has been changed in the *pas de fauteuil*, and Mlle Livry, from the moment of her entrance on the stage, flits with an ethereal grace and lightness about her young Scotsman, who wakes at the rustle of her wings. The second appearance of the Sylphide, on the window-ledge, her furtive steps, her sudden disappearances, her chaste allurement, her timid modesty, the whole love duet in which mime takes the place of the spoken word and music provides the idea, remain exactly as they were before, and M. Mazilier has my full approval for having permitted no alteration in this pretty interior scene.

"The *pas de trois*, which concludes the first act, is new,

not in its situation but in its arrangement—with the exception of the *coda*, not a bar of which has been modified. Mlle Livry brought the house down in prolonged cheering and acclamations when, in two prodigious jumps, she rose three feet above the level of the footlights. She returned after the *pas* to take her bow before the public, and from that moment it was easy to see that the success of this young artiste would assume the proportions of a triumph.

LOUIS MÉRANTE AND EMMA LIVRY IN "LA SYLPHIDE".
Caricature by Marcelin.

"In the second act, there has been inserted an entirely new *pas de deux*, for which I congratulate in all sincerity MM. Mazilier and Clapisson. The *adage* is designed with infinite taste; the two principal figures part on a lattice of young girls interweaving their rounded arms in a charming pose, reminding one of an antique bas-relief. All the other groups have as much originality as grace. The music is melodious and lively, full of verve and *brio*; in short, worthy of the composer of so many ingenious and popular pieces. Mlle Livry has three great *variations* in this *pas*: a first *écot*, in which she was loudly applauded for a *double cabriole* executed with unusual buoyancy; a second *écot*, more *tacqueté*, firmer, brilliantly crowned by a *double tour sur les pointes*; and finally, what raised the enthusiasm of the house to its highest pitch, a *coda* of *grands jetés*, marvellously successful, in which the *débutante* gave proof at the same time of her lightness, her elevation and her *parcours*.

"Now I foresee the objections, the criticisms and the reserves that will, according to all appearances, be voiced concerning this remarkable début. Perfection does not come at once. I have spoken of the precious qualities of Mlle Livry; I have given her age. Assurance, neatness, precision, are only acquired after much practice and toil, but what cannot be learnt is the marvellous lightness and the natural distinction which she possesses." [1]

Emma had been very nervous when the ballet started, for she not only had to introduce herself to the public, but to command the stage in a leading part and overcome an inevitable and what might well be an invidious comparison with Marie Taglioni. One critic, Albert de Lasalle, admitted that he had decided, before entering the theatre, to enliven his review with the fable of the frog whose ambition was to grow as big as the bull, but was completely disarmed by Emma's triumph. When she made her first entrance, she was trembling and very pale, and for a moment her friends feared that her emotion might be too much for her, but her nervousness passed, and as the warmth of the applause increased, so did she give fuller play to her powers until she was exerting herself to the utmost amidst a frenzy of enthusiasm.

Though Fiorentino had refused to consider the school to which her style belonged, other critics who gave the matter thought were unanimous in their opinions. "If the art of Taglioni was French", wrote Jouvin, " then Mlle Emma Livry is undoubtedly a French dancer in the fullest meaning of the term. On a stage where Ferraris and her predecessors have triumphed with *tours de force* of danced vocalization, rapid flashes, intricacies of notes, chromatic scales, the *débutante* tries to sing more simply, more correctly, more vigorously. Unconsciously and in obedience to her instinct, to her artistic temperament, she belongs to the neglected school of Taglioni. Like that celebrated ballerina, it is on her shoulders that she wears her sylphide wings, which the Italian virtuosi of to-day are accustomed to wear on their feet."

Saint-Victor concurred in this judgment. "Mlle Emma Livry

---

[1] The other members of the cast of the 1858 revival of *La Sylphide* included Louis Mérante (James Reuben), Berthier (Gurn), Adèle Villiers (Effie), Aline (Madge). A *pas de deux* in Act I was danced by Beauchet and Fanny Génat. Nine of the twenty-eight sylphides in Act II were "flying" sylphides, including Léontine Beaugrand. The witches scene in this act was omitted.

comes from the French school, the ethereal school", he wrote. "She rises like a feather that has been breathed upon, and when she alights, the feather becomes an arrow and pierces the stage with a point of steel. Her *entrechats* are clean; she covers the stage with fantastic rapidity. She has, in *temps penchés*, a marble-like poise that gives the impression of the curve of a statue. She has, above all, that chaste and correct elegance which distinguishes the French school. . . . The *dilettanti* of the ballet say that one day she will dance in the winged shoes of the great Sylphide. She has already, we are assured, something of her modest grace, of her incorporeal lightness. When, after a long absence, Mlle Taglioni returned to the Opéra in 1844 to dance in her great scene from *L'Ombre*, Alfred de Musset wrote these pretty lines in her album:—

> *Si vous ne voulez plus danser,*
> *Si vous ne faites que passer*
> *Sur ce grand théâtre si sombre,*
> *Ne courez pas après votre ombre,*
> *Et tâchez de nous la laisser.*

The shadow has remained. It has taken such a body as a shadow can take. It has grown, it will grow, and it is she whom we have seen dance so lightly the other night, by the light of the moon in the enchanted forest."

But Emma was still very young, and more than one critic voiced a word of warning in the fear that too much praise now might spoil the results to be expected later with experience. It is not in May, remarked one, that the vintagers gather their harvest. "Let us not forget", added Jouvin, "in spite of her success, that Mlle Emma Livry is only a child, a most promising child, nothing more. What accidents might happen on the journey between the promise of talent and final celebrity! What storms may break before the corn ripens! . . . At sixteen, one cannot know how to be the leader of a school, nor a rival to oppose the two great *danseuses* of exotic origin that the Opéra possesses. Indigenous dancers should be encouraged: nothing better. It is time to restore the French school."

Her extreme youth was particularly apparent in her miming. "Occasionally her expression remains serious when it should reflect passion", observed Théodore Anne. "The difficulty arises from giving her a lover's rôle at an age when she is not yet aware of the torments, the agitation and heartbreak of love. Here art must take nature's place."

    Having successfully steered his *protégée* through her début, Montguyon now prepared for the arrival in Paris of Marie Taglioni. He wanted her to see Emma dance as soon as possible, and he therefore wrote to Royer on Monday, November 15th: "With Mlle Taglioni coming to the Opéra on Wednesday, and the receipts of *La Sylphide* keeping up as they are, I thought it might be better to give *La Sylphide* on Wednesday and postpone *Marco Spada* until next week. The presence of Mlle Taglioni will, needless to say, pass unnoticed at a performance of *Marco*, but would, on the other hand, create a great effect at one of *La Sylphide*. I believe that this will be to the financial advantage both of the management and of Mlle Livry. I would be very grateful to you for seeing to this, especially as I know of no major reason against it." Royer was duly convinced, and at once gave orders for Wednesday's programme to be changed.

    The first person to call on Marie Taglioni after she had settled in her apartment at No. 45 Rue Laffitte was Emma Livry. The two Sylphides talked together for nearly an hour, and as Emma was leaving, Marie Taglioni said to her, "I shall return your visit to-morrow." The following evening, Wednesday, November 17th, she watched the seventh performance of the revival of *La Sylphide* from Dr. Véron's box. There seemed to be something symbolic in her reappearance after so long an absence, and indeed she was the object of no less interest than the young dancer who had attracted her back to Paris. "It is astonishing", wrote a spectator, "with what ease and bravery the ladies of her profession bear the attacks of time—the approach of age. Is it that their nimble step outruns the pace of the old enemy, or that he hesitates to touch with his dreaded weapons creatures so frail and graceful as they seem to be? Whatever be the cause, Taglioni is a living proof that dancing is not a fatiguing profession; for saving a still more serious cast thrown over her always melancholy countenance, she is as young and active as ever, having wonderfully preserved the elasticity of her figure and the grace of her movements."

    At the end of November, Emma Livry and Carolina Rosati

organized a banquet in the great dancer's honour at the fashionable restaurant of the Trois Frères Provençaux. More than fifty people sat down to table, including the guest of honour, the two organizers, Dr. Véron, presiding in the place of Royer who was indisposed and unable to be present, Fanny Cerrito, Adeline Plunkett, Joseph Mazilier, Lucien Petipa, and many of the leading personalities of the dancing world of Paris. During dessert, Gustave Vaëz declaimed some verses written by Royer for the occasion, and when dinner was over, a quadrille by Mazilier—called *Le Quadrille du Prince Impérial*, and dedicated, by permission, to the Empress—was danced by eight of the guests: Taglioni and Mazilier, Rosati and Petipa, Cerrito and Mérante, and Plunkett and Beauchet. An invitation to dance in this quadrille had been sent to Mme Montessu, who was living in Marseilles and had grown very stout, but she had been unable to make the journey to Paris. It was said that only the most tactful persuasion had overcome Rosati's reluctance to participate, because someone had referred to it in her presence as the "*quadrille des embaumées*".

Marie Taglioni was often seen that winter at intellectual and artistic gatherings in Paris, particularly the *soirées musicales* given by the elderly Rossini. There she met many of her old friends, including, one day, the great tenor, Mario. She was sure, she told him, that he had forgotten her.

"Ah! *diva*!" he replied in a murmur of friendly reproach.

One evening she was persuaded to dance. "Taglioni, in a small corner of the room about the width of a Paisley shawl and the length of a Manchester kerchief", described an English guest, "danced once more the *pas* from *Guillaume Tell* and the *Gavotte de Vestris*. . . . The space was small, the dress was heavy, the crinoline was expansive, the lights were close, the atmosphere sultry; in short, altogether the general cry was, '*Ce n'est plus ça!*' Who is altered for the worse, the dancer, whose name has reached us as the very Muse of her art, or we ourselves? Surely *she* cannot have grown old, and stiff, and pinched, and wrinkled! It must be ourselves whose souls have become crabbed and our spirits dulled, rendering us no longer capable of judging of her excellence."

Marie Taglioni's own *soirées* were well attended. At one which she gave in the spring of 1859, she, Emma Livry, Célestine Emarot and Amalia Ferraris took part in the quadrille, and at the end of the evening the hostess danced an *allemande* with Olimpia Priora "in a style which can never be imitated". In the summer she gave a party to celebrate her moving into a new apartment, at No. 80 Rue Taitbout. Among those invited were Emma Livry and her mother, Amalia Ferraris, and Louise and Nathalie Fitzjames. The hostess danced a *pas* of her own composition with Emma Livry, and the party ended at about midnight with a quadrille and finally a polka-mazurka danced by Marie Taglioni and her sixteen-year-old son.

Although she would dance before her friends, Marie Taglioni had taken a solemn vow never again to dance in public. This vow she observed strictly. Indeed she was censured for refusing an invitation to dance for the benefit of the distressed Italians in Paris, and another time her friend Scribe was unable to persuade her to dance for the poor of the second *arrondissement*.

On August 7th, 1859, she was appointed *Inspectrice de la danse* at the Opéra, at an annual salary of 3000 francs, a post which she held until the end of the Second Empire, and which entailed supervising the various classes of the *Conservatoire de Danse* and judging at the annual dance examinations. The following year she was named *professeur de la classe de perfectionnement*. In thanking the Emperor for this latter appointment, she told him that she owed her superiority "to her father's continual advice, to his rigorous teaching, and to his firm conviction that difficulties must be overcome to the point where the public has no suspicion of the effort made to conquer them and where everything appears to be of the utmost ease". Now she was passing on her inheritance to others. The value of her teaching was delicately recognized one day by the protector of one of the most promising *petits sujets*, who presented her with a model of the little watering-can which she used to lend her pupils, engraved with the words :—

Je fais naître les fleurs.

*   *   *   *   *   *

With the universal acclamation that greeted her début, Emma Livry soon discovered that success brings enemies as well as friends. Cabals began to form within the ranks of the *corps de ballet*, strengthened by the protectors of some of its less talented members. Ulterior motives were suggested to

Amalia Ferraris and Louis Mérante
in *L'Étoile de Messine*

Berthier in *L'Étoile de Messine*

L'Étoile de Messine, Act I, Scene I

L'Étoile de Messine, Act II, Scene I

L'Étoile de Messine, Act II, Scene III

Marie S. Petipa in *Le Diable à quatre*　　F. I. Kshesinski in *Le Diable à quatre*

Lucien Petipa in *Le Diable à*
quatre

Berthier and Zina Mérante in
Le Diable à quatre

Marie Vernon as Fenella in
La Muette de Portici

Laure Fonta in *La Muette de
Portici*

Léontine Beaugrand in *La Muette
de Portici*

Eugénie Schlosser and Eugène
Coralli in *La Muette de Portici*

explain Emma's success. The part played by Morny, at the behest of Montguyon, in furthering her interests was misinterpreted. Rumours spread until it was the Emperor himself whose influence was supposed to be behind Emma's triumph. In time these whispers reached the ears of the enemies of the régime, rabid Republicans who recognized no code of honour; not even Emma's death was to arouse any feelings of decency in their hardened hearts, and for many years they continued to scatter their vile libels insinuating a liaison between the Emperor and her.[1] The Emperor certainly had amorous propensities, but of the existence of such a liaison there has never been a shred of real evidence. Napoleon III reasoned that the extraordinary physical strain to which dancers' legs were subjected necessarily interfered with their intellectual development, and he was once heard to remark, "*L'esprit de la danseuse est dans ses jambes, et je n'aime pas les femmes bêtes.*"

On November 9th, 1858, just less than three weeks after her début, Royer fixed Emma's salary in accordance with his agreement with Montguyon at 10,000 francs a year, and her first contract, for a year's engagement, was signed. Soon afterwards, she began to rehearse the leading part in the *divertissement* in Félicien David's new opera, *Herculanum*, which was first given on March 4th, 1859. She played the rôle of Erigone in the bacchanal in Act III. It was a *divertissement*, described Saint-Victor, "stimulated by the clatter of *crotala* and the beat of tambourines. The Egyptians with their golden horns and the bacchantes, clad in panther skins, come running in, brandishing their *thyrsi*. *Evoe! Evoe!* There is something intoxicating in those intermittent cries, separated by silences in which the single note of the tambourine resounds with exhilarating monotony. The vast *amphora* of the vintage is trundled on to the stage. Two bacchantes take hold of it by the handles, while a faun clings to its rim, dipping into it a golden vase which he empties into the cups held out to him. *Evoe! Evoe!*

---

[1] An example of their scurrilous propaganda is to be found in Hippolyte Magen's *Les Deux Cours et les Nuits de Saint-Cloud: mœurs, débauches et crimes de la famille Bonaparte* (London and Brussels, 1868). ". . . So the heaven of our two spouses [the Emperor and Empress] darkened", reads a passage from this book. ". . . Emma Livry and others among [her] sweet companions were charged with the delicate mission of consoling H.M. the Emperor for the infirmity of his mate. They performed their task so well that when, in the morning, they quitted the couch of the hero of Strasbourg and Boulogne, the demi-god was done for and utterly besotted."

Then the bacchantes entwine themselves in a living bas-relief around the immense urn, which revolves as though intoxicated by the wine it contains."

Even the less fervent of her admirers, such as Jouvin, now admitted that Emma had made great progress. Fiorentino considered her improvement "unbelievable". "The charm and the excuse of the ballet", he wrote, "is the ethereal and chaste dancing of this child, this bird, this fairy, Mlle Emma Livry. She has a *variation* on *pointes* of unequalled strength and neatness; she rises, springs, takes wing; now she is here, now down there,

EMMA LIVRY IN "HERCULANUM".
Caricature by Marcelin.

now in the clouds, There would be no end to describing the cheering, the stamping, the calls." Saint-Victor was no less enthusiastic. "Her dancing", he wrote, "is distinguished by an ideal lightness regulated by the most classical correctness. Her elevation hovers like a flight, she covers the stage in three bounds, her sharp and delicate *pointes* skim over the boards like skates on the ice. . . . At last here is a French *danseuse* who will soon be the equal of the greatest! It seemed as though one were seeing a charming resurrection of Taglioni."

    •   •   •   •   •

Emma Livry's career developed quickly after her success in *Herculanum*. At the end of March her engagement was extended for a further three years from August 1st, when her first contract was due to expire, at a salary rising from 18,000 francs for the first year, to 24,000 francs for the second and 30,000 francs for the third, and with the promise of the principal rôle in the next ballet to be produced after *La*

Comtesse d'Egmont, which Rota was then preparing for Rosati. This ballet was commissioned very shortly afterwards, and the combination chosen—Saint-Georges as the scenarist, Offenbach as the composer, and Marie Taglioni as the choreographer—indicated the very high hopes that were officially held of Emma Livry's future.

At the same time there was some talk of giving her a rôle—inferior, naturally, to Rosati's—in *La Comtesse d'Egmont*, but as soon as Montguyon learnt of this proposal, he protested most vigorously to the Director. "As for the rôle in Rota's ballet", he wrote, "you know my views. I consider that to cast Mlle Livry, who is about to create a ballet by Mlle Taglioni, in a secondary rôle and in endless bits and pieces, would be as bad for the interests of the theatre as for her own. . . . If Mme Rosati is to appear in the ballet, then, as Mlle Livry does not deny Mme Rosati's superiority as a mime, she will consent to play the rôle, but with reluctance. But should it be *anyone else*, Mlle Livry will not consent to play in a secondary rôle, whether miming or dancing."

A few days later he wrote again: "We agreed that you would write to Mlle Livry, when her engagement was being renewed, on the subject of Rota's ballet, and tell her that her part would not be a disagreeable mime rôle and that there would be no dancing rôle in the ballet more important than hers. Further, it is understood that if Mme Rosati does not appear in the ballet or ceases to appear in it, Mlle Livry will be freed from her obligations if she feels so inclined. You are also to tell her that, so far as it lies within your power . . . her ballet will not be given in the summer."

Rota's ballet had to be abandoned a few months later, when Rosati terminated her engagement with the Opéra, and the preparation of the new ballet for Emma Livry was pressed forward.

Emma's prestige at the Opéra was now greatly enhanced, for she stood second in importance only to Ferraris. Her sudden success, however, had left her quite unspoilt and made no difference to her mode of living. She continued to live with her mother in their third-floor apartment at No. 22 Rue Rossini, which they left in 1861, after Emma's triumph in *Le Papillon*, for a slightly larger home on the third floor of No. 18 Rue Laffitte. There, for the first time, Emma enjoyed the luxury of a bedroom of her own—a small room with pink and white chintz hangings and muslin curtains, and, as the only ornaments, a crucifix over the head of her bed, a small figure of the Virgin, and her mother's portrait.

She was a very modest girl and, for her years, unusually mature, aware of her responsibilities, and appreciative of kind actions that others had done for her and being anxious to repay them. In March 1860, for instance, when she was given a well-placed box for a first night at the Gymnase and heard that Morny had not been so fortunate as she, she immediately offered to exchange her own box for his. "I hope, *monsieur le comte*", she wrote to him, "that you will accept, and give me the only opportunity that I shall perhaps have of doing you a favour in return for all the kindness you have shown me and all the help you have given me." There was gaiety in her nature, too, and she enjoyed life with all the simplicity of a child. After she had spent an evening at the Bouffes-Parisiens in January 1860, *Le Figaro* reported: "This time, the first prize for hilarity goes to our little friend, Emma Livry, who dances at the Opéra like the great dancer she is already—luckily for us—and who amuses herself at the theatre like the child she is still—luckily for her."

She spared no pains to improve her art, and made no pretence of hiding her natural pleasure at being applauded when she danced. But she was satisfied with the ovations of the public, and refused many of the costly presents that were offered her; after her death, it was found that she had accepted only three such gifts during her career—a bracelet and a golden chain, once the property of the Orléans family, from Montguyon, and a butterfly in precious stones from the Baron James de Rothschild. What she valued much more than jewels and trinkets were the portraits that Marie Taglioni and Offenbach had sent her while the rehearsals of the new ballet were in progress. The composer had written on his, "To the most poetic and the most zealous of butterflies, Emma Livry, from her unworthy and grateful musician, Jacques Offenbach"; while Marie Taglioni had inscribed on hers the advice, "*Faites-moi oublier; ne m'oubliez pas.*"

Marie Taglioni had grown very fond of Emma Livry, and the two were often together. In April 1860 they were both on the Jury at the annual dance examination; and on June 1st they were both invited by Dr. Véron to a sumptuous banquet at the Maison Dorée, where the menu included *Filets de canneton aux oranges rouges*, a dish invented by the host himself.

Meanwhile the rehearsals of the new ballet were continuing. In the spring of 1860, Marie Taglioni's eighty-one-year-old father, the choreographer of *La Sylphide*, came to Paris for an operation to restore his failing eyesight. He returned again in November and watched one of the last rehearsals of his daughter's ballet. He was severely critical. "Nothing is in time", he complained, although he admitted that the *pas* were "well arranged and very pretty".

The title of the ballet was decided upon only at the last moment. Saint-Georges had first suggested *Zaidée*, which was originally the name of the heroine, but this was altered at Marie Taglioni's request to *Farfalla*, the Italian word for a butterfly. Royer for his part preferred *Le Papillon et la Fée*, but those persons who were guarding Emma's interests objected that this gave too much prominence to a secondary character, and so the title was finally agreed simply as *Le Papillon*.

The aim of the authors of the ballet was to give Emma Livry a rôle with which she might become identified, just as Taglioni had with the Sylphide, and Carlotta Grisi with Giselle. In Saint-Georges' scenario, Farfalla—the part written for Emma Livry—is held in the power of the aged and wicked fairy, Hamza (L. Marquet), who is anxious for the Emir's nephew, Djalma (L. Mérante), to kiss her, for then she will be transformed into a beautiful young woman. Stopping to take refreshment at Hamza's cottage during a hunt, Djalma is charmed by her maid, Farfalla, and kisses her, to the great annoyance of Hamza, who, after the party has gone, turns the girl into a butterfly. In the forest, Djalma is given a butterfly that a member of his suite has caught, and pins it to the trunk of a tree. As he does so, the butterfly changes into a girl, whom he recognizes as Farfalla. She escapes from his grasp, only to be caught by Hamza. Patimate (Berthier), a woodman, has meanwhile recognized Hamza as the kidnapper of the Emir's daughter, and, seizing her magic crutch, frees Farfalla. Though the crutch is snatched away from him by an evil sprite, Farfalla manages to escape, for the other butterflies imprison Hamza with the net in which she had hoped to entrap Farfalla.

Hamza is brought before the Emir (Lenfant), and made to confess her crime and restore his daughter to him. Farfalla then returns to her father, attended by a rich suite, and is presented to Djalma as his destined bride. Djalma is overjoyed, but Farfalla, remembering the wound she has received at his hands, repulses him. As he tries to embrace her, Hamza

EMMA LIVRY IN "LE PAPILLON".
Caricature by Hadol.

steps between them and, receiving the kiss intended for Farfalla, is transformed into a beautiful woman. While the betrothal of Djalma and Farfalla is being celebrated, Hamza treacherously turns Farfalla into a butterfly and entrances Djalma, before whose eyes she conjures up a vision of an enchanted garden. It is here that she plans to marry Djalma herself. Her sisters—the Diamond Fairy (V. Maupérin), the Pearl Fairy (Simon), the Flower Fairy (Schlosser) and the Harvest Fairy (Troisvallets)—arrive for the ceremony. A young Hymen (C. Brach) appears with a lighted torch. Attracted by the flame, Farfalla darts forward, but approaches too close. As her wings shrivel with the heat, so Hamza's spell is broken. Hamza is turned into a statue by her sisters, who then conduct Djalma and Farfalla towards a magnificent palace that rises into the air beyond the garden.

The first performance of *Le Papillon*, given on November 26th, 1860, before the Emperor and a brilliant audience, almost overshadowed the important liberal reforms that had been announced only two days before. The ballet had been so long in preparation, the combination of choreographer, musician and dancer promised such exciting possibilities, that the standards by which the work was ultimately judged were unusually high. A certain amount of disappointment was therefore almost inevitable. Certainly *Le Papillon* had its failings. Its plot lacked simplicity and flow, and perhaps too much reliance was placed on the scenic effect, although indeed only one of the sets—the clearing in the forest, by Despléchin— was considered particularly noteworthy. There was criticism, too, of Offenbach's score, but this came mainly from purists who were shocked that a composer of popular music should be given a hearing within the walls of the Opéra. The more open-minded, who listened without having formed their opinions in advance, appreciated the skilful orchestration and the abundance of delightful melodies: the *Valse des rayons*— the vivacious mazurka, *La Lesguinka*—the *Bohémienne*—the charming pastoral march, to name but a few.

Of the choreography, little was said. Taglioni's *pas* were varied, her groups well designed [1]: she had, in short, accomplished her task of providing Emma Livry with the means of triumph. The effect of her influence was there for all to see, for the young dancer's style was now uncannily like hers in

---

[1] A document in the Archives of the Opéra contains a detailed description of a short *écot* arranged by Marie Taglioni and danced by Léontine Beaugrand in the *pas de trois* in Act II:

"Du pied droit. Un tour sur la pointe en attitude, tourner sur les pointes (2 fois).
"Un tour sur la pointe en attitude, remonter sur la pointe, poser, et deux tours sur le cou-de-pied.
"Recommencer du pied gauche un tour sur la pointe en attitude, tourner sur les pointes (2 fois).
"Un tour sur la pointe en attitude, remonter sur la pointe et remonter la scène.
"Une cabriole en quatrième oblique, retomber sur le pied gauche, jeté, jeté (3 fois).
"Glissade, jeté en tournant, soubresaut, recommencer de même de l'autre côté.
"Deux tours en l'air sur le cou-de-pied, poser sur la pointe du pied droit, quatre emboîtés sur les pointes (2 fois).
"Glissade. Jeté en tournant (4 fois).
"Pas de bourrée sur les pointes jusqu'à la fin (6 fois)."

her days of glory: even the gestures and the little mannerisms could all be recognized. When the performance was over, Taglioni and Livry took a call together, radiantly happy and almost in each other's arms, and the whole house responded with cheering even lustier than had punctuated the ballet throughout the evening.

EMMA LIVRY IN "LE PAPILLON".
Caricature by Marcelin.

Emma's progress astonished the critics. "It was a surprise and a revelation", wrote Fiorentino. "Only yesterday she was a child. . . . To-day she is a great dancer, a dancer of the first rank, *di prima sfera*, a star. . . . Mlle Emma Livry gives proof, not only of elevation, lightness and grace, but of great artistry, a complete talent, an unbelievable strength. She is hardly ever off the stage; she mimes wonderfully, and dances to perfection all the types of *pas* which Mlle Taglioni has been able to compress into a single ballet as though to display the hardiest and the most charming things that, I will not say her pupil, but her beloved adopted child, can do.

"See her first in the mazurka. What verve and originality!

Aline as Berthe and Martha Muravieva as Giselle in *Giselle*, Act I

Louis Mérante as Albrecht in
Giselle, Act I

Félix Rémond as Wilfrid in
Giselle

Eugène Coralli as Hilarion in
Giselle

Louis Lenfant as the Duke of
Courland in *Giselle*

Louise Marquet as Bathilde in
Giselle

Augustine Malot as a Peasant in
Giselle, Act I

Martha Muravieva as Giselle in
Act II

How precise, vivacious, playful she is! We had not seen Mlle Livry in a *pas de caractère* before. She seemed made for the impalpable, vaporous, ethereal dance, but here she is coming down to earth and, with much mischief and sprightliness, tapping her little heels on the resonant boards. She recalls the best performances of Fanny Elssler and Rosati.

"Her *valse des rayons*, so aptly named, shows her in various positions of exquisite charm and rare audacity. In the *adage*, which is composed of *pas de bourrée sur les pointes* and ends with a *pirouette en attitude allongée*, she performs a *développé en arabesque* astonishing for its steadiness, for she bends almost to the ground without deviating from the line or turning a hair. In her *variation* in this same waltz, she accomplishes a stupendous flight, once known as the *course Taglioni*, returning to traverse the stage with an impetuosity and ardour that nothing can stop; it is just a simple *glissade* and a rapid *assemblé*, but all so perfectly done, so exact, so precisely rendered, that the whole house burst into frenzied cheering. . . .

"Then there is her *grand pas de deux* with Mérante, with its first *variation* of *entrechats six* and *deux* and *soubresauts* taken from right to left, and that *variation* which so astonished the public, and in which she descended the stage with *temps piqués sur la pointe*, and those *jetés en tournant* which she performs with such rare assurance. This *pas* will be called the *pas Livry*; and with these three last *écots* alone, Mlle Livry could conquer the world."

"You were only a caterpillar", Montguyon said as he embraced her afterwards, "but I have turned you into a butterfly." Emma's success had been complete, but not easily gained, for a cruel attack of cramp had gripped her during the second act: "The contrast between her anguished face and her dancing feet was heart-rending", wrote Saint-Victor, "but she danced on nevertheless, although in considerable pain." Signs of her triumph were not wanting. The Emperor specially requested that *Le Papillon* should be included in the programme about a week later, so that he could see it a second time; the managers of London's two opera houses, Her Majesty's and Covent Garden, who had been present at the first night, both tried, unsuccessfully, to induce her to bring the ballet to England the following summer; and the sculptor, Barre, who many years before had fashioned statuettes of Taglioni and

Elssler, now asked that she should allow him to complete his select series by modelling her as Farfalla.

Emma did not forget those who had worked with her in her hour of triumph. She gave Marie Taglioni a bracelet adorned with a butterfly set in diamonds and turquoises; each of the principals received a box of sweets with a lithograph on the lid depicting her stepping over a waterfall, an incident in the last scene of the ballet, and bags of sweets were distributed among the rest of the cast; while those dancers who did not participate in her success were all given well-placed seats for the first performance.

At about this time, if the columns of *The Court Journal* are to be believed, the Baron de Chassiron, returning from his tour of the East, re-entered his daughter's life. The paper referred to him as "one of the French Dukes of the oldest régime, who, providing for [Emma's] education in the same career as that pursued by her mother, had deemed himself quit of all further obligation", and as having recently returned to Paris after being French Ambassador at a northern Court— a description that may well have been purposely misleading, so as to give as much of the story as possible without causing offence to the Baron. The "Duke", it was reported, visited the Opéra and saw Emma dance. "He sat transfixed with astonishment and delight . . . and [afterwards] hurried behind the scenes to compliment the artiste. How much was the delight increased by pride on learning it was his own daughter! Every day after this event was his carriage to be seen at her door, until, won over by the charm of goodness and nobility of soul displayed by the young dancer, he frankly offered to recognize her as his child, and to settle a portion of his princely fortune upon her. . . . The offer was peremptorily declined. The old Duke accepted this rebuff with ancestral philosophy, but they say he has often expressed his intention of acting with as much disinterested pride and dignity as the fair *danseuse*, and to perform all the promise made to her, without condition and without consent."

For many months *Le Papillon* appeared regularly on the play-bills of the Opéra. On October 18th, 1861, the thirty-seventh performance took place before the King of Holland. At the end of the first scene, when Farfalla, changed into a butterfly, leaps through the window, Emma caught her foot on the sill and fell heavily against a projecting piece of wood. It was her first fall before the public in more than a hundred appearances. While the stage was being set for the next scene, she was examined by the doctor. No ribs were broken, as was at first feared, and, with similar courage to that she had shown on the first night, she carried on to the end of the ballet, omitting only two of the more strenuous passages. A thorough examination followed the fall of the last curtain, and she was ordered to rest for several weeks. Her side was found to be badly bruised, and the application of leeches was prescribed. A month later, on November 23rd, she was examined again. "Mlle Emma Livry told us", the doctors reported, "that she experiences pain in the lumbar region and weakness in the knee-joints when she practises." A further ten to twelve days' rest was advised.

Some months earlier, in the summer of 1861, the Director had suggested to Emma Livry that she should play the dumb girl, Fenella, in a revival of *La Muette de Portici*, and asked whether she would give up a month of her holiday to begin rehearsing. In his record of the interview, Royer wrote: "Mlle Livry does not wish to consider giving up her August holiday. Before accepting the rôle of the dumb girl, she would want her contract renewed and to be guaranteed another ballet, so that she would not leave the Opéra after a negative success, as she foresees she may obtain in the rôle of the dumb girl, which in her opinion would not suit her at all. Mlle Livry wishes me to give her a reply as soon as possible. Basically, it is an engagement that Mlle Livry wants, and she has let me know that her present salary must be increased. This salary is 30,000 francs a year from August 1st, with three months' holiday without pay, *i.e.* 2500 francs for every month of her service. If *La Muette* is played, Mlle Livry could only rehearse from September 1st, because of her holiday. Allowing for only six weeks' rehearsals, the work could not be put on until about October 15th, a month or a month and a half before the first performance of Gounod's new work. This would be very bad business from the financial point of view. In these circumstances, I feel that Mlle Livry must not be thought of for this rôle. Mlle Livry's engagement ends on August 1st, 1862. But, since

Mlle Livry has three months' holiday, the engagement actually
ends at the end of April 1862."

The revival of *La Muette de Portici* was therefore postponed,
and Gounod's new opera, *La Reine de Saba*, in which Emma Livry
had been allotted an important part in the *divertissement*, went
into rehearsal. Meanwhile the negotiations for the extension
of her engagement were still continuing. "The Opéra is in a
state of revolution", it was reported early in January. "The
rehearsals of *La Reine de Saba* are being carried on most vigorously, but it is very much feared that there will be no *première
danseuse* for the *divertissement*. Mlle Emma Livry, whose engagement is on the point of expiring, positively refuses to take a
penny less than the 42,000 francs paid to Mme Ferraris. . . .
A decision must be come to. If the difficulty be not got over
in a couple of days, Mlle Livry will no longer be a member
of the Opéra company, and a telegram will be despatched to
St Petersburg for Mme Petipa." Another dancer who was
being considered as a possible replacement for Emma Livry, if
the worse should come to the worst, was Carolina Pochini,[1]
whose husband, Pasquale Borri, was then in Paris producing
L'Étoile de Messine for Ferraris. Fortunately the difference
between Emma Livry and the management was resolved: she
no longer pressed for an increase of salary, a new contract for a
further two years at an annual salary of 30,000 francs was
duly approved by the Minister of State, and she gave a refusal
to the Italian impresario who had been importuning her with
a tempting offer.

The *divertissement* of *La Reine de Saba* came in the third act,
and was being arranged by Lucien Petipa. The choreographer
was faced with several worries during the course of the
rehearsals. Paul Lormier, the costume designer, suggested that
the Sabine women should be chosen from among the brunettes
of the *corps de ballet*, in order to further the general colour
scheme, an interference which infuriated Petipa, who asked
heatedly, did Lormier not know that Eve was a blonde? A still
more serious crisis had to be surmounted when Jules Barbier,
one of the librettists, suggested suppressing the *divertissement* or
at least cutting it, but Petipa stood his ground firmly and the
ballet remained as it originally was.

---

[1] Roqueplan had offered Pochini an engagement at the Opéra in 1853, but she
had been unable to accept.

Emma Livry too had her wishes. "My dear M. Gounod, my good M. Gounod", she said to him sweetly, "I want a little flute accompaniment for my *pas*, as there is in *Herculanum*."

By the next rehearsal the gallant composer had such an accompaniment prepared.

"*Ah, mon Dieu!*" cried Emma, stopping after a few bars, "you have two flutes playing!"

"Well?"

"But M. Félicien David had only one in *Herculanum*."

"Bah!" replied Gounod, "these gentlemen play together so well that it might be only one. Let us continue."

"*Ah, mon Dieu!*" she cried again after a few bars more, "but, M. Gounod, there is a violin accompaniment too!"

"That is certainly true, and there was none in *Herculanum*, you are going to say. But never fear, I have told those gentlemen to play so softly that only the audience will notice it."

La Reine de Saba was given on February 28th, 1862, and proved a failure. Gounod was accused of Wagnerian tendencies, which was sufficient condemnation, with the recent fiasco of *Tannhäuser* at the Opéra still fresh in people's minds. Though Emma Livry and Zina Mérante were warmly applauded, the *divertissement* made little impression. "Mlle Livry is as light as a feather", commented one observer, "but that is no reason why M. Chapuy should carry her off as though she were a bundle of old clothes."

.　　.　　.　　.　　.　　.　　.

With the negotiations for the extension of Emma Livry's engagement successfully concluded, the management were now able to formulate plans for her future. She had at last been persuaded to accept the wholly miming rôle of Fenella in *La Muette de Portici*, and had even refused an offer to insert a *pas* specially for her; there was discussion about her playing Zoloé in a revival of *Le Dieu et la Bayadère*; and preparations were begun for a new ballet.

The 1862 budget contained an item of 20,000 francs for a one-act ballet, but this figure was later increased to 38,000 francs to provide another two scenes. Charles Nuitter wrote the scenario of this ballet, *Zara*, the first act of which was set in the gardens of a harem overlooking the sea near Algiers, and the second at Versailles in the reign of Louis XIV, first in the park, and then in the palace itself. The scenery of the first act was being designed by Cambon and Thierry, who were to make use of a new mobile panorama invented by an engineer named Raignard, while Despléchin was responsible for the two sets of the second act. The score, which originally was to have been composed by Théodore Semet, was finally entrusted to Ernest Boulanger. Among the projects of Marie Taglioni, who was devising the choreography, were a *tarantelle* and a *cachucha* in Act I and a *pas arabe* in the first scene of Act II.

Zara went into rehearsal on October 28th, 1862.[1]

.   .   .   .

Fire was a danger against which constant precautions had to be taken. The opera house was built largely of wood and plaster, and a strong and efficient fire service had to be maintained for its safety. Smoking was rigorously prohibited; the stage was isolated from the auditorium by a large metal grill after each performance; and when the artistes had left, every fire in the building was carefully extinguished. Further precautions were taken for the safety of the performers. In 1861 a new system of stage-lighting, invented by Professor Lissajous, was installed, in which the footlights were placed about two and a half feet below the level of the boards, and the light reflected to the stage through a plate of ground glass, so that the flames were effectively screened and the glare reduced.

While Professor Lissajous had been working on a system to prevent the flames from reaching the costumes of the performers, others had been searching for some method of making these costumes non-inflammable. A short while before, a M. Carteron had invented such a method, and had given such

---

[1] The scenario of *Zara* has not been traced. The cast was originally to have been as follows:

Zara .	Emma Livry
The Countess	Louise Marquet
A slave-girl .	Eugénie Schlosser
A negress .	Mme Dominique
Marcel	Louis Mérante
Achmed .	Alfred Chapuy
D'Hautefort	Eugène Coralli
De Verneuil .	Édouard Pluque

The mythological *divertissement* in Act II, Scene 2, was to have included three numbers:

1. *Daphné*: Laure Fonta, Louis Mérante and others.
2. *Iris*: Zina Mérante and others.
3. *Galathée*: Amalia Ferraris, Louis Mérante, Eugène Coralli and others.

(The *divertissement* was planned after Ferraris had been selected to take over the rôle of Zara.)

an impressive demonstration before the Emperor at Compiègne that, by a decree dated November 27th, 1859, carteronization of all scenery and costumes at the Opéra was made compulsory. The solution with which the stuffs were treated, however, made the dancers' dresses appear stiff and dirty, and a general outcry went up protesting against its adoption. Typical was the reaction of Eugénie Schlosser. "Bah!" she cried. "One only burns once, but one would have to wear dirty petticoats every night!" [1]

When Emma Livry had refused to submit to this order at the first performance of *Le Papillon*, the Director, in order to safeguard himself from liability, had required her to put her refusal into writing.

"I absolutely insist, *monsieur*, on dancing the first performance of the ballet in my ordinary ballet skirts", she had written accordingly on November 23rd, 1860, "and I take upon myself the responsibility for anything that might happen to me. In the last scene [in which Farfalla brushes against Hymen's torch] I will dance with my carteronized skirt. I cannot show myself in skirts which would be ugly or which are unbecoming. Since I consider that the management is right in the innovation it wishes to introduce, I will myself ask for the substitution to be made after a few performances, provided that it does not spoil the appearance of the costumes, as I fear it will."

The last few months of Emma's career contained several strange portents of the terrible fate that was approaching her. Strangest of all came when the writer, Ernest Feydeau, asked her to explain some technical dancing terms that he wished to insert in his novel, *Le Mari de la danseuse*. She gladly consented, and completed the lesson in the Foyer de la Danse by dancing the *pas* from *La Sylphide*, which the novelist wished to describe.

"In return", she then said, "tell me the story of your novel."

Feydeau did so, sketching briefly the adventures of his heroine to the climax of his book, in which her skirt catches fire from the footlights as she is dancing in *La Sylphide*, and she is burnt to death in full view of the audience.

When he had finished, Emma was silent for a moment. Then she turned to her mother and said: "To be burnt to

---

[1] The loathing with which carteronization was regarded even after Emma Livry's accident is reflected in the exclamation of Amalia Ferraris: "No! I would rather burn like Mlle Livry!"

death, that must be very painful." She paused. "All the same", she continued suddenly, turning to Feydeau, "it is a fine death for a dancer." [1]

Another portent had occurred some time before, during one of the dress rehearsals of *Le Papillon*, when the skirt of Maria Baratte, a *petit sujet*, had caught fire. The flames had fortunately been quickly extinguished by the prompt action of Saint-Georges, and she had been able to appear at the final rehearsal a few days later, the only evidence of the accident being what one critic touchingly described as "that dear little burnt hand, enveloped in bandages". Indeed the person who suffered most from this little incident was the unfortunate Offenbach, a very sensitive man, whom many people avoided, thinking he had the "evil eye" and brought bad luck.

Finally, early in November 1862, the mirror in Emma's dressing-room broke for no apparent reason. Her mother, who was superstitious, was frightened, but Emma merely smiled.

Emma Livry had reappeared at the Opéra in *Le Papillon* on September 3rd, after her three months' holiday. The preparations for *La Muette de Portici* had proceeded slowly. The tenor, Michot, was first selected for the rôle of Masaniello, but fell ill after a few weeks; rehearsals were suspended, and renewed again when, at Auber's suggestion, the part was confided to Mario. On Wednesday, November 12th, Emma danced for the last time, in *Herculanum*. A dress rehearsal of *La Muette* was fixed for Saturday evening.

Mme Emarot accompanied her daughter to the theatre as usual, and left her in her dressing-room, while she joined Montguyon in one of the *baignoires*. The first act passed without incident. During the second act Emma was to make her entrance after the famous duet, *Amour sacré de la patrie*, from a practicable rock on the O.P. side of the stage. She left her dressing-room early with the intention of listening to Mario. A stool was brought for her and placed on the practicable rock. When the moment approached for her entrance, she stood up

---

[1] A letter from Feydeau to the journalist, Henry de Pène, written from Trouville on August 5th, 1863, was published in *L'Entr'acte* on August 12th. In this letter Feydeau described the assistance that Emma Livry had given him in connection with his book, and stated that this conversation took place about six months before her accident. His novel first appeared in serial form in the newspaper, *L'Opinion Nationale*, beginning on October 5th, 1862, more than a month before the accident.

and shook out her skirt, forgetful of the wing-light alongside. The sudden movement of air caused a flame to dart over its guard and touch her skirt.

"Don't move, *mademoiselle!*" shouted a fireman, as he rushed towards her.

Hearing him shout, Emma looked back and saw the flames rising from her costume. Panic-stricken, she ran down from the rock on to the stage. Almost at once, the flames were rising into the air three times her height. Augustine Malot, a member of the *corps de ballet*, heedless of her own danger, approached her several times and tried to tear the blazing shreds from her costume. The other *danseuses* were not so courageous; when they saw Emma burning, they recoiled in fear of contact, and many fled out of the theatre into the street before realizing where they were. Enveloped in a searing column of fire, Emma screamed three times in her terror, "Cries", said Dr. Laborie, "that the ear could never forget." The male dancer, Pluque, made valiant efforts to save her. Then, from the wings, one of the firemen, Muller, ran out with the safety-blanket, caught her, threw her to the ground, and, by rolling with her on the boards, at last succeeded in extinguishing the savage flames. Before Emma lost consciousness, her form could be distinguished beneath the sodden blanket, in an attitude of prayer.

Dr. Laborie, one of the doctors attached to the Opéra, was in the orchestra stalls, and, as soon as the accident occurred, hurried to the stage. When he arrived, he found Emma lying senseless on the floor: the terrible incident had lasted only a few seconds. At his order she was taken to her dressing-room, where she regained consciousness. Her mother, in a state of collapse, was brought to her. "When I saw those flames", Emma told her, "I felt I was lost and quickly said a little prayer." Seeing that she was nearly naked, she modestly tried to cover her body with the scorched and tattered remains of her costume. With some difficulty the doctors removed these shreds, examined her quickly, and ordered her to be taken home.

Well wrapped up, she was carried on a stretcher from the Opéra, along the gas-lit streets—its was nine o'clock in the evening—to her home near by in the Rue Laffitte, followed by a curious and sympathetic crowd. Only once was she heard to cry out in pain. Her mother was in great distress, and Emma tried to comfort her by saying "Have no fear, it will be nothing."

Emma was then examined thoroughly by her own doctor and by Dr. Laborie, whom she asked to continue attending her. In the latter's report to the Director of the Opéra he wrote: "The fire had caused very extensive burns, covering both thighs, the loins, the back, the shoulders and both arms. . . . Her condition appeared very serious, not because of the depth of the burns, but because of their extent." Her face and chest were barely touched. Her burns were covered with cotton-wool, which was painfully removed thirty-six hours later.

There was a continuous flow of callers enquiring the patient's progress and inscribing their names in the visitors' book. On the Sunday, Comte Walewski called. Théophile Gautier, Auber, Camille Doucet, Prince Joseph Poniatowski also came. All Paris was anxious, humble folk as well as the famed and the wealthy: the Director of the Opéra received a letter from a tradesman of the Rue du Bac, suggesting that when Emma made her reappearance she should be led on to the stage by Muller in his fireman's uniform and with the *Médaille Militaire* that the Emperor had awarded him for his bravery [1] pinned to his tunic. Montguyon hardly ever left her side.

After her dressings had been renewed she relapsed into a violent fever, that night dreaming she was again surrounded by flames. She had to be held to prevent further injury. Her pulse frequency increased alarmingly and the doctors began to despair. Then she rallied, and on Tuesday night she was able to take a little food and sleep calmly. She was not out of danger yet, for another crisis followed nine days later.

She went through unbelievable suffering. For more than four months she remained lying face downwards with her arms outstretched, and every day the roadway below her window was covered with straw to deaden the clatter of the traffic. Lemon juice was applied to her burns, and attempts were made to graft flesh in the hope of preventing scars from forming. She was forbidden to speak, and even to groan or weep or make any movement at all, for fear that the feeble

---

[1] Muller also received a gratuity of 300 francs and Pluque a gratuity of 200 francs. In token of her gratitude, Emma Livry gave Muller a watch engraved with the date of the accident.

tissues that were being encouraged to cover her sores might be damaged. Her thoughts and her fears, all had to be contained within her, shared with no one, and when she could bear the anguish no longer, when her youth and strength revolted, an impassive voice warned her, "Keep calm if you want to live."

"I want to live", she murmured. "Please God, give me courage." And she would resign herself to silence and stillness once more.

"What went on in that young mind so fatally given over to suffering?" asked Paul d'Ambert, who had written of her triumphs and now had the sad task of recording her martyrdom. "What is certain is that not a murmur escaped her, and that during those terrible crises her greatest concern was to console her mother. In the convulsions of an agony which was renewed a score of times before carrying her off, she would smile at her and assure her that she was getting well."

Her piety and gentleness were remarked by all who saw her suffer. "Pray for me, pray for me, Sister", she would repeat. Albéric Second, who called to enquire after her, met the Sister of Charity coming out of Emma's room, where she had been sitting by her bedside. "*Monsieur, she is an angel*", she said softly as she passed him.

Another day Emma was visited by a little ballet girl whom she had befriended, and made her promise to visit her priest and pray for her recovery. Some days later, as the Abbé was leaving his church, his arm was seized by the young girl, breathless, her bonnet askew, her hair flying.

"What do you want, my child?" he asked.

"I have come to confess for Emma Livry", she replied.

The Abbé smiled. "You are welcome for whatever reason you come", he said, "only you should have arrived earlier, for confession time is over."

"I know", she interrupted. "I have run as fast as I could. I couldn't leave before the end of the rehearsal."

"Rehearsal?"

"Yes. Of the ballet I am dancing in."

"You are a dancer, my poor child?"

"Yes, Father. Does that surprise you?"

"No, it distresses me, for I feel that you could be doing something better."

"I don't know", replied the girl. "After all, I am able to

keep my poor widowed mother, pay for my sister's apprentice-ship, and send my little brother to a good school. Do you know how I could earn more at my age?"

The Abbé bowed his head in silence, and conducted the young penitent to his confessional.

In the spring, Emma's condition showed signs of improve-ment. The Emperor and Empress placed a house at Compiègne at her disposal, and when Prince Joseph Poniatowski came to tell her of their kindness she spoke to him of her art and her plans for the future. The Sister who was tending her, however, was not so optimistic. "Such hope disturbs me", she said to herself. "I know very well that this poor girl is lost."

As the summer advanced, Emma was allowed to receive a few visitors, and her doctors considered that she would be able to stand a short journey, though not so far as Compiègne. Her mother therefore rented a small country house near Neuilly, No. 10 Place de Villiers.

One day in July, Emma, in a white dressing-gown, and her head covered by a bonnet, was carefully brought downstairs from her room. She smiled at the friends and servants who had gathered in the hall to wish her a speedy recovery. "I will soon come back grown-up", she said to them. She was assisted into the waiting barouche. The doctor suggested that she should lie down, but she preferred to travel sitting, and was placed between him and a Sister of Charity, with her feet resting on the lap of her mother, who was sitting facing her. It was a beautiful summer's day and the roads were filled with people. Some gentlemen who recognized her raised their hats as she passed, and, touched by these marks of sympathy, she bowed and smiled back at them.

At the end of the journey Emma was helped out of the carriage and taken into a large room on the ground floor of the house, overlooking the garden. There she found some holy relics sent by the Empress, who had never ceased to enquire after her. Emma had stood the journey well, and for a few days her cure continued. Then, without warning, erysipelas set in. Montguyon kept constant vigil by her bedside, reading aloud from the Gospels and *The Imitation of Christ* as her condition grew rapidly worse. Weakened by her long illness, she no longer had the strength to resist. She had no illusions now. "I know I shall never recover", she told the Sister.

"I am going to God." She concerned herself with the details of her funeral, and distributed a few souvenirs among her dearest friends: one of them long treasured the Sèvres cup from which she used to drink iced coffee before going on to the stage.

On the Sunday, July 26th, her pain became unbearable, and the house resounded with her cries. "Oh, for pity's sake, let me weep", she gasped. "I cannot stop screaming. It is tearing me apart." Towards ten o'clock in the evening she became calmer. She was now so weak that she could no longer even groan. She took a little food, and at nine o'clock M. Nélaton, the Emperor's surgeon, came to see her. His expression was serious, and afterwards he did not conceal his opinion that the end was near. Only Mme Emarot remained blind to the hopelessness of her daughter's condition. That night another crisis seized the patient, and was followed by a further calm. Then, shortly before midnight, Emma murmured a few words, a happy smile played on her lips, two tears rolled down her cheeks, and all was over.

. . . .

The Requiem Mass was arranged to take place at the Church of Notre-Dame de Lorette at ten o'clock on the Wednesday morning, July 29th. That same evening the Opéra was to give the ballet, *Diavolina*; the Russian dancer, Martha Muravieva, begged the Director to excuse her from appearing, but he was unable to accede to her request at such short notice.

The body was brought from Neuilly early that morning in a closed hearse. The church soon began to fill, and by ten o'clock there was room for not one person more, and a crowd of many thousands had gathered in the streets outside. Attending the service were many famous figures of the political, theatrical, literary and artistic worlds: Alphonse Gautier, Secretary-General to the Ministry of the Emperor's Household and Fine Arts; Camille Doucet, the Superintendent-General of Theatres; Émile Perrin, the Director of the Opéra, Henri Duponchel and Alphonse Royer, two past Directors, and Hippolyte Cogniard, the manager of the Variétés; Auber and Prince Joseph Poniatowski, the composers; Théophile Gautier, Alexandre Dumas *fils*, Saint-Georges, Paul Foucher, Albéric Second; Eugénie Doche, the actress, and Mlle Cico of operetta fame; Mmes Vandenheuvel-Duprez and Gueymard-Lauters, sopranos of the Opéra; and among the many dancers, Marie Taglioni, Carolina Rosati, Adeline Plunkett, Mme Dominique, Zina Mérante, Laure Fonta, Louise Marquet, Marie Vernon, Fanny Génat, Adèle Villiers and Hortense Clavelle.

The Requiem Mass was said by the vicar of the parish. M. Vauthrot, the *chef de chant* of the Opéra, led a choir of the principal male singers in Plantade's *Libera* during the Offertory and Panseron's *Pie Jésu* during the Elevation of the Host. While the service was being held, the crowds outside waited in silence. Then the small coffin, covered with white drapings and flowers, was borne out of the church, placed on the funeral carriage, and taken slowly to the Montmartre Cemetery, where the burial was to take place. Six young girls from the *Conservatoire de Danse*, in white dresses and veils, held the cordons of the canopy, and eight others walked behind. Many of Emma Livry's companions were in the crowd that followed her on her last journey. It was a sad procession, and a little *rat* of the third quadrille was heard to observe pensively: "*Moi aussi, j'aurais bien aimé mourir sage! Mais je n'en avais pas le moyen.*" As a symbol of Emma Livry's brief career, two white butterflies were seen hovering over the coffin as the procession neared the cemetery.

So great was the crowd that the gates of the cemetery had to be closed, leaving many people outside who wished to hear Lucien Petipa deliver the funeral oration.

.   .   .   .

The critics then offered their last tributes to her memory.

"Emma Livry was barely twenty-one", wrote Théophile Gautier in *Le Moniteur*. "From her début . . . she had shown herself to be a dancer of the first order, and the public's attention had never strayed from her. She belonged to that chaste school of Taglioni which makes the dance an almost spiritual art by its modest grace, seemly reserve, and virginal translucency. Catching a glimpse of her through the transparency of her veilings, her foot barely raising the hem, one was reminded of a happy shade, an elysian apparition at play in a bluish gleam; she was possessed of imponderable lightness, and her silent figure darted through space without one hearing the quivering of the air. In the ballet—the only one, alas!—that she created, she played the part of a butterfly. This was no banal choreographic gallantry. She could imitate the charming, whimsical flight of a butterfly settling on a flower without bending its stem. She resembled a butterfly too closely, for she, too, burnt her wings in the flame, and, as though wishing to take part in the funeral of a sister, two white butterflies hovered ceaselessly over her white coffin during its journey from the church to the cemetery. This detail, which the Greeks would have seen as a poetic symbol, was remarked by thousands of people, for an immense crowd accompanied the hearse. On the simple tomb of the young dancer, what epitaph would be more apt than that written for an Emma Livry of antiquity by a poet of the Anthology: 'Oh, earth, rest gently over me, I trod so lightly upon thee.'

"In that lively and tender interest of a whole population, the talent, youth, and tragic death of the young victim, and her long suffering, counted, indeed, for much; but there was yet another cause—the desire to honour that pure life led in a career beset with temptations, that modest virtue in face of which slander held its tongue, that love of art and toil which asked no other allurements than the dance itself; the desire to show respect for the artist who respected herself. If anything can console a mother's grief, it would be that procession, so solemn, so touching, so religious in character, following the mourning carriage, in which, seated among the celebrities of the Opéra, were the two Sisters of Charity who had tended the poor girl during the agony borne so courageously and in so Christian a spirit."

Wrote Nestor Roqueplan in *Le Constitutionnel*: "Emma Livry was a great artist from the beginning. She was both noble and modest: chaste as a muse, she sought in her art only the charm of the art itself. In her honesty of heart, she did not consider herself separated by her profession from the classes that the Church admits to its offices and receives to its bosom. She never thought that there could be any inconsistency between her art and piety. And who knows if, on the day before her début, in her desire to do well, she did not let fall a prayer to God to give her the grace to succeed the next day."

Wrote Jules Janin in the *Journal des Débats*: "A few moments more, and Emma Livry would have been an incomparable dancer. She was light as a bird; she combined grace with intelligence; merely to see her slender, elegant, well-shaped figure made one realize that she was born to dance. 'It is true', said Mlle Taglioni, 'that I never saw myself dance, but I must have danced like her.' To see them together, one would have said they were mother and daughter. . . . She was the only artiste at the Opéra who deserved the attention and enthusiasm of good judges. She alone had a name in that crowd, a character in that ballet; she alone was always new for us. She sought and created, and the critics would willingly have done for her what they had done for Mlle Taglioni, her second mother. For ten years the critics spoke of Mlle Taglioni, always finding words of praise to bestow upon her, and they counted on Emma Livry for their days of enjoyment and leisure. The memory of the young dancer's funeral will long endure. The whole capital wished to pay her their last respects; the public accompanied that light coffin to the tomb. It was a unanimous ovation."

. . . .

Mme Emarot was plunged into inconsolable grief. Montguyon, too, was overwhelmed by the tragedy, and learning that Mme Emarot had had to pledge her jewellery to meet the heavy medical expenses incurred, and that the Opéra had ceased to pay her daughter's salary since May, he saw to it that her plight was brought to the notice of the Emperor. Napoleon III at once ordered the Minister of his Household, Marshal Vaillant, to draw up a document granting Mme Emarot a gratuity of 40,000 francs and a pension of 6000 francs a year to commence from July 27th, 1863. The Emperor signed it immediately. "If anything could soften the grief at the cruel bereavement I have suffered", Mme Emarot wrote to the Marshal, "it would be the interest that His Majesty is kind enough to take in me. My daughter, at the moment of her death, did not forget all the kindness of His Majesty, and, like her, I shall always remember it."

Seven years later, during the Franco-German War, the Emperor's authority was overthrown and a Republican régime set up. Forgetful of all the benefits the Second Empire had brought to the country, the self-appointed Government of National Defence refused to recognize many of the pensions granted out of the Emperor's Civil List, Mme Emarot's among them. After many protests, Mme Emarot appealed to the

Laure Fonta as Myrtha in *Giselle*   Louis Mérante as Albrecht in
Giselle, Act II

Louis Mérante and Martha   Eugénie Fiocre as Fenella in
Muravieva in *Diavolina*   *La Muette de Portici*

La Maschera, Act II, Scene II

Amina Boschetti in *La Maschera*   Eugénie Fiocre in *La Maschera*

Court, but her plea was rejected on the grounds that there was no question of the Opéra being under any liability in respect of the accident, and that the pension had been granted merely as an act of magnanimity by the Emperor.

Emma's father, the Baron Charles de Chassiron, died at Tarbes in 1871. A few years later, in 1876, her benefactor, Montguyon, his last resources spent and his will to live gone, killed himself in a Turkish bath. Mme Emarot, who had retired to a modest apartment in No. 19 Avenue de la Grande Armée, lived on, and, on October 7th, 1892, died there at the age of sixty-eight. She had outlived her daughter by nearly thirty years.

VII

THE LAST YEARS OF FERRARIS

THE departure of Carolina Rosati from the Opéra in the summer of 1859 left Amalia Ferraris as the sole representative of the Italian school and the highest paid dancer in Paris. Her only rival was Emma Livry, whose career was then just beginning, and whose talent was still in bud.

That winter, *Pierre de Médicis*, an opera by Prince Joseph Poniatowski, went into rehearsal, with Ferraris cast in the leading rôle in the *divertissement*. For her condescension in waiving the stipulation in her contract that she was not to appear in operas, she had been promised a new ballet by her countryman, Pasquale Borri, and was to be further rewarded by the gift of a magnificent bracelet from Napoleon III, after he had attended the first performance of the opera with the Empress.

The *divertissement*, entitled *Les Amours de Diane*, lasted some twenty minutes and formed an important part of the opera. Its plot told of Diane (Ferraris) and her lover, Endymion (L. Mérante), being surprised in the forest by Pan (E. Coralli), who kills Endymion in a bout of jealousy. Diane transforms herself into Hecate, and calls on her Furies to surround Pan. Pan eludes their grasp and vanishes. Finally, Endymion is restored to life by the timely arrival of Cupid (L. Fiocre).

The rôle of Diane was specially designed by the choreographer, Lucien Petipa, to bring out the rare qualities of Ferraris' style. Her dancing in the two *grandes variations* was masterly. "She rose to an incredible height", wrote Fiorentino. "She flew, like a shuttlecock between two racquets, from the hands of Endymion to those of Pan, turning, or beating *entrechats* in space. She literally hovered in the air, and if she consented to alight on the ground, it was to circle a group five or six times with marvellous rapidity on *pointes* as straight and firm as the golden arrows in her quiver." Then came *temps d'aplomb* on the *pointe*, during which she changed her position three times without lowering her other foot, before finally breaking into a sequence of rapid steps to a sparkling accompaniment on the flute.

The smaller rôle of Cupid served to introduce Louise Fiocre, the elder of the two sisters who were so renowned for their shapely figures. Born at Pau on July 10th, 1843, she had been persuaded to take up dancing by her one-time neighbour, Arthur Saint-Léon, and had entered the third quadrille as a child in 1856. Her plump little figure and arch expression won her many admirers. "*Je prendrais bien ce petit amour de Fiocre à l'heure*", quipped Xavier Aubyrat; and Nérée-Desarbres, the Secretary of the Opéra, meeting her in the street the day after her début, carrying a basket of vegetables, could not resist saying, "What! Cupid going marketing!"—a remark that confused the girl, who blushed, thinking he was being witty at her expense. Later, her charms paled before the wonderful vision of her younger sister, Eugénie, and she had progressed no further than the grade of *petit sujet* when she retired from the stage in 1868. She married the tenor, Colin, who died of pleurisy in January 1872, and, in her later years, lived at Courbevoie.

.   .   .   .

The hostile reception given to Wagner's opera, *Tannhaüser*, at the Opéra in March 1861, had several causes. Many people were unfamiliar with this new form of music drama that Wagner was seeking to evolve, a form far removed from that so familiar in the operas of Meyerbeer, Auber and Rossini which were the mainstay of the repertory. Others grasped at the opportunity of protesting against the influence of the Austrian Ambassadress, the Princess Pauline Metternich, who was known to be Wagner's champion and was believed to have used her position at Court to have the work put on at the Opéra. And not the least effective cause was the anger of certain men of fashion at not being given their ballet at the time they considered they were entitled to it.

During the many months that elapsed before *Tannhaüser* was presented, several hundred thousands of francs were expended, settings of great magnificence were designed and constructed, singers were specially engaged, and rehearsal followed rehearsal until their number reached one hundred and sixty-three. One of the many bitter wrangles that developed between Wagner and the management was concerned with the inclusion of a ballet, without which no full-length opera was deemed complete. Because a fashionable and influential section of the audience—members of the Jockey Club for the most part—were accustomed to arriving after the performance had begun, the *divertissement* was never placed earlier than in the second act, a practice that seemed absurd and artificial to Wagner.

The press sensed a difference between musician and management as early as June 1860. "Who will compose the ballet music?" was the question asked in *L'Entr'acte*. "You quite misunderstand the artistic temperament of Richard Wagner if you think he would allow the addition of even a single note that had not come from his pen. But where will the author of *Tristan und Isolde* find the lightness and the regular rhythm for a *pas de deux*? Just wait, and when a ballet is being given at the Opéra, glance round the house and you will see M. Wagner sitting motionless, attentive, all eyes and ears, eagerly following the evolutions and the movements of the choreography, listening and observing with that implacable conscientiousness and concentration which form three-quarters of his talent."

As a result of these visits to the Opéra, Wagner made up his mind to expand the Venusberg scene in the first act by inserting a bacchanal dance by the *corps de ballet*. Alphonse Royer, Lucien Petipa, even Comte Walewski, the Minister of the Household, pointed out the dangers that attended placing the *divertissement* so early in the opera; the services of the *premières danseuses* could not be expected, explained Petipa, although perhaps three Hungarian dancers could be engaged from the Théâtre Déjazet to play the three Graces. Wagner was obdurate, and refused to take account of a section of the audience who chose to arrive late; and since *Tannhaüser* was being given by order of the Emperor, and so much had been spent on it already, the management had no choice but to give way.

Lucien Petipa only began work on the *divertissement* at the last moment, when the new music for the scene was provided. At the same time he was arranging a new ballet for Ferraris, which prevented him from devoting his whole attention to *Tannhaüser*, as Wagner doubtless expected he should. When the composer tried to explain how he wanted the scene arranged, Petipa replied shortly: "Oh, I understand very well, but I should need all *premières danseuses* for that. If I said a word to my people about it, and suggested the poses you want, we should get the cancan right away, and be ruined."

"Little expense has been laid out for this entertainment", wrote Fiorentino of the finished result. "Twenty-four bacchantes walk from right to left, and raise their arms above their heads, a slow, gentle movement that is only amusing to these ballet girls. Then twenty-four fauns walk from left to right, raising their arms like the bacchantes. Sixteen nymphs follow the fauns, raising their arms in the same manner. Then sixteen youths, who were asleep on the rocks, wake up suddenly and raise their arms, as though stretching. Finally, twelve Cupids, not to be different, raise their little arms in the air, without knowing why. All these raised arms undoubtedly make a charming scene, but it lasts too long. There remain the three Graces—Mlles Rousseau, Stoïkoff and Troisvallets. One hopes for a moment that they will be excepted from the routine and do what they like with their arms; but soon one sees that they, no less than the fauns, the bacchantes, the youths and the nymphs, will not be allowed to lower them, and that they will end by catching cramp. Apparently the dance of the future only permits arms in the air. I admit indeed that this simultaneous elevation of all those assembled arms gives an impression of mysticism and devotion."

The three performances of *Tannhäuser* in March 1861, the first two of which were attended by the Emperor and Empress, occasioned hostile demonstrations that made any serious appraisal of the work impossible. Paul Scudo, the eccentric music critic of the *Revue des Deux Mondes*, openly encouraged the catcalls and whistling from his seat in the stalls, delighted at what he took to be a public rejection of Wagner's music. The real instigators, however, were not the champions of the old order of music, but the gentlemen of the Jockey Club, who arrived in strength after buying the entire stock of hunting whistles from a nearby armourer. Towards the end of the second act, they began tapping their canes on the floor and chanting, "*Le bal-let! Le bal-let!*"

The Princess Metternich, who had arranged that many of her friends should be present on the first night to lead the applause, was bitterly disappointed at the fiasco. It was said that she broke her fan in anger when the hissing started, and that, during an interval, she snatched a whistle from an aristocratic member of the hostile cabal and dropped it into her corsage.

After three performances the management was as anxious as the composer himself that the work should be taken off; and on July 19th the scenery and properties, which had been prepared at such great expense, were destroyed in the conflagration of the scenery-store in the Rue Richer.[1]

. . . . . .

The third and last performance of *Tannhaüser* took place on Sunday, March 24th, 1861. The following day, Amalia Ferraris created the title-rôle in *Graziosa*, a one-act ballet by Lucien Petipa, with music by Labarre and scenario by J. Derley. This latter name cloaked the identity of the Comte Roger de Sainte-Marie, a young and elegant member of the Jockey Club, who, needless to say, had caused a great stir among the *corps de ballet* during the rehearsals. Originally entitled *Marianna*, *Graziosa* had been hurriedly commissioned when it was realized that Wagner could not be persuaded to include a proper *divertissement* in *Tannhaüser*. The first performance had been planned to coincide with that of the opera, so as to appease the dreaded wrath of the Jockey Club; and the choice of de Sainte-Marie as scenarist was looked on as an added insurance against any hostile demonstration. Time being short, less than 10,000 francs were expended on the production, the set for the first act of *Marco Spada* and many of the costumes for that ballet being put into service again.

Even then, *Graziosa* was not ready in time to be given with the first performance of *Tannhaüser*, a misfortune that the superstitious attributed to the presence of someone with the "evil eye", namely a certain Italian gentleman who had been lent a box in the theatre. Ferraris was most anxious that the influence should be removed, and her anxiety, of course, had to be relieved.

Several attempts were made to recover the ticket for the box,

[1] The scenery of *La Sylphide*, *Orfa* and *Le Corsaire* was burnt at the same time. The only ballets whose sets and costumes were preserved were *La Vivandière*, *Le Papillon*, *Graziosa*, *Le Marché des Innocents* (these being in the theatre), *Giselle*, *Le Diable à quatre*, *Jovita* and *Sacountala*.

but all without success. Then someone had an inspiration. An enormous gibbet was taken from the property-store and placed at the back of the box, with the desired result that it was unoccupied when the first performance of *Graziosa* was given. It was then promptly forgotten by all except the elderly attendant, who had been warned not to touch it, but was unaware of the reason for its presence. It was not removed until the Secretary of the Opéra entered the box some six months later and discovered that it was still there.

The action of *Graziosa* passed in the public square of a small town near Naples, in the days of the Spanish rule. A quarrel between two Spanish noblemen over a masked lady, whom one is escorting, leads to a duel. Graziosa (Ferraris) and her sweetheart, Pietro (Chapuy), hear the clash of swords. After vainly trying to separate the duellists, Pietro goes to fetch help, but while he is away, Graziosa, unobserved by the two noblemen, changes places with the masked lady, and then, by unmasking herself before them, puts an end to the fight. When Pietro arrives with the soldiers, the square is deserted, and he is arrested and ordered to be imprisoned by the Podesta (Dauty). Returning, Graziosa is surprised to hear her sweetheart calling to her from a prison cell, and facilitates his escape by fascinating the sergeant (Berthier) and the soldiers with her dancing. The Podesta threatens to have the sergeant shot unless the prisoner is recaptured. The square then fills with people coming to see the bull-fight. Pietro arrives with Graziosa, but he is recognized by the Podesta, who orders his arrest. But the Governor (E. Coralli), who was one of the duellists, recognizes Graziosa as his benefactress, and, by commanding Pietro to be set at liberty, reunites her with her lover.

"Perhaps Mme Ferraris has never been received—even in her grand ballets—with greater enthusiasm", wrote Fiorentino. "It can be said that her talent was revealed in quite a new light. . . . She is a young girl of the people, carefree and gay, abandoning herself to that exuberance of life, youth and happiness that can be felt in the pleasant climate of Central Italy." Lucien Petipa had given her several effective dances, including a *pas de la charmeuse* and a *pas de la fiancée*, the latter a charming and original composition that displayed her strong *pointe* .work and her wonderful elevation and *ballon*. A particularly colourful passage was the bull-fight scene, *La Corrida de los toreros*, led by Louise Marquet, who enacted "the episode of the *espada* with a superb swagger, planting her sword between the horns of an imaginary bull". At the end of the ballet, the stage was covered with a profusion of bouquets of camellias, white lilac and Parma violets, most of them thrown from the boxes occupied by the Jockey Club—a tribute to both the ballerina and their fellow member, and also, perhaps, a display of relief at being given something more readily comprehensible than the strange *divertissement* in *Tannhaüser*.

．　　　．　　　．　　　．　　　．　　　．　　　．

That summer, Marius Petipa, Lucien's younger brother and a rising choreographer in St. Petersburg, arrived in Paris with his wife, to produce a ballet at the Opéra. Having little time at his disposal, he decided to adapt a ballet he had produced at St. Petersburg two years before, *Le Marché de Paris*, a work which entailed comparatively little preparation, since it comprised only one act, and his wife was perfectly familiar with the leading rôle, which she had in fact created. An old set, that had once served Adam's opera, *La Bouquetière*, was brought out of store, and further economies were made, so that little more than 6000 francs were expended on the production. The ballet, re-entitled *Le Marché des Innocents*, was first given at the Opéra on May 29th, 1861.

For the French production, the period of the action had been transposed from the reign of Louis XV, in which the original version had been set, to the time of the Directory, as the former epoch had been used very recently for *Graziosa*. The slight plot was woven round the characters of Gloriette (Mme Petipa) and her lover, Simon (L. Mérante), and Lindor (Dauty), an *incroyable*, and his mistress, Denise (L. Marquet). After Lindor has tried to flirt with Gloriette, Denise intervenes and finally persuades her protector to give the lovers a handsome dowry. The score, by Pugni, matched the flimsy nature of the scenario.

The main interest of the production was the Paris début of Marie Petipa. The illegitimate daughter of a St. Petersburg milliner, Maria Sergueyevna Surovshchikova was born in 1836 and married Marius Petipa in 1854. She was now, in 1861, in the prime of her voluptuous beauty. Paris saw her, in the rôle of Gloriette, as a fine comedienne, with an

Saint-Léon rehearsing *Néméa*

Néméa, Act I

Martha Muravieva as Néméa   Eugénie Fiocre as Cupid in *Néméa*

Louis Mérante in *Néméa*   Dauty in *Néméa*

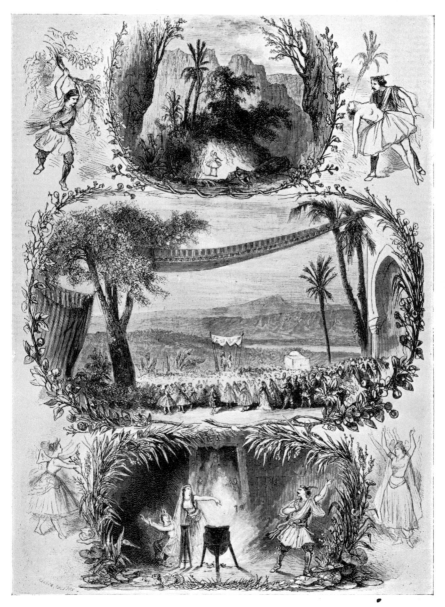

Scenes from *La Source*

Eugénie Fiocre in *La Source*
Oil-painting by Degas

inexhaustible fund of vivacity, and a dancer whose style was so natural and spontaneous that at times it seemed as though she was dancing just as her inspiration moved her. Her style was strongest in her firm, delicate and rapid *pointe* work, and weakest in *temps d'élévation*; her dancing was very assured, her sense of rhythm very exact. She possessed a serpentine suppleness, and commanded arm movements so flowing and graceful that more than one critic was reminded of the wings of a bird. "She is truly Russian", it was written of her. "She aspires neither to the fine classical effects of the French style, nor to the warm and powerful fantasy of Italy, nor to a Spanish fury. She is a delightful caprice, ever floating between a heedless folly and a graceful melancholy, a strange mixture resulting from her Slav character." "This gipsy mocks at your rules", added Fiorentino. "She prefers the curved line to the straight, and dancing for pleasure to dancing of the *haute école*. Her small feet commit many solecisms, and her agile, flexible arms curve gracefully despite the rules of grammar."

Her husband's choreography brought into relief all the originality of her style. The scene in which Gloriette repulses the advances of Lindor led to an amusing *variation* in which she jumped and turned and pirouetted and raised her arms in the air, as though unable to contain her mirth at having made a fool of the ridiculous old man. Then there was a mazurka in which she advanced from the back of the stage on her *pointes*, turning sharply at every step, the haughty set of her head and her provocative little smile giving her interpretation a wonderful swagger. Another *pas de caractère* was the *Ziganka*, a Bohemian dance that began with "twistings, *parcours, pirouettes* of a frolicsome gaiety", then developed into a slow passage when the orchestra seemed to lull her to sleep with "the sound of a brook rippling through a wood", and ended, as it began, with an exhilarating turbulence.

Among the *pas d'ensemble* were a *pas de guirlandes*, somewhat forced in conception, which gave Marie Petipa time to change her costume, and a very spirited *pas des dames de la Halle*, led by Eugénie Schlosser.

Le Marché des Innocents caused less of a stir at the theatre than in the law courts, where it gave rise to two actions. First, a M. René Lordereau, who had translated Marius Petipa's scenario, unsuccessfully sued the management of the Opéra for not having included his name on the bills; and the following year, the courts heard what was probably the first lawsuit concerning the infringement of copyright in choreography— the case of *Perrot v. Petipa*.

Jules Perrot had arrived in Paris in the summer of 1861, at about the same time as the Petipas, whom he had met at the wedding of Louis Mérante and Zina Richard in July. Marie Petipa had then asked him if she could dance his *pas*, *La Cosmopolitana*—originally arranged for his ballet, *Gazelda, ou les Tsiganes*—but he had refused his consent. Shortly afterwards, in August, a friend informed him that his *pas* had nevertheless been incorporated into *Le Marché des Innocents*, very thinly disguised as *La Cosmopolite*. Perrot visited the Opéra to see for himself, and then immediately complained to the Director. Receiving no satisfaction, he finally had recourse to litigation. The case was heard in the first chamber of the Tribunal Civil de la Seine, before M. Benoit-Champy, on July 11th, 1862.

Maître Carraby, counsel for Perrot, explained: "[Perrot's] case has presented some difficulty from the outset, and the defendant doubtless relied on that. How is it in fact to be established that a *pas* danced in St Petersburg is the same as a *pas* danced in Paris? Some choreographers commit their *pas* to writing, others memorize them. . . . Unfortunately Perrot improvises his works and does not write them down." To strengthen his case, counsel put in a declaration made by Saint-Léon attesting that the two dances were the same, and asked the Court to award his client 10,000 francs damages.

Maître Chaix d'Est-Ange, for Marius Petipa, pleaded that the Franco-Russian copyright treaty did not extend to dramatic works. He would not dispute that copyright could exist in the scenario of a ballet, but the steps were of a different nature, because, as he explained, "it is the artiste herself who is everything, it is her grace, her strength, her expression, all the play of her body and features that make up the success". Many other ballets—he cited *La Péri* and *Le Corsaire* in particular—had included *pas* such as the one in dispute. As for Maître Carraby's argument that it was plagiarism because the same music had been used, Pugni had expressly authorized his client to use any of his music he pleased for *Le Marché des*

Innocents. Counsel concluded by remarking that Perrot himself had produced many ballets at St. Petersburg that had originally been the work of other choreographers, and taken the credit himself.

The Court found for Perrot, holding that although the *pas* was based on certain well-known national dances, their combination could nevertheless constitute a composition in which copyright might exist. The plea that no treaty existed between France and Russia covering copyright in works of art was rejected because, although the *pas* had been originally given in Russia, it was the work of a Frenchman. Perrot was awarded 300 francs damages.

. . . .

L'Étoile de Messine—the ballet by the Milanese choreographer, Pasquale Borri, promised to Ferraris as a recompense for her appearance in *Pierre de Médicis*—went into production in the summer of 1861, and was presented on November 20th. It was a revised version of the same choreographer's *La Giuocoliera*, which had been produced in Venice, with Adeline Plunkett, in 1856, and in which Ferraris had first danced at Bologna in the winter of 1857. The Paris production was conceived on a very lavish scale, more than 80,000 francs being expended; there were five new sets, four of them being exterior scenes, and some six hundred new costumes, while more than a hundred and sixty persons were taking part in three of the six scenes.

At the dress rehearsal, in the interval between the two acts, someone recognized Rossini in one of the boxes. The news of his presence rapidly spread through the audience, who began to applaud, whereupon the orchestra took up their instruments and played the overture to *Guillaume Tell* as they had seldom played it before. When they had finished, clapping and cheering broke out afresh. The old composer, deeply touched by this spontaneous tribute, came to the front of the box and bowed, smiling. He was at a loss for words, and Alphonse Royer, who was with him, had to step forward and speak his thanks.

Paul Foucher, the scenarist, had set the action of the ballet in Messina, during the seventeenth century, when Sicily was ruled by a Spanish viceroy. The curtain first rose to show a casino, with a masked ball in progress. Two noblemen appear among the revellers, Don Flaminio (E. Coralli), an elderly

roué, and Don Raphael (Chapuy), a younger man, simply
dressed. A masked lady approaches them, and asks to be shown
the medallion that Don Raphael gazes at so lovingly. When
he refuses, she unmasks and reveals herself as his *fiancée*, the
Countess Aldini (L. Marquet). He tries to follow her out of
the casino, but a masked cavalier bars his way. Gazella
(Ferraris), the leading dancer of a troupe of strolling players,
then appears, and Don Raphael recognizes her as the original
of the medallion. Thinking that he is of her own station,
Gazella accepts his simple flower in preference to the
magnificent bouquet offered by Don Flaminio, before dancing
a *pas de deux* with her brother, Gianni (L. Mérante). When
the dance is over, the masked cavalier reappears and reveals
himself as Don Raphael's father, the Governor of Messina
(Lenfant). He reproaches his son, and reminds him that he is
to sign his marriage contract the following morning.

The scene changes to the inn where the strolling players
are lodging. Gianni returns from the casino in a sad and
pensive mood; he is burdened with a secret that only Jacinta
(Aline), the oldest member of the troupe, shares with him.
Gazella then enters, and asks to be left alone. To reassure
herself from fears which she cannot explain, she plucks the
petals from a marguerite, but the oracle is unfavourable. She
contemplates the flower that Don Raphael has given her,
when suddenly he appears and declares his love, begging her
to come away with him. She tells him that she cannot desert
her companions. A knock sounds at the door, and Gazella
hurries Don Raphael out of the room. Don Flaminio enters,
and tries to tempt her with jewels. As his attentions become
pressing, Gianni and the other dancers appear. Don Flaminio
explains that he has come to engage them for the wedding
festivities of the Governor's son. To tantalize him for his
insulting advances, Gazella dances a polka with her brother
that so excites the passions of Don Flaminio, that he tries to
follow her movements, but soon sinks exhausted into a chair.
He rises to follow her out of the room, but Jacopo (Berthier),
the leader of the troupe, stops him and ejects him from the inn.

The next scene takes place by the coast. An inn stands in
the foreground, and anchored off the shore is a small boat.
The flower-girl, Rosetta (Morando), is joined by her lover,
Momolo (Beauchet), a fisherman. Then Gianni appears with

Gazella, telling her that they are leaving the island after the festivities because he fears that she has lost her heart. Later, when Don Raphael again begs her to go away with him, she consents, and he tells her that he will send a man, who will disclose his identity by showing her the medallion, to take her to his boat. Momolo is entrusted with this task, but Don Flaminio, who has overheard Don Raphael giving his instructions, bribes the fisherman to hand over the medallion and lies in wait for Gazella himself. His plot is foiled by the timely appearance of Gianni, who unmasks Don Flaminio, reproaches Gazella for having given way to a mercenary passion, and raises his hand to strike her. But the crowd which has gathered will not see their idol assaulted, and turn on Gianni and would kill him but for the intervention of Gazella. They beg her to dance a *tarantella*, and all join in the frenzied dance as the curtain falls.

The curtain rises again on the second act to show another curtain, that of the private theatre in the Viceregal palace. The Viceroy (Estienne), the Governor, Don Flaminio, and the Countess are seated, waiting for the entertainment to begin, but Don Raphael has not yet arrived. Don Flaminio tells the Countess that she has been betrayed, and shows her the medallion. The *divertissement*, entitled *La Révolte des fées*, begins. The Countess immediately recognizes Gazella from her portrait, and starts from her seat. As the *divertissement* is drawing to its close, Don Raphael enters and kisses the Countess's hand. Seeing him for the first time in his rich raiment, Gazella realizes that she has been deceived. She gives vent to her anger, and is carried away fainting by Gianni and Jacopo. Don Flaminio tells the Countess to follow him.

He takes her to the inn, where they find Jacinta awaiting the dancers' return. Flourishing a warrant bearing the Viceroy's signature, Don Flaminio orders Jacinta to hide the Countess so that she can see all that takes place in the room. Gianni and Gazella enter. Gianni declares his love, and tells her his secret, that she is not his sister, but that he had found her abandoned as a baby. Don Raphael comes in search of Gazella. Enraged, Gianni draws his sword. They fight, and Don Raphael is disarmed. The Countess then emerges and reminds Don Raphael of his vows. Gazella tells him that all is over between them.

The scene changes to a square near the port. The wedding
procession passes, Don Raphael searching sadly among the
crowd for Gazella, the Countess walking proudly by his side.
As they enter the church, Gazella arrives with Gianni and
Jacopo, surrounded by girls begging her to dance. Sad at
heart, she refuses, but when Don Flaminio comes to taunt her
with having lost her opportunity by spurning his advances,
she forces back her tears, and, with a supreme effort, begins to
dance. Her movements become more and more frenzied,
until the bells announce that the ceremony is over. As the
bridal couple come out of the church, her steps at last falter,
and, heartbroken, she falls into Gianni's arms. Don Raphael
runs to her, but Gianni forbids him to approach and covers
her dead body with his cloak. The ship that is to bear the
dancers to the mainland comes into view. The bells are still
chiming as the curtain falls.

  L'Étoile de Messine was a triumph of choreography. Hailed
by Saint-Victor as "an artist of the great school of Taglioni
and Viganò", Pasquale Borri was one of the most celebrated
Italian choreographers of the day. Like his other ballets,
L'Étoile de Messine was remarkable above all for its ably handled
crowd scenes. Borri had taken as much trouble in drilling the
corps de ballet and the supers as he had in coaching the principals,
and with rewarding results, for never before had crowds been
manœuvred to such brilliant effect on the Opéra stage. "What
places him above his rivals", wrote Fiorentino, "is his understanding of design and colour, which he possesses to a supreme
degree. The difficulty is not to huddle two or three hundred
people on the stage at one time, but to distribute them, separate
them, bring them together again with discernment, to trace
patterns and dispose figures, match and blend colours, vary
positions, shade distances and effect perspectives—that is the
secret of choreography." Such scenes had entailed infinite
pains and patience, and long preparation; every detail was
planned, yet the underlying design was never so apparent as
to dull the profusion of colour and movement.

  The casino scene, which opened the ballet, made other
bals masqués seem tame by comparison, so cleverly were the
colours of the costumes blended in the choreography; the
stage was a constantly changing kaleidoscope of pierrettes in
red and black, and sky-blue, slender follies in red and blue,

shepherds in green, and shepherdesses who might have stepped from a picture by Watteau or Boucher. Contrasting with this turbulence, there followed the *pas de deux* by Ferraris and Mérante, with its classic poses and its breath-taking climax, when, resting her hand lightly in her partner's, Ferraris executed a brilliant sequence of *pirouettes sur la pointe* upon an upright tambourine. Her other *pas* differed widely in style from each other. The *polka comique* was a light and witty composition, in which she expressed a mischievous delight in tantalizing the elderly *roué* with her charms; the *tarantella* so thrilled the audience by its speed and fury that they insisted on seeing it again; and her *pas* in the *divertissement* brought out her grace and her ethereal lightness, her movements being followed by the *corps de ballet* in the same way, said Fiorentino, that a chorus accompanies the *prima donna* in an opera. But the most impressive passage of all occurred during the last few moments of the ballet. The scene in which she danced herself to death was unforgettable; it was said that she died in the grand manner, with such dramatic power as was possessed by few of her contemporaries. "Without seeing her in that final attack of madness", wrote Fiorentino, "pallid, exhausted, broken . . . dancing that dance of agony, unconscious of movement or thought, mechanically, instinctively obeying an unknown force—without seeing all that, nobody can understand to what degree the greatest grief, the most moving and most dramatic moments can be expressed by look and gesture alone."

Unfortunately the distinguished choreography and the brilliant interpretation were hampered by a disappointing score, the work of another Italian, Count Nicolò Gabrielli. The scenario, with its Sicilian setting, its masked ball and wedding procession, its faery *divertissement* and its tragic climax, might well have inspired a masterpiece, but all Gabrielli could produce was a patchwork of tunes that might have served almost any *divertissement*. The music critic, Paul Scudo, was rightly indignant. "Now what has M. Gabrielli done to deserve the honour of having his *pots-pourris* heard in the Opéra?" he asked. "Paris has twenty composers more learned and more inspired than he, who would gladly have so charming and inventive a ballerina as Mme Ferraris dance to their tunes. Why apply to incompetent aliens, when there are men of talent at hand, and French and Christian born, as the moralists say!"

.   .   .   .

Marie Petipa paid her second visit to the Opéra in June and July 1862, for which she was engaged at 4000 francs a month. She reappeared in *Le Marché des Innocents* on June 4th, and on the 20th first played the rôle of Mazourka in a revival, with new sets and costumes, of *Le Diable à quatre*. Once again she gained a great triumph with her "bold and simple, brilliant and rebellious dancing, touched with Slav caprice and French wit", as Saint-Victor put it. "A childlike playfulness mingles with her womanly grace", he continued. "She has also a child's infinite mobility of expression, for her pretty face is never still for a moment. . . . And her arms have the skill of her legs, a rare quality at the Opéra."

The second act had been expanded to include a brilliant *polski mazur*, in which she was partnered by a well-known male dancer, specially engaged from St. Petersburg at the enormous salary, for a man, of 1800 francs a month, Felix Ivanovitch Kshesinski. "It is an equestrian, martial dance", described Saint-Victor, "its rhythm beaten by spurs and the rattling of a sabre in its scabbard. Tapping his heel, the cavalier provokes the *danseuse*, who is first rebellious, almost savage. He walks away in defiance, twirling his moustache. Softly, like an amazon surrendering her sword, she goes to him, and rests her head lovingly on his shoulder. Then the couple throw themselves into a boisterous, frenzied dance, that evokes thoughts of a galloping elopement across the steppes."

The rôle of Mazourka afforded Marie Petipa the opportunity of bringing into play her talent as an actress. "Her least movements, her most fleeting gestures, which seem so spontaneous, are calculated to produce certain effects, not one of which is left to chance", wrote Fiorentino. "She was applauded in the charming passage when she admires herself in a mirror, dazzled and almost frightened by her metamorphosis, and again, when, trembling before the angry look of her boor of a husband, she protests indignantly with her lively little feet and her whole person against so terrible a tyranny."

Paris saw her as Mazourka for the last time on July 30th, but before returning to Russia she appeared at the benefit performance in aid of the pensions fund on August 9th, in a

Guglielmina Salvioni

Adèle Grantzow

Angelina Fioretti and Blanche
Montaubry in *Hamlet*

Blanche Montaubry in *Faust*

Marie Taglioni (*c.* 1860)

Madame Dominique

Émile Perrin

Arthur Saint-Léon (*c.* 1870)

new *pas* by Lucien Petipa, interpolated in *La Juive*. This was to be her last season in the French capital. Though she had paid only two fleeting visits, she was at least said to have introduced one innovation at the Opéra, that of scattering resin on the floor of the Foyer de la Danse to obviate the danger of slipping. She continued her career in St. Petersburg until 1869, when she retired. In 1881 she made an unsuccessful début on the legitimate stage, and the following year died of virulent smallpox at Novocherkassk, on the river Don.

. . . .

On September 22nd, 1862, shortly after Marie Petipa's return to Russia, another Marie, Marie Vernon, made her début as Gloriette in *Le Marché des Innocents*; on October 24th she appeared in *La Vivandière*, and on December 8th took over the rôle of Mazourka in *Le Diable à quatre*. Her real name was Renon, and she was of Anglo-French extraction and, according to Janin, the goddaughter of Théophile Gautier. She was about seventeen, a typically English beauty, gentle and elegant, with regular features, blue eyes and ash-blonde hair, a strong contrast in fact to Marie Petipa, whose rôles she was assuming. She had been attached to the Opéra for some years, being taught by Gosselin, Marie Taglioni and Mme Dominique, and had been under a year's contract since August at a salary of 3600 francs.

"She is of the charming age of the month of May and the dawn", wrote the poet, Théodore de Banville, after seeing her début. "She is a joy, a fairy, a grace. . . . Why did Mme Petipa leave? Why did she absent herself for one minute? At play, and deservedly, has this child snatched the finest diamond from her crown. Yesterday the pretty name of Gloriette was synonymous with that of Mme Petipa, but to-day, and for evermore, one will think of Marie Vernon."

Some two months after her début, the accident to Emma Livry during the rehearsals of *La Muette de Portici* made necessary the casting of another dancer in the rôle of Fenella, and the choice fell on Marie Vernon. At the same time her engagement was extended to the end of July 1866, and her salary increased to 12,000 francs a year, rising to 15,000 francs for the last year. She had little more than six weeks in which to learn the part, and was very apprehensive lest disappointment at Livry's absence might tell against her. "For you, I shall make a very great effort", she wrote to the Director before the dress rehearsal. "Count on my zeal and my willingness for this evening. I crave all your indulgence."

She appeared as Fenella on January 19th, 1863, in a costume inspired by a painting by Hébert; the conventional ballet skirt had been discarded in favour of a loosely hanging ankle-length dress—the unusual length had caused her to trip at the dress rehearsal—and on her head she wore the traditional *magnosa* of Neapolitan peasant-women. She was so anxious to succeed, that her miming was somewhat forced, but it had the merit of being clear and comprehensible, for her features were surprisingly mobile and expressive for a beauty such as hers. She played the rôle regularly for two years, also filling the title-rôle in *Diavolina* and taking part in the *divertissements* in *Les Vêpres siciliennes* and *Moïse*. At the end of 1864 she asked for her engagement to be annulled, and retired from the stage to marry a M. Gaiffe.

Making her début as a *sujet* in the *divertissement* of *La Muette de Portici* was a young pupil of Lucien Petipa, Laure Fonta, a girl of about eighteen, who had been appearing in the *corps de ballet* under her real name of Poinet ever since she was a child, and who was said to have originally taken up dancing to cure a nervous ailment. Auber, noticing her one day at class, had been so impressed that he had written some new music specially for her to dance to in the revival of *La Muette de Portici*. The aged composer often attended Petipa's classes to see how his *protégée* was progressing, and whenever he was present, she would concentrate so hard to give of her best that her expression became set and over-serious. One day, Auber called her to him.

"I am very pleased with you, *mademoiselle*", he said, "but now will you do me the favour of dancing for *me*?"

She looked at him in astonishment, for that was just what she had been doing for the past hour.

Auber then explained kindly: "When you dance for me, you must always smile."

Despite this advice, her seriousness became almost legendary; the critic of *Le Nain Jaune* once spoke of her "composure that would be the envy of a Quaker", and asked, "Now who has ever seen Mlle Fonta smile?"

Laure Fonta's success in *La Muette de Portici* took her by surprise, no less than the public, to whom she further endeared herself, when she took her call, by bowing a little awkwardly, obviously delighted but very confused. "She has the frankest and most sympathetic smile", wrote Fiorentino, "a gaiety that is a charm in itself, and an unusual and effortless lightness and elevation."

. . . .

A few weeks before the revival of *La Muette de Portici*, Alphonse Royer had been succeeded as Director of the Opéra by Émile Perrin. Perrin, who had managed the Opéra-Comique and the Théâtre Lyrique, was by nature autocratic, holding himself aloof from his staff, as he considered befitted his dignity. He was deeply conscious of the squint with which Nature had afflicted him, and was always careful to show his profile as often as possible. Though an able business man and an experienced administrator, he often appeared unsympathetic and abrupt in manner, was obstinate and unresponsive to reason once his mind was made up, and inclined to be tight-fisted in money matters. He lacked charm, and made few friends.

Shortly before his appointment, Ferraris had agreed very reluctantly to take over Emma Livry's rôle in *Zara*, which she had begun to rehearse with Marie Taglioni on December 5th. Early in the New Year, Perrin demanded certain changes in the ballet of which Ferraris disapproved. Relations between the dancer and the Director worsened rapidly. Ferraris' contract was due to expire on June 4th, and both parties refused to compromise on the terms of a new engagement, Ferraris demanding 60,000 francs and no less, and Perrin refusing to consider one sou more than 50,000 francs. Their difference came to a head on February 8th, when Perrin informed Ferraris that Zina Mérante and Laure Fonta were to be given important parts in the *divertissement*. Ferraris thereupon asked that her contract should be annulled as from February 10th. On the 10th, Marie Vernon was chosen to take over the ill-fated rôle of Zara. Rehearsals were begun anew, but had to be suspended once again in the middle of March so as to leave the stage free for the revival of *Giselle*, in which Martha Muravieva was to make her Paris début. *Zara*, although almost ready for production, was shelved indefinitely, and in vain did its aggrieved authors complain to the Minister of State.

The half-benefit performance, to which Ferraris was entitled under her contract, took place on March 21st, the programme including *Graziosa* and the casino scene from *L'Étoile de Messine*. At her own request the prices of admission had not been increased, as was usual on such occasions. The Emperor and Empress were among the audience who gathered to bid her farewell, and the former sent a magnificent pair of emerald and diamond ear-rings to her dressing-room during the performance. She was loudly cheered when she first appeared, and was recalled many times during the evening; a rain of bouquets fell at her feet, and a crown of laurel leaves was thrown from the Jockey Club box, as she stood, deeply moved, before the curtain to receive her last ovation from the Parisians.

That summer she appeared in London, and the following spring fulfilled an engagement in Brussels. For several years more she danced in the towns of Italy before finally retiring in 1868. Later, she returned to Paris for a time to teach. She died at Florence on February 8th, 1904, and bequeathed her entire fortune, which amounted to more than 600,000 lire, to charity.

VIII

MURAVIEVA AND BOSCHETTI

ÉMILE PERRIN had assumed the management of the Opéra
at a critical moment, for Emma Livry's accident had occurred
only a few weeks before and Ferraris' engagement was
approaching its end. Faced with the task of finding suitable
replacements for these two dancers, Perrin lost no time, and
within a month of his appointment offered a contract to a
well-known Russian ballerina, Martha Nicolayevna Muravieva.
The daughter of a liberated peasant, Muravieva had made her
début at St. Petersburg in 1848, when she was ten, in Perrot's
Le Délire d'un peintre; Fanny Elssler, who was playing the
leading rôle, had been greatly impressed by the child's promise,
and was seen to embrace her in the wings during the performance. Since then, Muravieva's artistry had been developed
and polished by the teaching of Frédéric, Eugène Huguet and
Marius Petipa, until she had now become one of the most
popular dancers in Russia.

Application for permission for her to accept Perrin's offer
was made, in accordance with formal procedure, through
the Minister of State in Paris to the Minister of the Tsar's
Household. Almost at once, a plot—hatched by Marie Petipa,
who was hankering after another season at the Opéra and
hopefully expecting to obtain from Perrin a monthly salary
of 6000 francs—was set in motion to prevent Muravieva's
Paris engagement. Count Borkh, the Director of the Imperial
Theatres, for a time took Marie Petipa's part, and tried to
persuade Muravieva to withdraw her acceptance of the offer.
Even the French Ambassador in St. Petersburg was drawn into
the intrigue, being induced to telegraph to Paris that there
might still be time to treat with Marie Petipa. Finally, when
it was realized that Perrin was interested in Muravieva alone,
the plot collapsed; Muravieva was granted leave from early in
March, and a six months' contract, stipulating a salary of
2632 francs a month, was drawn up and signed.

"On Sunday next, she begins her journey, so that you will
see her on Thursday or Friday", wrote Huguet, Muravieva's

teacher and adviser, to Perrin on March 3rd. "She is very shy and terribly frightened at the thought of soon being in a strange country. She would have liked very much to have known which *maître de ballet* she is to work with for the new ballet to be produced for her. She is very anxious . . . that you should choose Perrot or Saint-Léon; they have already composed for her in St. Petersburg. She could see herself working under Lucien Petipa."

The short duration of her engagement made it imperative that she should make her début as soon as possible after her arrival, and at an early stage in the negotiations Perrin decided to introduce her, not in a new ballet, which was to come later, but in a revival of *Giselle*, a ballet with which she was already familiar. "Mlle Muravieva is quite willing to make her début in *Giselle*", Huguet told him. "She has obtained much success in it here, and hopes to do the same in Paris. She would have preferred to make her début in the new ballet, but, as I tell her every day, that would take too long. She is afraid that *Giselle* is too old a ballet."

Muravieva reached Paris on March 16th, shortly before the last appearance of Ferraris, whose dressing-room she was to take over. She soon had cause for complaint. "Will you be so good as to give instructions for the dressing-room assigned to me to be put in order", she wrote to Perrin on April 7th. "Not only is it unfurnished, but there is no chair for me to sit on, and it is dirty. At the same time, I would ask you to place a dresser at my disposal, and everything necessary for my toilet. I am told that I am occupying the dressing-room of Mme Ferraris, who had her own furniture. You will appreciate that, coming from Russia, I cannot drag furniture around with me, and that I should expect to find everything ready for me, as otherwise there would be delays interfering with the rehearsals."

Ten years had passed since *Giselle* had last been given at the Opéra. Perrin had entrusted the revival to Lucien Petipa, creator of the rôle of Albrecht, and had authorized a liberal expenditure. New sets had been commissioned from Despléchin (Act I) and Cambon and Thierry (Act II) to replace the scenery which Ciceri had painted in 1841; nearly a hundred and fifty persons were to take part in the first act, including about ninety peasants and a hunting party of nearly forty courtiers, with horses; and fifty Wilis, including their Queen and Giselle, were to appear in the second act. The choreography probably differed only slightly from that of the original production.

The widow of Adolphe Adam wrote to Perrin after attending the dress rehearsal: "I was unable to congratulate you after the rehearsal of *Giselle*. I wanted to thank you for using your good taste to give this revival all the brilliance of a novelty."

The first night took place a few days later, on May 8th, 1863.[1] The double attraction of Muravieva's début and a revival of such a popular ballet as *Giselle* ensured success; the receipts over the first ten performances averaged 8160.95 francs.

Muravieva was very small and slender, with a compact figure and well-shaped legs, of a type, said one critic, that might be called "sparkling". There was a great attraction in her frank expression and wide smile, but her features were too irregular to be beautiful; Jouvin likened her profile to that of "the Duchess at Versailles whose aquiline nose curving over two rosy lips resembled, according to a chronicler of the time, a parrot eating a cherry".

She showed no unusual aptitude as a mime. It was, therefore, solely on her ability as a dancer that her success depended. Though possessing neither the ample elegance of Ferraris, nor the graceful mastery of Emma Livry, her nervous tension and the rich variety of technical resources at her command imparted to her style a brilliance that made up for her lack of grace and charm. Her acute sense of rhythm was displayed in the remarkable precision of her *pointe* work and in *petits pas* repeated with astonishing speed and agility: "There are moments", it was said, "when her legs move so rapidly that the eye can only distinguish a blur."

Nestor Roqueplan could find only one fault with her interpretation of Giselle. "She should", he wrote, "tone down certain *temps de sablier*, which are somewhat reminiscent of the *Jaleo*, and, from the point of view of style, are unsuited to Giselle, whose well-conceived and well-drawn character should not be altered." In the first act she was loudly applauded at the

---

[1] The cast was as follows: Muravieva (Giselle), Louis Mérante (Albrecht), Eugène Coralli (Hilarion), Aline (Berthe), Lenfant (Duke of Courland), Louise Marquet (Bathilde), Rémond (Wilfrid), Fonta (Myrtha), Savel (Zulmé), Élise Parent (Moyna), Zina Mérante and Chapuy (*pas de deux*, Act I).

end of her *pas de deux* with Mérante, which had included an exciting moment when the fury of her dancing suddenly calmed, and, in the words of Jouvin, "she broke measure with a *rallentando* such as singers use at the end of an aria". The *danse de folie*, culminating the first act, was competently performed. "She has so tender a look, so sweet a passion", wrote Janin, "and she suffers in the true Taglioni manner."

In the second act, continued Janin, "this little Muravieva shows a perfect understanding of fantasy and fascination. Shadow and mist, she is like a dream come forth from the ivory gates, whose whiteness she retains." The romantic atmosphere of this scene, set by a moonlit pool in the forest, was heightened by an ingenious arrangement of mirrors to represent the water. These mirrors were mounted sloping upwards towards the back of the stage, one being placed behind and on a higher level than the other, so that a dancer on the platform placed in the gap between them would appear to the audience to be standing in the middle of the mirror and reflected in it. The Queen of the Wilis made her first entrance on a trap in this platform, seeming to rise out of the waters; and instead of the flights which had been used in the original production, the Wilis darted across the surface of the pool as though possessing no mortal substance. The storage of these enormous mirrors presented a difficult problem, which was solved so satisfactorily that there was not a single breakage during the five years that this production was given.

The magical effect of this scene prompted Gautier to devote a whole *feuilleton* to the stage designer's art. "The few lines of explanation in the scenario could not have been understood and expressed more poetically", he wrote of this set. "Great ash trees, their satiny trunks mottled with patches of brown moss, spread their trembling foliage in the blue mist, framing a marvellous undergrowth which Narcisse Diaz would have envied. Masses of trees, of a humid, glaucous green silvered by the pale light, are reflected in the calm, sleepy waters of the pool, on which float the large heart-shaped leaves of the water-lily. The reflection has so magical a depth that it might be a submarine forest. Do not imagine that this astonishing effect is produced by the mirrors, for they only repeat the part of the pool painted above them. They merely add to the tone, by means of their polish, a sombre limpidity, a damp transparency, which distemper could not obtain. By reflecting the will-o'-the-wisps, the white shadows of the Wilis flying across them, the mirrors give the impression of real water, and when they are caught in the white gleam of electric light, the illusion of the spangled tremble of a moonlit lake is complete. But what we admire even more is the painting of this nocturnal landscape, so cool, so melancholy, so dream-like, of so fascinating and charming a sadness, wherein can perhaps be found all the poetry of the lake over which Gendron made his round of Wilis whirl."

Shortly after the first night the Minister of State received a letter from the lawyer of a Mr. Callcott, complaining that his client's patent had been infringed by this use of mirrors. Mr. Callcott's rights, it was claimed, had been assigned to the manager of the Châtelet, who had employed the system in a spectacle entitled *La Prise de Pékin*, and by whom Mr. Callcott was now in fear of being sued. The Opéra considered the wording of the patent unreasonably wide, and pointed out that Mr. Callcott was by no means the first person to use mirrors in the construction of theatrical sets, that Servandoni had used them in the eighteenth century, and that more recently they had created a sensational effect in *Den Hama-dryaden*, a comic opera by Adam, produced in Berlin in 1840. In fact, Adam had brought the models to Paris the following year, when he had suggested them for the original production of *Giselle*, and only practical difficulties had caused the proposal to be abandoned. In 1851, a similar arrangement of mirrors had been projected, but again not adopted, for *Pâquerette*.

Another device invented for this revival of *Giselle* was a sliding trap, on which Giselle and Albrecht were to glide to the sanctuary of the Cross in Act II, but difficulty was experienced during rehearsals in keeping the mechanism greased, and the projected group may have been abandoned before the first performance.

When Muravieva returned to Russia, Zina Mérante took over the rôle of Giselle, which she played for the first time on September 30th, 1863, being "very cordially greeted"; on November 13th, 1865, Nadezhda Bogdanova made a single appearance in the first act; and, the following May, Adèle Grantzow made her Paris début as Giselle, which she danced exclusively until the ballet was dropped from the repertory in

October 1868, not to be revived again at the Opéra until 1924.

.   .   .   .   .   .

For the new ballet in which Muravieva was to appear, Huguet had suggested to Perrin one of Saint-Léon's recent works produced at St. Petersburg. The latest of these was *Théolinda l'orpheline*, but as its plot had been taken from *Le Lutin de la vallée*, an opera-ballet that Saint-Léon had staged at the Théâtre Lyrique in 1853, Perrin considered that it would not have the appeal of a novelty. Saint-Léon himself suggested *Météora*, which, he told Perrin, "suits [Muravieva] perfectly", and "if the changes are not too great, could be ready, so far as I am concerned, in a fortnight". This suggestion was not acceptable either, and finally Saint-Léon travelled to Paris to stage an entirely new ballet, *Diavolina*, which was presented for the first time on July 6th, 1863.

It was a short work, in one act, set in the outskirts of Caserta in about the year 1805. The plot was very slight. Diavolina (Muravieva) is about to marry her fisherman lover, Gennariello (L. Mérante). There are many charming and comical incidents before the wedding repast comes to an end, but, after a lovers' quarrel and reconciliation, the marriage contract is finally signed. The score which accompanied this was the work of Cesare Pugni, who had served Saint-Léon so often before; it was remarkable only for the number of melodies—Neapolitan airs, soldiers' songs, and a polka-galop by Graziani—that the composer had borrowed.

In conception, *Diavolina* was a comic ballet. Some critics, like Janin, appreciating the invention and novelty in Saint-Léon's choreography, saw it as a masterpiece in miniature. Others were a little shocked; in the olden days, they said, such clowning as Saint-Léon had devised for the scene of the wedding repast would have been confined to the Porte-Saint-Martin, if not to the Funambules. Saint-Victor dismissed the ballet as a "*sauterie d'occasion et de circonstance*".

Discussing Saint-Léon as a choreographer, Nestor Roqueplan wrote: "In the dance, as in music, two contrasting schools can be distinguished. . . . French choreographers have a perfect understanding of the essence and development of a scene, being able to introduce comic effects of great delicacy even into a moving situation. Italian choreographers, having few scruples in the choice of subjects (some reach the utmost depths of stupidity), see in a choreographic idea, apart from two or three violent scenes, merely excuses for *ballabili* and the manœuvring of crowds. Although a Frenchman, M. Saint-Léon belongs to the Italian school. Neither logic nor probability must be sought in his ballets, but only his own particular qualities—the greatest dexterity in handling masses, and a feeling for rhythm which is due to his talent as a musician. His ballets have always lacked foundation: nothing now remains of those brilliant spectacles, those *divertissements* arranged with so easy a touch, and to which the co-operation of Mme Cerrito brought a charm which vanished with her."

The choreography of *Diavolina* was inventive, varied, and never dull. In the *scène de filet*, by Muravieva and Mérante, the ballerina displayed great dexterity in executing the original, although not always graceful, movements that Saint-Léon had devised for her. This was followed by two *pas d'ensemble*, *La Scarpetta* and *La Niania*, both danced by Muravieva and Mérante with eight other couples: the former, a lovers' dance in which the girl has to put on a slipper that her partner has placed on the ground, "a sequence of oscillations executed in unison and *sur place*, a real orgy of laziness"; and the latter, a very comical dance to a monotonous and irritatingly infectious rhythm. Then came a *pas de quatre* by Muravieva and Mérante, with Maria Baratte and Léontine Beaugrand; and the ballet ended with a military *divertissement*, entitled *Le Bon vieux temps*, which included a *pas de tambour* danced by Muravieva. In Jouvin's opinion, this military *divertissement* spoilt the good impression that the earlier part of the ballet had created; "Diavolina, dressed up as a *cantinière*", he wrote, "has led the Opéra into the street, and turned its principal dancer into a virtuoso of the crossroads."

Muravieva's style did not please everyone. Saint-Victor, while admitting her strong *pointes* and good elevation, thought that she lacked "the mimetic power and the polish of execution of the great virtuosi of the dance", and continued: "She seeks effect, and finds it by means that are eccentric rather than graceful. Her dancing, at its best moments, has something dry and artificial about it." Jouvin was more sympathetic. "I must mention one imperceptible fault in her dancing", he wrote. "In the way in which she throws out her feet and her hands, there is a coquetry and an impishness that are quite adorable; she might be a spoilt child with an infatuation for dancing. But the abuse of soft *cabrioles* becomes tiring to the audience, and makes the ballerina exaggerate effect to restore freshness. Originality then becomes lost in eccentricity, and in the fear of not appearing at her best, the dancer comes to resemble a puppet whose wires are being jerked too violently. . . . Nevertheless, Muravieva's style is very firm and very picturesque, bringing to our ballet a new vitality of which it was in great need. . . . She has not the intrepidity of Zina, nor the prettiness of Marie Petipa, her two compatriots; less irreproachable in her execution than the former, less feminine than the latter, she has a more marked individuality than either. . . . I will not say of this frail and delicate dancer, with her sharp features, that she is a phantom fashioned of muscles, nerves, and a little bone, for the image would not be quite true nor very gallant. I would rather compare La Muravieva to a musical box displaying its cylinder turning and striking the hammers. At first, you are absorbed by the mechanism and distracted from the music, but the poetry of its sound finally captivates you. So it is with Muravieva; the poetry of her dancing only triumphs at second viewing."

. . . .

Early in 1863, when it had seemed probable that Muravieva would be prevented from visiting Paris in the summer, Perrin had approached Amina Boschetti, who had been recommended to him by the Italian Ambassador. Amina—or, more properly, Anisa—Boschetti was the prima ballerina of the Scala, Milan. The daughter of a general in the Austrian army, she had begun her career at the age of nine by being chosen by Marie Taglioni for a small part at the Scala, and was a pupil of Blasis. She was now about twenty-six.

Having somewhat prematurely declined all offers of engagements for the summer on the strength of Perrin's approach, she was not a little embarrassed to learn that the six months' engagement he was offering would not start until September. She found herself faced with the choice of either refusing the contract, which she was very reluctant to do, or else renouncing a winter engagement in Trieste, which would subject her to a heavy penalty. She asked if Perrin would assume half this liability, but, on his refusing, raised no further objection and signed the contract he had sent her, which fixed her salary at 2650 francs a month.

For her début in Paris, she had suggested *Ariella*, a ballet by Antonio Pallerini, with music by Giorza, which had been recently produced for her at the Scala, but the composer had dissuaded Perrin by telling him that its subject resembled those of *La Fonti* and *L'Étoile de Messine*. "Giorza would rather compose the music for a new ballet", was Boschetti's comment. However, her disappointment soon gave place to delight when she was told that she was to make her first appearance at the Opéra in a new work by the great Italian choreographer, Giuseppe Rota.

She arrived in Paris in July 1863, to prepare for her début under the guidance of her friend, Adice, one of the teachers at the Opéra. Adice, who had nearly thirty years' experience of the Opéra behind him, was anxious that she should not be prejudiced by the ill-feeling that existed between himself and Perrin, and hastened to enquire whether she had paid her respects to the Director. He was astonished to hear that she had only visited the leader of the *claque*, a personage whose power had by this time dwindled out of all recognition since the days of the great Auguste, and advised her to call on Perrin without delay. She did so that very day, and found the Director quite courteous, although she was a little surprised when he said, as she was leaving, "Did they not tell you I was a hard, coarse sort of fellow, and treated my artistes badly? *Mais, moi, je m'en f——!*"

Having spent the previous six months convalescing in Naples after an illness, Boschetti was very much out of practice, and her figure had grown to such proportions as to make Adice fear the reactions of the French audiences. For very good reasons, he decided to coach her behind locked doors, and subjected her to a special course of gymnastic exercises to reduce her weight. "Spying through the keyhole, underneath the door, through the cracks of the windows . . . the gossips, especially the women, who were always loitering round the class-room in the Rue Richer", he explained, "would eventually discover that Mlle Boschetti was short and of an enormous girth, and would spitefully conclude that consequently she could no longer dance as well as she had done in the past."

Though the slimming exercises proved disappointing, Boschetti's powerful technique was gradually restored. Adice was astounded; difficulties no longer existed for her. "There had never been seen before, and perhaps would never be seen again," he wrote, "*tours de pirouette sur l'extrémité de la pointe* executed with such assurance, ease, and incredible precision. Then no one had ever seen a complete *variation* of twenty-four bars' length composed of an *enchaînement* of *ronds de jambe* and *petits battements sur le cou-de-pied* executed on one toe and *en tournant. Entrechats six, sept, huit, de face, de côté, en tournant.* The most difficult poses are rendered without the slightest hesitation and always with precision. In my experience, not one of the great executants of my time ever performed the groups of her *pas de deux* so precisely and so perfectly as she did."

Giuseppe Rota arrived in Paris in the autumn, and at once began to prepare his new ballet, for which Saint-Georges had provided a scenario, and Giorza, an adequate, if somewhat unimaginative, score. It was the custom of Italian *maîtres de ballet*, who seldom stayed very long in any one town or with any one company, to begin their work by rehearsing the *pas d'ensemble* with the *corps de ballet*. There was a double advantage in this, for not only were they able to weigh up quickly the merits of the company, but it also gave the *corps de ballet* time to accustom themselves to the choreographer. Rota therefore devoted his first rehearsal to the *mascherata*, a scene of great difficulty, depending for its effect principally on the male dancers. He soon made an appalling discovery; the men, unaccustomed to appearing in the forefront, were deplorably lacking in ability, and many were no longer young. Rota stopped the rehearsal and turned his attention to the *pas des fleurs*, for which Berthier had selected twenty-four of the ablest girls in the *corps de ballet*. Yet another shock awaited him; the girls were little better than the men; they could not keep time with the music or with each other, even in the simplest arm movements, and complained that his choreography was too difficult and too complicated for them. Rota was faced with an arduous task, but he did not despair.

Boschetti began studying her rôle about November, rehearsing alone with Rota. She did not appear with the whole company until the first general rehearsal. Perrin, then seeing her dance for the first time, was astounded at her prowess and complimented her warmly.

The difficulties that Rota had encountered retarded the production by several weeks. Perrin was forced to prolong the duration of Boschetti's engagement by three months, increasing her monthly salary to 4000 francs, so as to obtain some benefit from her contract, while Rota obligingly risked postponing his return to Milan until the last moment, barely allowing time enough to complete a new work for the Scala. Even then, he had to leave Paris before the first night on February 19th, 1864.

The new ballet, *La Maschera*, was set in eighteenth-century Venice. The first act takes place in a piazza on the bank of a canal. Donato Rizzi (L. Mérante), a successful painter, is returning to his native city with his pupil, Pier Angelo (E. Fiocre), and his friend, Squarcione (Dauty). His aunt Catherina (Mme Dominique) and his *fiancée*, Marietta (Sanlaville), are waiting to greet him. As he steps off the gondola, a bouquet falls at his feet. He quickly picks it up, and looks to see who has thrown it. Count Campagnano (E. Coralli) then approaches, ordering servants to bear gifts to the ballerina, Lucilla. Seeing Donato Rizzi's health being toasted, he enquires his identity, and, on being told, asks him to paint his portrait. Instead, Donato Rizzi prefers to sketch an old beggar, but does so so skilfully that the Count is lost in admiration. A band of gipsies, led by a woman in a mask (Boschetti), dances into the piazza. The Count, having thrown the beggar a purse, is about to take away the picture when the masked dancer gives the beggar a ring and takes the picture herself. She approaches Donato Rizzi to tell his fortune. When she says that he is in love, he points to Marietta's house, but she then asks why he has kept her bouquet. She begs him to paint her portrait, but he will do so only on the condition that she removes her mask. Seeing the Count watching closely, she tells him that a guide bearing her scarf will conduct him to her that very evening. Daylight fades, and Donato Rizzi is left alone in the piazza. Marietta appears on her balcony. Remorseful, Donato Rizzi starts towards her, but at that moment two pages arrive with the scarf. They blindfold him and lead him to a gondola. The Count, suspecting the identity

CARICATURES OF "LA MASCHERA" BY MARCELIN.

Model by Daran for *Coppélia*, Act I, Scene I (1875)

Model by Daran for *Coppélia*, Act I, Scene II (1875)

Design for the Bell in Act II of *Coppélia* (1870)

of the masked dancer, runs to the bank of the canal shaking his fist, while Marietta reappears sorrowfully at her window. The canal sparkles with illumined barges, and the far-away songs of gondoliers come across the water as the curtain falls.

The second act opens in Lucilla's boudoir. Donato Rizzi is admitted and his bandage removed. The goddesses of Air, Water, Earth and Fire—all impersonated by Lucilla—dance before his gaze, and finally the message "*Au Lido*" appears on the wall. After he has left, the Count arrives, mad with jealousy, but Lucilla angrily orders him to leave. She then places her hand to her heart, and indicates the words on the wall. The scene changes to the Lido, where Donato Rizzi and Lucilla meet in the crowd. The Count sarcastically compliments her on her choice. A quarrel ensues, and when a fight seems imminent, Lucilla removes her mask. Realizing who she is for the first time, Donato Rizzi leaves her with the Count. Lucilla runs off, and the dancing recommences.

The curtain rises on the third and last act to reveal Donato Rizzi's studio. After Marietta has dissuaded him from his intention of provoking the Count to a duel, the artist tries to banish the thought of Lucilla from his memory by painting, but her image seems to appear on every canvas. He runs to the door, only to find Lucilla herself before him. She asks why he is displeased with her, then flings her jewellery to the ground, telling him that she has only herself to offer. Spellbound, Donato Rizzi embraces her and leaves, promising to elope with her at the ball that night. Marietta, who has observed this scene, begs Lucilla to renounce Donato Rizzi. When Lucilla refuses, Marietta leaps through the window into the canal below. The scene changes to a road by the canal. Two gondoliers appear, carrying Marietta whom they have rescued. Lucilla runs to her assistance. Realizing the depth of Marietta's love, she has decided to sacrifice her own, and tells Marietta to accompany her to the ball. The final scene takes place in the ballroom, where Donato Rizzi is surprised to be faced with two similar dominoes. Bidden to choose between them, he feels their hearts to see which beats the more rapidly. It is Marietta's. Lucilla unmasks and joins in the ball. As she is carried round the room in triumph after a brilliant *variation*, she bids a last farewell to Donato Rizzi and Marietta.

The ballet lasted three hours at the first performance,

which many thought too long. It was saved from failure—
indeed, triumph was almost achieved—by the distinguished
choreography of Rota, who, in common with other Italian
choreographers of his time, was a master at arranging crowd
scenes. In the several months of preparation, he had succeeded
in drilling into the Opéra *corps de ballet* a competence that
satisfied him. The final scene—including the *pas des fleurs*, in
which flower-girls open the ball, and the *mascherata*, with its
motley collection of pierrots, harlequins, pantaloons and
punchinellos dressed in the style of the *Commedia dell'Arte*—
ended the ballet on a thrilling pitch.

"No Italian choreographer since Viganò has had a fuller
and more brilliant career", wrote Fiorentino. "At the Scala
alone, within the space of nine years, Rota has composed
twenty-five ballets [1] . . . works for the most part in three or
five acts, entailing a complicated production, and containing
at least four *ballabili*. At the same time—for he has the gift of
ubiquity—Rota's ballets were being played at other theatres
in Italy. . . . So fertile are his resources, so powerful his
invention, so great the number of his works, so rich and
inexhaustible the variety of his patterns, his groups, his figures,
that other choreographers cannot help borrowing from him,
often unwittingly; in Borri's *La Giuocoliera*, which we have seen
here as *L'Étoile de Messine*, many of the *pas* and effects were
Rota's. His great originality and talent lie in his manner of
manœuvring crowds, grouping, separating, and bringing them
together again with such symmetry and in so perfect an order
that the eye is continually offered· the most charming and
harmonious aspects. He plays with line and colour like an
able painter. . . . He is especially careful to give his dances
the savour of their country and their period. No detail, however
insignificant, is left to chance in his ballets, whose execution
must be as exact as their conception; in this respect, the
Italian dancers, who are much more disciplined than ours,
render the choreographer's intentions with scrupulous fidelity
and irreproachable precision."

Amina Boschetti appeared to the Parisians for the first
time as a short, stocky woman of rather generous proportions.

---

[1] This is an exaggeration. Cambiasi, in *La Scala, 1778–1889*, lists eight ballets
by Rota (one of which was revived by another choreographer) staged between
1853 and the Paris production of *La Maschera*, and two staged afterwards.

Her features were finely chiselled and of a mobility that seemed able to convey every shade of emotion; her lips were full and firm, her chin well moulded, her eyes small but bright.

The great strength in her back and legs, combined with a surprising agility, enabled her to perform the most difficult and audacious feats with great ease. Her *pointe* work was very rapid and precise, and her elevation astonishing for one of her shape; her *cabrioles* seemed sometimes to be beaten almost horizontally, and her *jetés*, too, were very brilliant. Her stumpiness, however, which was emphasized by the meagre figures of the *corps de ballet*, and caused Janin spitefully to dub her "Malagamba", put her at a disadvantage in scenes requiring grace or tenderness. Her miming was very much in the Italian manner, appearing so exaggerated to French eyes that she had to tone it down after the first performance.

A few weeks after her début, Saint-Léon and Muravieva returned to Paris, and Boschetti at once began to observe a change in Perrin's manner towards her. One evening, when she was watching the Russian dancer in *Giselle*, she noticed the Director in the box immediately opposite. "At each *pas*, at each pose, at the simplest movement and the most insignificant gesture that [Muravieva] made", she complained to Adice, "I saw him making contortions with his body and his head, like a man fascinated, and exaggerated to such an extent as to make me leave my box in exasperation, because, at every writhe, at the end of every insipid twist, he never failed to look me scornfully in the eye as though to say, 'There's dancing for you! There's a real dancer!'" Adice told her that Perrin's strange behaviour was due to Saint-Léon having said that her dancing was nothing but a series of *tours de force*.

Boschetti had to contend not only with Saint-Léon's partisanship of Muravieva, but also with the animosity of those who admired slender dancers and disapproved of the influx of Italians that had heralded *La Maschera*. Discovering that she was not billed to appear in the annual benefit performance for dramatic artistes, which was to take place on April 30th, she consulted Adice and, on his advice, visited Perrin. Perrin pretended to know nothing about the programme, which he said was being arranged by Saint-Georges; but Saint-Georges told her he had been informed that she did not wish to take part. Her name was inserted on the bills at once, but when she appeared in the performance a week later, hissing began in a box occupied by two dancers and was taken up immediately by the *claque* in the pit. The applause of her admirers drowned the hissing, but did not prevent two minute bouquets of the cheapest flowers from being thrown on to the stage. Despite the obvious insult, she picked them up and curtsied gracefully, betraying no sign of her true feelings. The next day, she complained to Perrin, who listened politely but took no action. Adice, well-informed as always, explained that Perrin had not wished her to appear on the same evening as Muravieva, whom he feared might be compared unfavourably with her, and had therefore given orders that she was to be badly received. Moreover, Adice went on, Muravieva was protected by "a personage of her own country, of high station and consequently very influential, through whom Saint-Léon had obtained the cross of some order. . . ."

Boschetti had gained many admirers during her brief stay in Paris, including the Duke Ernst of Saxe-Coburg-Gotha, who hoped that she would play the leading rôle in his projected ballet based on the Second Angel's story from Moore's *Loves of the Angels*. Nevertheless, she was not offered a further extension of her engagement at the Opéra, nor, in view of Perrin's unjust treatment of her, would she have been likely to accept such an offer, if one had been made. She made her last appearance at the Opéra on May 30th, 1864, in *La Maschera*. She finally left the stage about ten years later, and retired to Naples, where she died of a heart attack, at about the age of forty-five, on January 2nd, 1881.

Shortly after her success in *Diavolina*, Muravieva had signed a contract to dance at the Opéra during the summers of 1864 and 1865 at an increased salary of 4000 francs a month. Perrin was anxiously awaiting her return all the following winter. "The moment is drawing near when you will be returning to Paris", he wrote on December 20th, "and I can assure you that your return will be a great occasion for us." Four months later, on April 22nd, 1864, she reappeared at the Opéra in *Giselle*. "How welcome she is!" cried Janin, who no doubt was of the same mind as Perrin. "To begin with, may she send the Italian 'Malagamba' back to her own country!"

Saint-Léon had also arrived in Paris, and was soon at

work preparing *Néméa*, a shortened version of his ballet, *Fiammetta*, which he had arranged for Muravieva in St. Petersburg the previous winter. Shortly before the first night, a vivid description of Saint-Léon at rehearsal appeared in *La Vie Parisienne*, written probably by Ludovic Halévy, one of the scenarists.

"About a hundred people, men, women and children, nearly all the women in ballet dress, are on the stage. Here and there, bodices of varied and brilliant hues break the monotony, like red and blue specks amid a swarm of white skirts. . . . All is noise and bustle before the rehearsal starts, the elders running hither and thither, laughing and gossiping, and the children, perched in clusters on the scenery, fidgeting and clapping their hands for no apparent reason. Above this hubbub, the *régisseur* calls the roll. Bantering voices answer him, and if anyone is absent, a thousand reasons are put forward, accompanied by whispered confidences and meaning smiles and glances. All around, framing the picture, are the firemen and the mothers. . . .

"On a platform erected over the orchestra pit are the authors of the scenario and, behind them, two violinists. A little in front, wearing a costume that allows him to demonstrate the steps, stands the *maître de ballet*, considered to be one of the ablest we have, a remarkable and much applauded artist, whether his hand holds a violin bow or brandishes that formidable stick which he uses to beat time, and with which, when the roll-call is over, he gives the signal by striking two or three times on the boards.

"The rehearsal begins. The peasants make their entrance, forming themselves into line, or, rather, not doing so when they should. Violent taps on the floor. 'Stop! Stop!' The violins stop playing, and the *maître de ballet* frowns and gently asks the ladies and gentlemen to begin again. They do so, but nothing goes right. Sometimes it is the fault of the men, sometimes of the women. Soon the *maître de ballet* stops tapping his stick, and throws it to the ground, swearing that he might as well give up everything. The girls shriek with laughter. 'All right, we will begin again.' 'You will indeed, so long as you do not do what you ought to do.' Tap, tap. The musicians groan, and scrape their violins. The tapping marks the rising temper of the *maître de ballet*. When he tires of swearing in

French, he swears in Russian. Everything goes wrong, horribly wrong, but finally turns out perfect."

Néméa, ou l'Amour vengé was given its first performance on July 11th, 1864. Although in mourning for the King of Württemburg, the Empress Eugénie hurried into town from Saint-Cloud to be present. Also in the audience were many dancers, including Marie Taglioni, Pauline Montessu, Fanny Cerrito, Marie Petipa, Marie Guy-Stéphan, Mme Dominique, Zina Mérante and Marie Vernon.

The scenario of the ballet had been written by Henri Meilhac and Ludovic Halévy, who later were to write the libretti of many of Offenbach's most successful operettas. The curtain rose to show a clearing in a Hungarian forest, with a statue of Cupid, half hidden in flowers, on one side, and a terrace marking the boundary of Count Molder's estate on the other. The villagers are celebrating the marriage of Hermiola (Sanlaville) and Kiralfi (Rémond); only Néméa (Muravieva) takes no part in the general rejoicing. Count Molder (L. Mérante) then arrives with his friends, and tries to pay court to Hermiola. The girl's father appeals to Cupid, but Molder pushes him roughly aside, and in so doing knocks the figure from the pedestal. Later, when Néméa comes to confide her sorrow in Cupid, she finds the pedestal occupied again, but not by a stone image, for after she has whispered the name of the man she loves, she looks up to see the god (E. Fiocre) smiling at her. She is told that the man she has mentioned is guilty of a terrible offence. As night falls, nymphs, fauns and glow-worms dance in the glade, but vanish at the return of Molder. He sees the statue still lying on the ground, but when he has gone, Cupid appears again and points menacingly to Molder's castle.

The second act takes place in a magnificent room in the castle, leading into another where a table can be seen laden with the remains of a banquet. It is dawn, and Molder and his friends have been carousing all night. Strange music is heard. A troupe of strolling players is passing, and Molder summons their leader, who is none other than Cupid in disguise, and demands to be entertained with beautiful girls. When Néméa is at last brought in, Molder falls in love with her, but she eludes him, and Cupid declares that he will never possess her. Angry at being thwarted, Molder draws his sword,

but Cupid strikes him motionless. Néméa implores the god
not to exact revenge. The castle wall then dissolves to reveal
the Temple of Love with the statue restored to its pedestal.
All bow in homage; Molder craves forgiveness, and when
Néméa joins her prayers to his, Cupid smiles and pardons him.
The curtain falls.

Néméa may not have been a masterpiece, but it was certainly
more than "much ado about nothing", as Jouvin described it.
The score, by the Hungarian composer, Ludwig Minkus,
though not evenly inspired, was praised by most critics:
"It is, to the platitudes of *La Maschera*, what a strophe by
Musset is to a vaudeville couplet", Jouvin conceded; and
Gautier, remarking its "haunting, dreamy quality", was
reminded of the songs of gipsies, and observed that "the
harmonies introduce those sweet and somewhat effeminate
falterings, whose secret Chopin and Glinka knew so well".

The choreography was distinguished, wrote Roqueplan, by
Saint-Léon's "imagination and originality, his ability to
handle masses, his research in seeking motifs for his *pas*, his
talent in achieving variety of effect, and the fertility he shows
in making use of all the resources of the company". The
first act contained the *berceuse*, a *pas seul* by Muravieva; an
hongroise; a *pas de dix* by Mme Dominique's pupils, "performing
ballonnés with comical conscientiousness"; and a *pas des lucioles*,
danced in electric light by twenty-four girls wearing miniature
oil-lamps attached to their foreheads. The second act was not
so interesting by comparison with the first, including a *pas de la
pomme* by Dauty, Eugénie Fiocre and Marie Pilatte; a *pas de
cinq*, in which Muravieva was partnered by Chapuy; and
finally a *chanson à boire*, danced by Muravieva.

Though she was very warmly received, Muravieva's
technical shortcomings did not pass unnoticed. "*Parcours,
cabrioles*, and ample movements are denied her", wrote
Roqueplan. "Her worn-out *pointes* scrape the stage without
stabbing it, except when she is supported by a partner who
gives her the perpendicular line and rigidity. She has no
batterie; her feet have never known the feeling of an *entrechat six*.
Finally, her arms, which are never fully extended and move
jerkily, allow of no fullness of movement. Nevertheless, the
impression Mlle Muravieva creates on the audience cannot be
denied, although it can be explained. It is her preparation and

intelligence that make Mlle Muravieva an artist; she is a dancer by reason only of her feeling for rhythm, her respect for tempo, and an understanding of effect so exact that she succeeds in hiding an imperfect anatomy, an absence of natural aptitude, and a very incomplete training."

Jouvin again remarked on her lack of grace, and described her style as birdlike in its mobility and impetuosity. "If she did not originate that charming and truly novel manner of throwing her arms above her head and lowering them gracefully, of beginning a step and finishing it with a play of her features, a toss of her head, and a flash of a smile", he continued, "she has at least perfected it. The *pas de la berceuse* gives the most complete idea of her style. She rouses herself from a voluptuous drowziness with sudden bounds, almost immediately repressed, that burst out like a note on the brass amid a murmuring of muted violins, or like the flash of a shooting star in the slumbering heavens."

The effect produced by Muravieva was almost overshadowed by the *succès de beauté* obtained by Eugénie Fiocre in the rôle of Cupid. When she suddenly appeared for the first time, standing on the pedestal against a background of green foliage, a spontaneous gasp of admiration rippled through the house. Even the Empress was unable to restrain an expression of delight. "Certainly Love was never personified in a more beautiful, more graceful, or more charming body", wrote Gautier. "Mlle Fiocre has managed to compound the perfections both of the young girl and of the youth, and to make of them a sexless beauty which is beauty itself. She might have been hewn from a block of Paros marble by a Greek sculptor, and animated by a miracle such as that of Galatea. To the purity of marble, she adds the suppleness of life. Her movements are developed and balanced in a sovereign harmony. Every position gives ten profiles that an artist would regret not to catch. What admirable legs! Diana the Huntress would envy them! What an easy, proud and tranquil grace! What modest, measured gestures, always keeping a sculptural line, never forcing the expression, yet conveying everything! So correct, rhythmical and noble is her miming that, like that of the mimes of old, it might be accompanied by two unseen fluteplayers. If Psyche saw this Cupid, she might perhaps forget the original."

Giuseppina Bozzacchi as Swanilda and Eugénie Fiocre as Frantz in
Coppélia

Caricatures by Marcelin

Giuseppina Bozzacchi in *Coppélia*
Top left, Act I, Scene I; top right and bottom left, Act I, Scene II;
bottom right, Act II

Designs by Alfred Albert for the Costumes of Coppélius and Frantz in *Coppélia*

Designs by Alfred Albert for the Costumes of Dawn and the Hours of Morning in *Coppélia*

The secret of Eugénie Fiocre's great attraction lay in the combination of a perfectly proportioned figure and a regal carriage with features that were far from being classical. For her tip-tilted nose and mocking expression gave her an irresistible allure, but it was the allure of a *grisette*. She had entered the third quadrille in 1858, at the age of thirteen, and appeared in *Néméa* in all the freshness of her nineteen years. Her promotion to *sujet* a few days before the first performance was amply justified by the sensation she caused.

From the band of gentlemen who came forward with offers of protection, she selected one who had till then shown little interest in romantic adventures, Baron Soubeyran, a fabulously wealthy banker. But, recorded a collector of anecdotes, "the artful angel (counselled to do so by the famous Dr. Véron— Mimi as he was called) kept him waiting, since hope deferred maketh the cheque thicker". When a group of financiers wished to embroil Soubeyran in a quarrel with the Spanish banker, Salamanca, who had the misfortune of being afflicted with webbed toes, they could think of no better plan than to take the latter to the Opéra to see Eugénie as Cupid. Salamanca's passions were duly roused, and he sent Isabelle, the flower-girl of the Jockey Club, to tell the dancer that "he would send her a blank cheque to fill in if his webbed foot might hope to climb her balcony". Isabelle, who was also in the plot, divulged the secret to Soubeyran. Very soon, Salamanca was threatened with ruin if he persisted in his pursuit, and prudently withdrew to London, leaving Soubeyran still in possession.

Eugénie Fiocre's talent as a dancer was never outstanding, but she had little occasion to show her shortcomings in the travesty rôles that she made her speciality. She became very rich, and began to hold herself aloof from her companions. Perhaps she found other pursuits more congenial than dancing: the paper, *Le Sport*, reported in September 1872 that she had returned to Paris from Sologne, where she had been seen taking part in a shoot and bringing down pheasants, quail and pigeons with an unerring aim. She retired from the stage in 1875, when she was only just thirty, and went to live in the country.

She apparently considered herself worthy of a more illustrious husband than a mere millionaire. "She was very well off, and aspired to marry an 'English Milord'—a Duke for choice", wrote the same recorder of gossip. "Seeing me one day on the racecourse at Chantilly with the very tall Lord Pembroke, she asked me if I knew an English Duke who would be willing to gild his strawberry leaves with her £8000 a year; but at the moment I had no such biped in view." According to Charles Bocher, an *abonné* of many years' standing, she became the Marquise de Créqui de Courtivron. This marriage, if in fact it ever took place, did not last long, for in 1892 the Comte de Maugny wrote that she was independent and was to be seen on winter evenings in a *baignoire* at the Opéra, always the centre of an admiring circle of visitors. She died in 1908.

.   .   .   .

Muravieva returned to Russia shortly after her last appearance of the season on September 23rd, 1864. Her contract obliged her to return to Paris the following spring, but as the time approached, the news seeped through that she was retiring from the stage, and later a rumour began to circulate that she had become a Carmelite nun. Her piety was well known, for she had attended the Russian church regularly while in Paris, and one day, when a friend had asked her what she would do when she could no longer dance, she had replied, "I shall enter a convent." It was probably from this chance remark, which Albéric Second recorded in *L'Entr'acte*, that this persistent, but unfounded, rumour sprang. However, the truth was that her emotions had conflicted with her career, and the choice with which she was faced had brought on a nervous and physical crisis.

In March 1865 Perrin received a disquieting letter from Eugène Huguet in St. Petersburg, telling him that Muravieva had made up her mind not to visit Paris in the summer. "The person with the greatest influence over Mlle Muravieva," Huguet confided, "is now insistent on her remaining in Russia, perhaps in order to marry her and make her leave the stage." A letter from the dancer herself followed a day or two later to say that she had been ill, and enclosing a doctor's certificate. A fortnight later another letter arrived from Huguet, containing further news of "this young ex-sylphide". "The future husband—for her marriage has been officially announced to take place after Easter—is a certain M. Seifert, a very bald and, it is said, very rich young man," Huguet wrote. "His mother, a most aristocratic old bird, insists that our young artiste should appear no more on the stage. That, I believe, is the secret of this great illness. . . . In my opinion, she deserves a good lawsuit brought against her."

Added to Muravieva's troubles was the worry that Perrin might invoke the penal clause in her contract. Not having received a reply to her letter, she feared he might have reacted unfavourably, and begged the French Ambassador to appoint doctors to examine her again. The Ambassador informed Perrin of her approach, and Perrin wrote immediately to put her fears at rest, explaining that he had not replied sooner because he had understood that her decision was not final; if in fact she was retiring, he was prepared to consider her engagement as terminated by *force majeure*, but should she return to the stage, he would reserve the right to hold her to the terms of her contract.

Muravieva was twenty-seven, and in the prime of her talent, when she retired. After her marriage, when she visited the theatre as a member of the audience, she seldom stayed until the end of the performance, and often returned home in tears. She died of consumption in 1879.

IX

YEARS OF DECLINE

THE departure of his four principal ballerinas, Boschetti, Muravieva, Zina Mérante and Marie Vernon, all within a few months, confronted Perrin with the unwelcome task of replacing every leading feminine rôle in the repertory at a time when all energies were being directed to the production of Meyerbeer's last opera, *L'Africaine*. This task was accomplished, but not satisfactorily: the artistes chosen were either immature or mediocre, and the position of ballet relative to opera sank progressively lower. Later, Adèle Grantzow was to raise its prestige a little, and later still, the early promise of Giuseppina Bozzacchi was to stir further hope. But the loss of Emma Livry was sadly felt, and nearly proved fatal to French ballet.

Another Italian ballerina, Guglielmina Salvioni, a pupil of Augusto Hus, was imported to replace the unfortunate Boschetti, but her début at the Opéra in a shortened version of *La Maschera* on December 21st, 1864, caused little sensation. She had an advantage over her predecessor in being tall and slender, but she lacked Boschetti's classic beauty of feature, being herself a little hard-featured and, it was said, given to keeping her mouth open when dancing. She was a faultless technician, very lively, with good *ballon*, and excelling in *pointe* work and *temps de batterie*; but her style was not particularly distinctive. Nevertheless, with the company so depleted, Perrin felt justified in attaching her to the Opéra until the summer of 1867.

Salvioni became the inseparable companion of Angelina Fioretti, who had been engaged a year previously, after Marie Taglioni, while on a tour of Italy in search of talent, had seen her dance at the Scala, Milan, and had recommended her to Perrin. Fioretti had made her début at the Opéra at the age of seventeen on December 28th, 1863, in the revival of *Moïse*; on February 7th, 1864, she had taken over the rôle of Gloriette in *Le Marché des Innocents*, and on May 26th, 1865, she added the title-rôle in *Néméa* to her repertory. She was a pupil of Carlo Blasis, "a product of the Italian school, ever ready to dance, essentially graceful and supple, and often given to laughter"; her miming was expressive, without appearing exaggerated.

The two rôles left vacant by the retirement of Marie Vernon—Fenella and Diavolina—were respectively allotted to Eugénie Fiocre, the ravishing Cupid of *Néméa*, and Léontine Beaugrand, who was to serve the Opéra with devotion until she was retired, unjustly and prematurely, in 1880.

Léontine Beaugrand, whose parents kept a shop in the suburb of La Villette, had entered the dancing school of the Opéra at the age of eight in 1850, and had ascended the hierarchy to the rank of *grand sujet* more slowly perhaps than she deserved. She knew that her plain features impeded her promotion, but persevered conscientiously at her studies with Théodore, Mathieu and, later, Marie Taglioni, until she had acquired a rare mastery of execution. Her talent was at last recognized: in the summer of 1864, Mme Dominique began instructing her in the title-rôle of *Diavolina*, which she danced for the first time on November 27th, 1864. "Yesterday there was nothing", wrote Gautier, "but to-day a bud is unfolding which in a few days will become a charming flower." According to Albéric Second, she brought a new sparkle to the ballet. "When Mlle Beaugrand dances Diavolina", he wrote, "there is rejoicing in the house, and still more on the stage. Do you know the reason? It is because she brings real bottles of real champagne which is joyfully swilled during the wedding repast."

Eugénie Fiocre succeeded Marie Vernon in *La Muette de Portici* on February 17th, 1865, portraying Fenella as a happy, carefree girl, embroiled in events which she cannot comprehend, and rebelling indignantly against misfortune. Her carefully conceived interpretation showed that she was gifted with intelligence as well as beauty. "As for her figure", wrote Gautier, "if the picturesque costume of the daughters of Nisida, with its heavy skirt, rough cloth blouse, and thick, gaily striped apron, become her sculptural beauty less than the short tunic of a Greek Cupid, at least it allows us to follow the harmonious lines of her fine body without the delusion of corset or crinoline. Every movement of Mlle Fiocre's miming might . . . provide a subject for a drawing or a statue. She does not seek this effect; it comes to her unwittingly, through the natural elegance of her limbs, the perfection of her proportions, and the purity of her form. . . . Apart from her beauty, we much admired Mlle Eugénie Fiocre's perfect simplicity of gesture and pose."

.   .   .   .

Considering the weakness of the company at the time, Perrin's lack of enthusiasm at Nadezhda Bogdanova's request to dance again at the Opéra, in *Giselle*, might have seemed strange to anyone who was unaware of the undercurrents that influenced the Director's opinion. He did not refuse her request, but would only agree to her appearing in the first act. Jules Janin tried to persuade Perrin to give her the opportunity of appearing in the whole ballet, but his intervention was of no avail: the decision was already made. Bogdanova's reappearance, on November 13th, 1865, passed almost unnoticed: most of the critics gave it a bare mention in their *feuilletons*, and even Janin only devoted a few uninspired lines to her.

The feel of the Opéra stage after an absence of more than ten years kindled in her a desire to appear there again, and she tried to enlist the support of Auber to obtain an engagement. "Dear M. Auber", she wrote to him, "looking at your charming photograph, at your dear portrait, gives me courage to address this little letter to you. You wrote beneath it, 'To my little Nadezhda Bogdanova.' Well, this is *your* little Nadezhda daring to beg you to take her into the sweetest little corner of your heart, and to speak to M. Perrin to ask him to grant me the honour of a revival or a creation at the Opéra. I would like to owe this happiness to your special protection. You know him well, and he will believe you when you tell him what you think, what you know of my talent. . . . Oh, I beseech you, dear M. Auber, stretch out your sweet little finger-tip to me, *your little Nadezhda!* My last appearance at the Opéra in the first act of *Giselle* made me known to M. Perrin. M. Auber, if (at this very moment) you would only say one little word about *your little Nadezhda*, there she will be, doing the *grand pas*, light and bounding, from St. Petersburg to Paris. The thought of seeing you again, of being near you, fills my eyes with tears and my heart with joy and gratitude. Oh, M. Auber, do, do perform this miracle for your little Nadezhda Bogdanova."

Auber gallantly forwarded her letter to Perrin, but unfortunately a stronger influence than his had been working against her, that of her former teacher, Saint-Léon, who wrote to Perrin on January 4th, 1866: "Mlle Bogdanova has written to M. Suvarov, Governor of St. Petersburg, and to the Minister Adelberg that her success in Paris was enormous and would have been greater still if I had not said so much against her talent. However, I do not think I was far from the truth when I qualified her as impossible for a serious stage. Perhaps in Berlin she will triumph over the wrong I was able to do her in Paris."

．　　　．　　　．　　　．　　　．　　　．　　　．

1865 had been a lean year for the ballet: Meyerbeer's posthumous opera, *L'Africaine*, had been produced at the end of April, and was played throughout the summer and autumn almost to the exclusion of everything else. But with the approach of winter, Perrin began to consider adding a new ballet to the repertory. In selecting the author and musician to be commissioned, he remembered the private theatricals at Compiègne that autumn, when he had helped design the costumes for a little revue by the Marquis de Massa which had been performed by members of the Court, with the Austrian Ambassador, Prince Richard Metternich, accompanying on the piano. It was therefore no coincidence that Perrin should choose Massa to write the scenario of the new ballet, and Prince Richard Metternich to compose the music, which, however, was to be orchestrated and attributed to Théodore Labarre; an advance notice in *Le Figaro* of October 22nd, 1865, added that Count Solms of the Prussian Embassy, an excellent musician, also had a share in the score. The choreography was to be by Lucien Petipa. Unfortunately the Marquis de Massa, a soldier by profession, was posted at his own request to the theatre of war in Mexico only a few days before his ballet was given its first performance on December 28th, 1865.

The scenario of the ballet, *Le Roi d'Yvetot*, was inspired by the poem by Béranger:

> *Il était un roi d'Yvetot*
> *Peu connu dans l'histoire:*
> *Se levant tard, se couchant tôt,*
> *Dormant fort bien sans gloire . . .*

The scene is laid in the public square of Yvetot; on one side
stands the house of Maître Crochu, the notary, and on the
other, Gros Guillaume's tavern, *Au roi d'Yvetot*. It is the village
custom once a year to elect a "King", and Gros Guillaume
(E. Coralli) is chosen, to the great annoyance of his rival,
Crochu (Dauty). While the men of the village follow Gros
Guillaume on a tour of his kingdom, the womenfolk prepare
for the evening's festivities. Rosette (Fonta), the daughter of
Gros Guillaume, and Thérèse (Fioretti), the daughter of
Crochu, each offer a bouquet to Jeannot (L. Mérante), who,
unable to decide which of the girls is the more charming,
accepts both. A squadron of Hussars arrives. Their young
Colonel (E. Fiocre) has specially chosen this day to visit
Yvetot, knowing that all the men will be away from the village.
Jeannot, who has remained behind, is discovered by the
soldiers, set upon, and locked up in Crochu's cellar. The
Hussars then choose their billets by lot, Thérèse arranging that
the Colonel should pick her ribbon out of the drummer's hat.
Rosette, whom no one has chosen, is walking away sadly,
when she hears Jeannot's cries. She unlocks the cellar door and
releases him. The menfolk, who have been warned of the
soldiers' arrival by Gros Guillaume's maid-servant, Jeanneton
(C. Brach), then come hurrying back to the village, but the
Hussars are too quick for them, and they find their wives
lined up with their forks ready for action. Gros Guillaume
tells Jeannot to choose a wife, and when both Rosette and
Thérèse put forward claims, blindfolds the boy. Jeannot picks
Rosette, but meanwhile Crochu has found Jeannot's cap in his
cellar and declares that the boy has compromised his daughter
and must marry her. Jeanneton then accuses Thérèse of having
allowed the Colonel to kiss her. There is a general uproar,
which ends with the abdication of Gros Guillaume, who has
had quite enough of it all and simply wants to go back to sleep.
Thérèse, on the Colonel's advice, cedes Jeannot to Rosette, and
finally Gros Guillaume places the crown on Crochu's head and
sinks to sleep in Jeanneton's arms.

"To this gay, amusing and lively scenario", wrote Gautier,
"Petipa has devised some charming *pas* and graceful *ensembles*,
accompanied by a brisk and sprightly score . . . full of rhythm
and melody, which it would be a pleasure to listen to on its
own, without the charm of the dances, pink tights, gauze

CARICATURES OF "LE ROI D'YVETOT" BY MARCELIN.

skirts, and pretty faces. The elegant uniforms of the Hussars contrast happily with the gay costumes of the villagers, and all stand out sharply against a coquettishly rustic set by MM. Cambon and Thierry, who have caught the light blue tints of one of Boucher's pier-glasses. Mlle Fioretti and Mlle Fonta are both delightful, and we should be as embarrassed as Jeannot was if we had to decide which is the prettier or the better dancer. Colonel Eugénie Fiocre, with her slender figure and proud bearing, seems like an Amazon Queen disguised as a gallant Hussar."

Roqueplan added that the choreography was "brilliant and original", and the final *ballabile* arranged with precision and clarity. "Mlle Fonta", he continued, "danced very well the *variation* beginning with *pas de bourrée* and *jetés* and finishing with *cabrioles en avant*."

.   .   .   .   .   .

For some years there had been talk of reviving the old opera-ballet, *Le Dieu et la Bayadère*, for which Filippo Taglioni had arranged the choreography when it was created in 1830. It was considered more than once for Emma Livry. In October 1859 the Minister of State had suggested that it might be staged with Ferraris as the Bayadère, but Royer had objected that the work was too short to be given on its own, and that the addition to the programme of *Le Papillon*, which was then in rehearsal, would make it seem that Ferraris was dancing in a curtain-raiser before the appearance of Emma Livry. Zina Mérante's name had also been mentioned, and Perrin had thought of reviving it for Muravieva in 1864. But all these plans had come to naught, and it was not until the autumn of 1865 that rehearsals were at last begun with Salvioni.

Though planned to be given at the same time as *Le Roi d'Yvetot*, *Le Dieu et la Bayadère* was not ready until more than three weeks afterwards, January 22nd, 1866. The revival was not a happy one; Saint-Victor said that the work had been exhumed only to be massacred by its interpreters, explaining, however, that he was referring principally to the singers, whose performance had been "deplorable".

The dancing was not remarkable. Although Salvioni had been instructed in the rôle of Zoloé by Marie Taglioni, who had created it, her interpretation was very different from the original. One looked in vain for the suggestion of gentle indolence which Taglioni had expressed, and instead was treated to an exhibition of *tours de force* inappropriate to the part. "Some of her movements", observed Roqueplan, "borrowed, we think, from *La Maschera*, were executed with a certain energetic violence. We still advise her to persist in those rapid turns which are in dancing what the final notes of an aria are in singing, and which caused some sensation among the audience; but . . . we are sorry that these turns are not enriched with *pas de bourrée, jetés en tournant,* or any other difficulty. At present, Mlle Salvioni appears to us as a beautiful person turning with a shattering rapidity; but such rotation has nothing to do with dancing."

Eugénie Fiocre, who played Fatmé, wore a costume that showed off her figure to great advantage, and was very well received. "She began", wrote Roqueplan, "with an excellent *adage*. All that followed was well done, and remarkable especially for the bold precision of her *pirouettes*, the style of her *développés*, the brilliance of her *tours renversés*, the assurance of her *tours sur la pointe*. The young dancer also knows how to finish, with her legs well placed and steady, her weight divided equally between them."

After ten performances, *Le Dieu et la Bayadère* disappeared for ever from the repertory.

.   .   .   .

In November 1865, Saint-Léon sent two long and enthusiastic letters to Paris, one to Perrin and the other to Mme Dominique, telling them of the recent triumph of Adèle Grantzow in Moscow. Saint-Léon was eagerly looking forward to returning to France. After sending messages to "Louise [Marquet], Baratte, Beaugrand, and my poor little sick Ribet [1]", he ended his letter to Mme Dominique with the words, "*Adieu*, Dominique, we shall see each other again in 2 months, 18 days, 14 hours, and 57 minutes, and I hope to find you both hale and hearty." Then, as a postscript, he

[1] Antonia Ribet, then a *coryphée*, had fallen ill with chlorosis that summer. She was a promising young dancer who had entered the third quadrille in 1861. She had risen to the rank of *grand sujet* when she created her last rôle, that of Hymen in *Coppélia*, in 1870. She died in Algiers, in 1871, at the age of about twenty-three.

added: "I find that *Néméa* is not given often enough. How shall I be able to buy my cigars? Reduced to *Crapulados!!* *Oh! patrie!*"

His latest *protégée*, Adèle Camille Grantzow, was the daughter of Gustav Grantzow, *maître de ballet* at Brunswick, in which city she was born on New Year's Day, 1845. Her introduction to ballet came at a performance by the Viennese Children which so impressed her that afterwards she could hardly sleep for excitement. The following day she left home without anyone knowing, to pay a visit to the director of the little troupe, Josephine Weiss. Frau Weiss, a very stout lady with a red face and a brusque manner, was having lunch with her menagerie of pets when the little girl arrived, and when she had finished eating, took her to watch a class of her pupils. Adèle was a little shocked by the tawdriness of the surroundings, but not enough to make her rebel against her father's decision that she was to become a dancer. The lure of the theatre captured her very early: her favourite game as a child was to devise little operas, with melodramatic plots and tragic endings, which she played by herself at home. She was a strange, melancholy child, spending long hours rapt in her dreams, speaking to no one, and prone to sudden outbursts of tears for no apparent reason.

She learnt quickly under her father's tuition, and was soon proficient enough to appear at the Brunswick Opera House, There she was noticed by the Duke, who began to treat her like a spoilt child and to give her presents—a bracelet for Christmas, a pair of ear-rings for her first Communion—until another dancer, the ducal favourite of the moment, objected strongly to this drain of jewellery, and Adèle's engagement was terminated. Her father then took her to Hanover, where she was given a contract as *première danseuse* and, it was said, first attracted the notice of Saint-Léon when he passed through the city on his travels.

When she was nineteen, Adèle realized that she could not afford to remain any longer in Hanover if she was to fulfil her ambitions, and persuaded her father to let her visit Paris. She paid her own fare, and travelled with her mother. Immediately on her arrival, she wrote to Mme Dominique, who took her *en pension*. Mme Dominique perceived her new pupil's promise at once. Having dissuaded her from accepting an engagement to dance at the Gaîté, she insisted that Saint-Léon, who was on the point of returning to Russia, should come and see her before his departure. He did so, with the result that when, the following year, 1865, the position of *première danseuse* in Moscow fell vacant, he put forward her name. She was engaged, and on November 27th made her début at the Bolshoi Theatre in *Fiammetta* with the success that Saint-Léon was enthusiastically relating to his friends in Paris.

"She had to contend with a severe and impatient public and the memory of Muravieva and Lebedeva, the idol of the Muscovites," he told Perrin, "and furthermore, she was the first foreigner for twelve years to attempt to overcome the obstacle of nationality. . . . The poor girl was dancing in *a ballet* for the first time: hitherto her repertory had consisted only of the Abbess in *Robert*, Fenella, and isolated *pas*. Despite these handicaps and much nervousness, she carried away the public to a pitch of enthusiasm as in the greatest days of her predecessors. In truth, I have never seen a talent more complete, or as varied and excellent in so many types of dancing. Her appearance is charming. I thought of your words when I heard her spoken of as a young Elssler—yes, but Elssler never had her suppleness nor her *ballon*; as well as this, she has astonishing *pointes*, *tacqueté*, *batterie*, an expressiveness in her miming and dancing worthy of a great artiste, and an assurance as though she had danced in grand ballets for twenty years. She was as light, delicate and lively in the fourth act as she had been in the first. Her wildest admirers followed her carriage back to her hotel, applauding. . . . I would hasten to show her to Paris in all her freshness; she would be suited to play all Muravieva's repertory, which would entail no delay in the projects you might have in mind . . . I will supervise her début with great pleasure, and for nothing."

Perrin was grateful to Saint-Léon for his recommendation, and asked when she could be available and in what ballet she should make her first appearance. "For her début, *Néméa* or *Giselle*, as you wish", replied Saint-Léon. "She is charming too in *La Fille mal gardée*, which I made her study before my departure from Moscow. This ballet, refurbished with new *pas*, would perhaps be an agreeable and inexpensive revival while preparing something new, if you think fit. I do not mention

Diavolina, since Beaugrand plays it, but she is very good in that too."

Within a few weeks terms had been agreed: Adèle Grantzow was to be at the disposal of the Opéra from April until the middle of September 1866, receiving a monthly salary of 2000 francs for the first three months and 2500 francs for the remainder of the engagement.

Saint-Léon arrived in Paris some weeks before his *protégée*, and at once set to work devising the dances for Mozart's *Don Juan*, which was given on April 2nd. The *divertissement* suggested the flirtation of roses and butterflies, the music accompanying it consisting of the well-known *Alla Turca*, in a new orchestration by Auber ("only Auber can touch Mozart without making it heavy", wrote Gautier), and other pieces selected from Mozart's works. Saint-Léon's choreography was brilliant. Angelina Fioretti danced to the *Alla Turca*, and Léontine Beaugrand was given a *variation tacquetée* which long remained celebrated at the Opéra as "*la variation de Beaugrand*".

Adèle Grantzow reached Paris shortly afterwards and made her début in *Giselle* on May 11th, 1866. "Mlle Grantzow", wrote Gautier, "is neither blonde nor blue-eyed like Carlotta. Her hair is black, her eyes the same colour, but her features are none the less charming and have an innocent and tender expression, such as the rôle demands. She has a gentle suppleness, a facility, and a sort of voluptuousness in her dancing which we ourselves prefer to those more or less disgraceful *tours de force* that never fail to be applauded. She knows how to find natural and graceful poses for her arms. Her miming is intelligent, expressive, without violent gestures; her features interpret well the workings of her soul. At the *dénouement*, when the tomb claims its prey and Giselle vanishes beneath the flowers, she was very moving and evoked an emotion that ballets seldom produce. The success of Mlle Grantzow grew with each scene; she was applauded during every *pas* and recalled. Not for a long time has a dancer been so warmly welcomed at the Opéra."

Not all the critics were so enthusiastic. Roqueplan recognized that she had lightness, *ballon*, a feeling for rhythm, and a wide command of technique, but, he added, "limited means, *pointes* which are strong only when she is supported by her partner, little expression, little grace".

She followed her success in *Giselle* by appearing in *Néméa* a fortnight later, on May 25th. "She is a pleasing dancer", commented Gautier. "Her features are not lacking in expression, and she mimes with truth and feeling. Her dancing is correct and light, and appears to cost her no effort, although she executes extremely daring and rapid *renversés*."

Her biographer, George Japy, in an attempt to describe the essence of her style, likened her dancing to tea, as compared with the mocha of Carlotta Grisi, the champagne of Muravieva, and the milk of Emma Livry. Her style reflected her character. She was a young woman of serious but simple tastes, with a sincere Lutheran faith, and unaffected by her sudden success. Unassuming, generous, anxious to befriend and help others, she made herself liked by everyone. She dressed simply, usually in black or mauve, relieved by a fresh carnation. Reading poetry, visiting the theatre, and improvising on the piano were among her greatest pleasures. She liked to pass the evening in her garden, amid the scent of acacia and roses, and to go down to the lake when the moon was shining on the water; and she took a strange delight in the fury of a storm.

.   .   .   .

La Source, the first grand ballet to be produced at the Opéra since *L'Étoile de Messine* five years before, went into rehearsal in the summer of 1866. It was originally planned as a two-act ballet, with scenario by Charles Nuitter, the archivist of the Opéra, score by Ludwig Minkus and Léo Delibes, and choreography by Saint-Léon. Adèle Grantzow was cast in the leading rôle of Naïla, which she began to study under Saint-Léon early in June. There were several delays: first, Grantzow twisted her foot during a rehearsal, and then it was decided to add a third act. As Grantzow was only engaged until the middle of September, it became clear that, at the earliest, the ballet would be ready only two or three weeks before her departure. Although it was hoped that the Russian authorities would grant an extension of her leave, Perrin prudently gave instructions that Salvioni was to study the rôle of Naïla simultaneously with Grantzow, a wise decision as it turned out, for both Grantzow and Saint-Léon were needed in Russia to take part in the festivities in honour of the wedding of the Tsarevitch.

Saint-Léon left Paris for St. Petersburg in the middle of

August, leaving Lucien Petipa to conduct the rehearsals in his absence. He hoped that personal persuasion might succeed where formal application had failed, but unfortunately he fell ill on the journey, and the negotiations for an extension of Grantzow's leave had to be abandoned.

Saint-Léon was thus forced to watch over the last weeks of rehearsal of his ballet from a distance of more than a thousand miles. Fortunately, however, he had in Nuitter not only a devoted friend, but a prolific correspondent who kept him fully informed of the progress of the work.

"My dear Nuitter," he wrote on September 11th, shortly after his arrival. "Since everything is against us, there remains only M. Perrin's good taste, your watchful eye over everything, and perhaps a little of my lucky star to preside over the production. Ask me anything you want. I will try to be as clear as possible. . . . Remember me to all the principal interpreters of *La Source*, not forgetting Mathieu and Pluque, to whom I entrust the *ensembles*. . . . I suggest to Mlle Salvioni and Delibes a *variation tacquetée*, to a violin solo, if she does not dance that of the second act: in the Mayseder style—I could even send a sketch. . . . Please give my respects to M. Perrin (together with a long sigh). If you only knew how tormented I have been during my illness! In my delirium I seemed to be rehearsing continually. . . . But *holà*, my brain is tired, my eyesight troubles me, and anger is making me perspire as once I used to after a *pas de deux*!"

On September 21st, when he learnt definitely that he could not be spared from St. Petersburg, Saint-Léon received another letter from Nuitter. "Of all you tell me", he replied the next day, "there is only one thing upon which I absolutely insist. That is my *groupe glissé* in the fourth scene. . . . It is not easy to find something new; therefore, if Mlle Salvioni cannot reproduce it as it was, I beg her at once to replace it *entirely*. At least I can use it another time. What effect does she create as a dancer? . . . Keep me in touch with everything until the ballet is given, make me this sacrifice. You must understand my anxiety. . . . My health is improving slowly. Still a weak and disordered stomach."

Early in October, Nuitter sent Saint-Léon a list of the characters. "The names seem to me very good", the choreographer replied, "but I think that in such a case the fairy being [Naïla] should not be *baptized*. The Sylphide had no other name than that of the title. But you are the master in such matters, and all you do will be *ben fatto*. . . . Last Monday, when we were working on the new ballet [1] at Minkus's house, we thought that *La Source* was being given. We stopped from time to time and paced the room. It was obvious that the Siberian authors were worried. We parted at ten minutes past two in the morning—it was midnight then in Paris. All this was premature. Mlle Salvioni must allow her foot to get quite better again—it seems to trouble her at times. To stop after the first night would, as you say, be very unfortunate. . . . I have heard nothing about Mlle Montaubry: please let me have news of her, because when I left, her eye was bad. My best wishes to my beautiful Nouredda [E. Fiocre], to my superb gipsy [L. Marquet], to Beaugrand, Baratte, Sanlaville, and *tutti quanti*. Minkus and I send our regards to Delibes."

A few days later, Nuitter wrote to Saint-Léon again about the concern felt for the weakness of Salvioni's foot. Saint-Léon was now deeply involved in the wedding festivities of the Tsarevitch and the Princess Dagmar. "I was unable to reply to your letter sooner", he wrote apologetically on the evening of October 30th. "I have not been out of Court dress for a week. I am at Tsarkoie Selo giving La Dagmar dancing lessons, and in the morning I rehearse the new ballet here. This does not prevent my giving serious thought to your questions. The solution is not easy. Obviously, if Salvioni's foot offers no guarantee for a series of performances, the simplest solution would be to make *La Source* the Exhibition ballet. Frankly I believe that the ballet could only gain by this, and would come at a splendid moment. The season here ends on March 12th. Grantzow could be in Paris a week later."

Perrin, however, had decided that the production could be delayed no longer, and the ballet was given its first performance on November 12th, 1866.

Nuitter's scenario, which more than one critic found "poor", gave the ballet an Oriental setting. The first act took place by a

---

[1] *Le Poisson doré*, ballet fantastique in 3 acts and 7 scenes by Saint-Léon, after a story by Pushkin, with music by Minkus, produced in St. Petersburg. Act I alone, with Lebedeva and Kantsireva, was included in the programme of a Gala Performance on November 20th, 1866, the eve of the Tsarevitch's wedding, but the work was not given in its entirety until October 8th, 1867, when Guglielmina Salvioni appeared in the leading rôle.

spring flowing amid the rocks of a mountain defile. Djémil
(L. Mérante), a hunter, having quenched his thirst at the
spring, prevents Morgab (L. Marquet), a gipsy, from throwing
some poisonous weeds into its water. A caravan then approaches,
bearing the lovely Nouredda (E. Fiocre) on her way to the
Court of the Khan. Nouredda implores the gentlemen of her
escort to pick for her a beautiful flower that is growing high
among the rocks. None will dare take the risk, but Djémil
scales the dangerous rock-face and brings the desired flower to
her. As a reward, he asks to be allowed to see Nouredda's face,
and for his insolence is left, bound hand and foot, to die, as
the caravan moves on. A great thirst seizes him, but Naïla,
the Spirit of the Spring (Salvioni), appears and frees him.
She is grateful for his having protected her from the gipsy,
but reproaches him for picking her talisman. His wish to rejoin
Nouredda and avenge himself is granted, and he sets forth on
his journey, armed with the magic flower and accompanied
by the goblin, Zail (Sanlaville).

In the second act, the Khan (Dauty) is impatiently awaiting
the arrival of Nouredda. Djémil, with the aid of the magic
flower, commands Naïla to appear. The Khan is captivated,
and begs her to become his bride, but she will accept only if
Nouredda is dismissed.

Forced to leave the Court, Nouredda is offered shelter by
the evil Morgab, who tries to ensnare Djémil into her tent.
The timely appearance of Zail enables Djémil to escape with
Nouredda. The scene changes back to the mountain defile.
Naïla is overwhelmed with sadness, for Zail had shown her
Djémil and Nouredda in the tent. She commands the lovers
to appear before her, and tells Djémil that Nouredda, who is
asleep by his side, will never love him. Djémil replies that she
could remedy this if she wished. Naïla explains that the magic
flower is linked to her existence, but then, with an effort of
generosity, places it on Nouredda's heart. As the lovers depart,
Naïla grows weaker and the water of the spring gradually
ceases to flow.

Salvioni was at a disadvantage in creating a rôle that had
been conceived in the first place for Grantzow, for their styles
were very different. "Mlle Salvioni dances and mimes the
rôle of the Spirit of the Spring with much talent; she is pure,
correct and lively", wrote Gautier. "Considering the nature

of the character, one would like to find something a little gentler, more fluid, more pliant in her charm and her poses. That would suit her type of beauty, which is rather that of Diana than of a naiad." Salvioni made up for her lack of grace by feats of great strength that seemingly cost her no effort. "She excels", said Saint-Victor, "in those daring *pas* and vehement poses reminiscent of the violent design of Florentine painting." It was remarked that at times the brilliance of her style was a little dimmed by faulty timing, but this was possibly caused by fatigue and anxiety about her foot. Her miming, like her dancing, was very Italian in flavour.

The two French dancers, Eugénie Fiocre and Léontine Beaugrand, also made a deep impression. Eugénie Fiocre, in the rôle of Nouredda, appeared to Gautier as "the prettiest blonde houri ever to have worn the bonnet and corset of pearls in the Mohammedan paradise. Her charming body", he continued, "shaded by light gauze specked with gold, is displayed with an exquisite grace in the *pas de la Guzla,* one of the prettiest in the ballet." Other critics were less kind: one remarked that she had now nearly learnt how to dance, and another described her *pas* as "a kind of Oriental cancan" and was greatly shocked by her costume, which, he said, "could not have been more disgraceful". The young artist Edgar Degas was more impressed by her beauty in repose, and his painting of her as she appeared in the first act, sitting pensively by the spring, was to be the first of his many famous pictures of the Paris Opéra ballet.

Beaugrand's part was very small: she appeared in a short *variation* in the *pas des voiles* in the beginning of Act II, but danced it so perfectly that the whole house burst into applause. "Mlle Beaugrand had only one *variation,* but she made of that simple *pas* a little masterpiece of finesse and precision", wrote Saint-Victor. "An ornamentist would be eager to design her *tacquetés* and her *pointes.* It is exquisite, dainty, delicate, like lace-work."

Minkus and Delibes had each composed the music for two scenes, Minkus for the first and fourth, and Delibes for the second and third. Léo Delibes, now a man of thirty, had studied composition at the Conservatoire under Adolphe Adam, and had entered the Opéra as second chorus-master in 1865. There were many delightful melodies in his contribution to the score, which was his first essay at ballet music. In Jouvin's opinion, his music was "vivacious and especially lively", contrasting to advantage with the plaintive melodies of Minkus. Gautier wrote that Delibes "has no less talent by being a Frenchman, and has acquitted himself well of the task set him. We seem to recognize in the score some reminiscences, perhaps not sufficiently disguised, of Mendelssohn's *Midsummer Night's Dream* music. Nevertheless they fit in there very well: is not a ballet a mimed symphony?"

The greater part of the 33,446.21 francs laid out on the production was expended on the sets. Of the three used, only one had been taken from store—the second, depicting the gardens of the Khan's palace, which had originally been painted by Cambon and Thierry for Act I of the unperformed *Zara*. The most praised was that for the first and last scenes, designed by Desplechin and constructed under the guidance of Sacré, the chief machinist. It was largely formed by a practicable mountain built upon the stage, with a spring of real water gushing from its side. In the first act, this spring flowed, limpid and abundant, amid lush undergrowth and exotic flowers, bathed in the first rays of a morning sun, simulated by electric light: when the curtain first went up, the set was applauded on its own account, although some criticism was raised that the natural water contrasted too harshly with the painted rocks. In the last scene, the spring dried up, leaving nothing but a wasted crater at the foot of the bare, arid rock. Another scenic effect had been successfully employed in the third scene, in Morgab's tent, when the gipsy had thrown a handful of herbs into her brazier and a bluish mist had been seen to rise—an illusion created by raising a gauze curtain.

Although Salvioni's foot caused no more anxiety, and she was able to appear in the ballet regularly during the winter, *La Source* did not obtain the success expected of it, and, in St. Petersburg, Saint-Léon was eagerly looking forward to the day when Grantzow could take over the rôle of Naïla. "I have great hopes for the revival of *La Source* with Grantzow (even if the ballet is on its last legs in France)", he wrote to Nuitter at the end of January 1867, "for what it has lacked is certainly the woman, the *danseuse*."

That winter, both in Moscow and St. Petersburg, Adèle

Grantzow had been gaining a triumph such as no other
ballerina had obtained there since Fanny Elssler. The Tsar
had personally congratulated her on her Giselle; when,
during a performance of *Météora*, she had struck her head on
a piece of scenery and fallen unconscious, the Grand Duke
Constantine had rushed anxiously to her assistance; and after
her farewell performance in St. Petersburg the Tsar had stood
up in his box to applaud her.

Fresh from these triumphs, Adèle Grantzow arrived in
Paris in April, and appeared in *La Source* on May 10th, 1867.
"This ballet . . . had collapsed without a sound", wrote
Roqueplan. "Mlle Grantzow has just put it on its feet again,
given it body, relief, meaning; she has not revived a rôle,
she has created one." "There are sopranos, mezzo-sopranos
and contraltos of the dance", added Gautier. "Mlle Salvioni is
a contralto, and Mlle Grantzow a soprano. Naïla was a little
high for Mlle Salvioni; Mlle Grantzow performs it without
transposing it. . . . Mlle Grantzow acted the rôle of Naïla
with much grace and feeling. She is supple and light, executes
marvellously *temps penchés* and *renversés*, and *retraites sur les
pointes*. Her movements are harmonious, well-linked, infused
with a gentleness that is voluptuous as well as being modest.
It is plain that she comes of a good school. She has talent and
charm, and her success was not for a moment in doubt."

On December 23rd, 1867, a third dancer interpreted the
rôle of Naïla, Angelina Fioretti. "She mimes with intelligence"
Gautier wrote of her, "for she not only dances her rôles, but
acts them, a quality that is becoming rarer and rarer."

. . . . .

Another revival of *La Muette de Portici* followed *La Source*
on January 18th, 1867, with Salvioni, whose contract was due
to expire on May 31st, in the rôle of Fenella. It was also the
occasion of the début at the Opéra of Henriette Dor, who had
been engaged through the Milanese agent, Albino Marini, on
the recommendation of Marie Taglioni.

Salvioni, wrote Eugène Tarbé, "gives to this poetic figure
[Fenella] quite a new colour. She restores the importance
that this rôle, the most prominent in the opera, had lost when
it was entrusted to a player incapable of bringing out its true
value and underlining its dramatic content. Mlle Salvioni has
more energy than her predecessor [Eugénie Fiocre], and it

could be said that her nationality is the cause of the deep feeling with which she mimes her rôle. She is an Italian dancing the rôle of the dumb girl, and I sincerely believe that at certain moments she is inspired by patriotism. The new Fenella is both an able dancer and a distinguished tragedienne: her face is expressive, and her gestures, perfect to understand, have the great merit of reflecting an individuality. Mlle Salvioni imitates no one, but stands out as one of those artistes who must herself be taken as a model." Salvioni had discarded the simple, but more accurate, costume worn by Marie Vernon and Eugénie Fiocre, and instead appeared in a blue ballet skirt of the conventional shape, with golden bodice and sleeves.

Henriette Dor made her appearance in the *divertissement*, dancing with Louis Mérante a new *pas*, *L'Uccellatore*, arranged by Lucien Petipa. She was a pupil of her father, Louis Dor, and danced with a typically French style. Perrin, however, was dissatisfied with her performance. He notified her that he would exercise his option to terminate her contract at the end of April, and apparently vented his spleen on Marie Taglioni, who had recommended her. Marie Taglioni in turn wrote complaining to the agent, Marini.

"Dear Mme Taglioni", Marini replied, "I cannot tell you how surprised I was by your letter of the 22nd, telling me of the non-success at the Opéra of Mlle Dor and the little merit you grant her. I will tell you why I am so astonished. First, because I received a telegram from M. Dor on the very day of her début giving me news of his daughter's great triumph. . . . The second reason is that you tell me that Mlle Dor is a dancer lacking in distinction and grace, that she is generally disliked, and that M. Perrin is furious at having engaged her. Let me say that before Mlle Dor was engaged, you went to see her dance . . . and were so satisfied that she expressed a wish that M. Perrin might allow you to revive *Le Papillon* for her. I was therefore persuaded that you found Mlle Dor very talented, and if M. Perrin engaged her, it was admittedly through my agency, but it was also on account of the encouraging information you gave him about this artiste."

.   .   .   .

To have lived in Paris in 1867 was an unforgettable experience. The Universal Exhibition, staged that summer with great pomp and magnificence on the Champ de Mars, marked the *apogée* of the Second Empire. Visitors from every corner of the globe flocked to Paris in their thousands to see the spectacle that was offered, and a succession of Royal and Imperial potentates arrived to be entertained and fêted by Napoleon III.

One of the greatest occasions of the year was the Gala Performance at the Opéra on June 4th in honour of the Tsar of Russia, Alexander II, and many other illustrious guests. As the day drew on, great crowds began to gather along the route that the procession was to take. The streets surrounding the Opéra were closed to the public; and omnibus services along the Boulevard des Italiens were suspended from eight o'clock. Lancers and Gendarmerie of the Imperial Guard lined the Rue Le Peletier, where the Opéra stood like a brilliant jewel, its façade ablaze with illuminations and decorated with flowers and French and Russian flags.

The Emperor and his guests, with an escort of Cent Gardes and Lancers, reached the theatre at about half-past nine. They were received by Perrin, who, observing an ancient custom of the Monarchy, walked backwards before them, branched candlestick in hand, up the stairway to the State Box. The Imperial Box at the side of the stage was much too small to accommodate all the guests of honour, and instead the nine centre boxes of the first tier had been combined to form a State Box, as had been done before on the occasion of Queen Victoria's visit in 1855. The house was lit by a dazzling galaxy of chandeliers.

As the Emperor and his guests entered the Box, sitting down in one long row [1] with their suites standing behind them, the audience rose to their feet and the orchestra played the Imperial Russian Anthem, specially arranged for the occasion by Delibes. The curtain then rose on Act IV of *L'Africaine*, which was followed, after an interval, by Act II of *Giselle*, with Grantzow as Giselle, Fonta as the Queen of the Wilis, and Beaugrand and Fioretti as Zulmé and Moyna. The audience, who had taken little notice of the opera, being far more

[1] Seated from left to right (viewed from the stage): Prince Joachim Murat, the Duke of Leuchtenberg, Princess Evgenia Maximilianovna, the Grand Duke Vladimir, Princess Ludwig of Hesse, the Tsarevitch, the Crown Princess of Prussia, Napoleon III, the Tsar, the Empress Eugénie, the Crown Prince of Prussia, the Grand Duchess Marie, Prince Ludwig of Hesse, Princesse Mathilde, Prince Friedrich of Hesse, Princesse Lucien Murat, the Duke of Saxe-Weimar, and the brother of the Tycoon of Japan. (*See* Frontispiece.)

interested in the occupants of the State Box, were considerably more attentive to the ballet, and although etiquette precluded applause, murmurs of appreciation were continually heard from all parts of the house. The performance ended at midnight, and the Boulevard was still crowded an hour later. "Paris", wrote Ludovic Halévy, "is nothing more than an enormous *guinguette*—but what a *guinguette*!"

The second act of *Giselle* was repeated with the same cast on June 10th for the King of Prussia, and again on July 5th for the Sultan of Turkey. Abdul Aziz, Halévy observed, "appeared completely bored by the opera, but the ballet on the other hand obviously pleased him: he peered at our dancers through his opera-glasses with the greatest curiosity."

Strangely enough, no new ballet had been commissioned for the year of the Universal Exhibition. Instead, Perrin had planned, somewhat belatedly, a revival of Mazilier's *Le Corsaire*, which, although the most successful ballet within recent memory, had been dropped when Carolina Rosati had left the Opéra, for want of a suitable successor in the rôle of Médora. The original choreography having been largely forgotten, Mazilier agreed to come out of retirement to supervise the production, and began rehearsing in May. He completely rearranged much of the ballet, adding to the second act a *pas des fleurs*, danced by Médora and Gulnare, to music by Delibes. New sets, no less splendid than the old, which had been burnt together with the costumes in 1861, were painted by Cambon (Act I), Rubé and Chaperon (Act II), and Despléchin (Act III).

Perrin's decision to stage a revival rather than a new work was not made for reasons of thrift, for when the final account was taken, an expenditure of over 72,000 francs was shown:

New music by Delibes . . .	1,497.40 francs
Cost of rehearsals (including 6000 francs paid to Mazilier)	9,220.95 ,,
Properties (including 12 mechanical fans, costing 433 francs) . . .	1,745.05 ,,
Costumes	23,818.82 ,,
Scenery	35,754.96 ,,
TOTAL . . .	72,037.18 ,,

It was Adèle Grantzow who was chosen for the rôle of Médora; Angelina Fioretti was cast as Gulnare, Louis Mérante as Conrad, Coralli as Birbanto; and Dauty, Petit and Louise Marquet played the rôles they had created in 1856. The work was not ready until well into the autumn, being first given on October 21st, 1867, and proving nearly as great a financial success as it had done originally: the receipts exceeded 10,000 francs on the second and third nights, and, over the first ten performances, averaged 8,174.56 francs.

Adèle Grantzow, who had been suffering from a badly bruised foot, disregarded her doctor's orders by dancing on the first night. By the end of the first act, her foot was so swollen that she had to slit her ballet shoe from end to end. She bravely continued dancing, betraying no sign of pain until, when the final curtain had fallen, she could hold back her tears no longer.

In rendering the rôle of Médora, she had wisely not taken as a model the performance of her predecessor, who had owed her triumph to her extraordinarily eloquent and impassioned miming. Grantzow had given much thought to her interpretation, and succeeded despite the memory of Rosati, though admittedly to a lesser degree. "Without showing those flashes of genius which carry away a whole audience, she acts with infinite feeling and intelligence", wrote Eugène Tarbé. "An able rather than a passionate mime, she leaves nothing to the inspiration of the moment."

Fioretti's performance as Gulnare was also praised. "Gentler and wittier dancing cannot be imagined", wrote Saint-Victor. "Her *pointes* and *entrechats* have the volubility of gay chatter. She has more than skill, she has a roguish delicacy in her legs. And what mocking eyes! What a piquant smile! She must be seen as she teases and mystifies her pasha: it is Rosina in the harem testing her malice on the head of a Turk."

Adèle Grantzow bore the pain in her foot for seven performances, before fever set in and forced her to take to her bed. She appeared again after ten days' rest, but there was time then for only three performances more before she returned to Russia early in December. She danced the rôle of Médora five times more in Paris the following summer, after which the ballet was finally dropped from the repertory. At about the same time, on May 19th, 1868, its choreographer, Joseph

Mazilier, died in Paris at the age of seventy from the effects of an operation.

.   .   .   .

In the last few years of Perrin's management, the ballet sank to a very low ebb in France, to be revived only by Saint-Léon's last work, *Coppélia*, in 1870. From 1866 to 1869 the number of ballet performances dropped steadily from 43 in 1866, to 32 in 1867, 28 in 1868, and only 6 in 1869. Not one new ballet was added to the repertory between *La Source* in November 1866 and *Coppélia* in May 1870; during these three and a half years the only choreographic novelties were opera *divertissements*.

The long-awaited production of Verdi's *Don Carlos*, given on March 11th, 1867, included a *divertissement* by Lucien Petipa in Act III, called *Le Ballet de la reine: la Peregrina*. Its slight plot told of a fisherman (L. Mérante) who visits a grotto in search of the most beautiful pearl of all for the King of Spain. The Queen of the Waters (L. Marquet) shows him many different pearls—a white pearl (Beaugrand), a pink pearl (Annette Mérante), a black pearl (Ribet)—but none of these satisfy him. He then combines the beauties of all the pearls, and from a golden shell there emerges the Peregrina, destined to become the finest gem of the Spanish crown: this wondrous stone is personified by the Queen of the Waters, who comes forth in a glittering chariot as the Spanish Anthem rings out and everyone bows in homage.

Lucien Petipa was also responsible for the small *divertissement*, entitled *La Fête du printemps*, in Thomas' opera, *Hamlet*, produced on March 9th, 1868. Its main attraction was a polka danced by Fioretti and Eugénie Fiocre, in travesty as a huntsman.

On June 29th, *Herculanum* was revived for the first time since the death of Emma Livry. Laure Fonta had the difficult task of filling the rôle of Erigone. "Like Emma Livry, she is slender, tall, and serious", wrote Gautier. "Her dancing has the character of classical correctness, and she has not needed to change anything of her predecessor's *pas*." "The main quality of her dancing", added Roqueplan, "is a quite unusual power of *parcours*, agreeably tempered by an easy precision."

That summer, Lucien Petipa met with an accident while out hunting, and as he had still not recovered by November,

Perrin decided that he should retire. Mme Petipa begged the Director to reconsider his decision. "The doctors prescribe rest", she told him, "and he will soon be cured. But to tell him at this moment that his post is lost would *kill him*. M. Perrin, I appeal to your good nature in requesting two months' leave for a talented artiste who has been and always will be your devoted and zealous servant." But her prayer was in vain.

Lucien Petipa was succeeded as *premier maître de ballet* by Henri Justament, formerly of the Porte-Saint-Martin, who was himself to be replaced by Louis Mérante in the winter of 1869.

Justament's test came when Gounod's *Faust* was produced at the Opéra on March 3rd, 1869, with a ballet inserted in the Brocken scene of the last act. Méphistophélès shows Faust a vision of a great palace, where Cléopâtre (Fonta), Hélène (Fioretti), and other courtesans are seen seated at a banquet. Cléopatre and Hélène display their charms before Faust. Then Phryné (E. Fiocre) enters, and joins in the dancing, letting drop her veils one by one until she appears in all her radiant beauty. Faust is captivated, and extends his cup to her. The vision fades.

The rôle of Hélène was the last to be created at the Opéra by Angelina Fioretti, who was to be succeeded in it by Léontine Beaugrand. On July 18th, 1870, she married Napoleone Verger, a baritone of the Théâtre Italien, at the Kensington Registry Office in London, and afterwards left the Opéra.

A curious scene was enacted at the Opéra on June 28th, 1869. *Le Prophète* was revived with two English professional roller-skaters, Mr. Elliott and Miss Frederika, in the *quadrille des patineurs*. Their technique was formidable; "two whirlwinds dancing in English", commented Achard. "How awkward and heavy the other dancers seem in comparison", remarked Gautier, who, like everyone else, was unable to resist the charm of Miss Frederika's pretty figure, with her long blonde hair floating loose about her shoulders.

Such was the level to which the ballet had sunk by 1869. Several factors had contributed to this decline: the illness of Grantzow; the delays hindering the production of Saint-Léon's new ballet; the retirement of Lucien Petipa and the failure to replace him with a choreographer of sufficient talent. According to Adice, Perrin refused to engage Jules Perrot, saying that he was "old . . . rusty . . . worn-out". In answer to protests, it was announced late in 1869 that several revivals were planned: *Giselle*, *Le Corsaire* and *La Source* for Grantzow, who was expected in 1870; *Diavolina* for Beaugrand; *Néméa* for Fioretti; and a ballet that, despite its success, no one had before had the heart to revive—*Le Papillon*. It was never announced who was to take the rôle of Farfalla, nor afterwards for certain known, for nearly all these hopes were to remain unfulfilled. But in these last few months of peace, Perrin must have been forming plans in his mind for the young Italian girl who was being coached so carefully for Saint-Léon's new ballet—Giuseppina Bozzacchi.

X

"COPPÉLIA"

"I HAVE seen many *maîtres de ballet* at the Opéra", said Perrin in his old age to the writer, Antonin Proust, " but of them all, Saint-Léon was the only one who could build up a ballet or a *divertissement* to perfection, and render it clear, concise and intelligible."

By the summer of 1867, Perrin had been Director of the Opéra for nearly five years, and of the five new ballets staged there during that period, three had been produced by Saint-Léon. When the question then arose of the next ballet to be created, Perrin's choice of choreographer fell naturally on Saint-Léon, Nuitter and Delibes being commissioned to provide the scenario and the score. These three men were a tried team : they were also the best of friends, having worked together with the utmost harmony and confidence in each other when devising *La Source* a short while before.

It was said that in writing his scenario, Nuitter had Léontine Beaugrand in mind as the model for his heroine, but that Perrin, a shrewd and prudent business man, had shrunk from the risk of launching the ballet with a star of only secondary grandeur. When, in the summer of 1868, work on the scenario and the score had sufficiently progressed to allow Saint-Léon to begin arranging the choreography, Adèle Grantzow had already been selected for the leading rôle.

The reports submitted to Perrin by the *régisseur de la danse*, Eugène Coralli, indicated the progress of the rehearsals :

"July 9th. M. Saint-Léon continues to rehearse.
"July 21st. Mlle Grantzow is to place herself at the management's disposal to-day, and to start rehearsing the new ballet to-morrow.
"July 30th. M. Saint-Léon, having no more music, has been obliged to suspend his rehearsals of the new ballet until M. Delibes gives him some more.
"August 11th. This morning, M. Saint-Léon continues his rehearsals, still the first scene.

"August 13th. This morning, M. Saint-Léon is rehearsing
the second scene of his new ballet for the second time.
"September 8th. M. Petipa has had to interrupt the
rehearsals of *Le Corsaire* and give room to M. Saint-
Léon to finish the second scene of his ballet."

Shortly afterwards, Saint-Léon returned to St. Petersburg,
leaving the ballet to be completed during his next visit to
Paris the following summer. For some time now he had been
in ill-health, and he hoped that a change of climate would
alleviate his pain. "I was deceived", he told Nuitter soon
after his arrival in Russia. "I suffer like the damned." As the
winter advanced, his condition grew alarmingly worse. "I have
just spent seventy-one nights out of my bed in unbelievable
suffering", he wrote on January 11th, 1869. "I could rest
neither lying down, nor sitting, nor standing. The only position
which comforted me was hunched up in a specially made
arm-chair, and even then I could not bear that anti-choreo-
graphic exercise for long. The cause of this disaster to me is
that I have been given in Paris and here a treatment entirely
unsuited to my illness. I have a complicated disease of the
kidneys and the intestines. But happily I have realized that
there is a God. An artist came to see me and recognized the
same symptoms from which he had been suffering. He brought
his doctor to me, and after a fortnight's treatment, I slept
in my bed for the first time on January 8th. I feel a definite
improvement, and he hopes to cure me."

When the time came for Saint-Léon to return to Paris in
1869, Adèle Grantzow was ill too, and the possibility of her
being well enough to dance that summer was so remote that
Perrin decided that the rehearsals of the new ballet must
continue with another dancer in the principal rôle. Perrin
and Saint-Léon approached Delibes and asked him to go to
Italy and search among the dancing schools there for a
ballerina to replace Grantzow.[1] Delibes returned to Paris a
few weeks later disappointed, but during his absence Perrin

---

[1] Antonin Proust, in an article, "La Danse à l'Académie Nationale de Musique"
(*Le Théâtre*, December 1898), quoted Delibes as having said: "I had written
Coppélia for Fioretti. But Fioretti was about to leave the stage, and someone had
to be found to replace her . . . etc." Although Angelina Fioretti would have made
an excellent Swanilda, the Archives of the Opéra contain no evidence that she
was ever considered for the rôle. She did not in fact retire until more than a year
after Bozzacchi had been given the part.

and Saint-Léon had found the answer to their problem just round the corner, in Mme Dominique's class in the Rue Richer. Soon Perrin was introducing Delibes to his discovery—a little brown-haired girl with laughing black eyes, called Giuseppina Bozzacchi.

.   .   .   .

The news of Perrin's decision reached Adèle Grantzow at Blankenburg, in the Harz Mountains, where she had gone to convalesce. "Mme Dominique has informed me", she wrote to him, "that you want to give the ballet, *La Poupée de Nurnberg*, this winter with Mlle Joséphine, and I am praying for the greatest success both for the young and talented girl and for the ballet itself, although I am very sorry that I have not been chosen for the rôle."

Perrin replied tactfully a few days later. "You speak of the ballet which M. Saint-Léon had composed for you, and which I am having rehearsed with Mlle Bozzacchi, so that he can complete his work", he wrote. "Although the young artiste has shown very real qualities at these rehearsals, I have as yet come to no definite decision as to the time when the ballet will be produced or the cast. . . . There can certainly be no possible comparison between an artiste of your standing, and as well placed as you with our public, and a young person who is indeed remarkably talented, but has neither the stage experience nor the authority necessary to create a rôle. . . . The greater part of the ballet has been composed for you, and no one can forget how perfect you were in it. But it has been completed for another, and perhaps Saint-Léon has not given this latter part of it as much importance as he would have done had he been working for you. Also, you know the character of the ballet—it is somewhat light and comic; and after your long absence, I would rather you reappear in a work of a more elevated and more poetic character . . . which would give your talent the opportunity of being applauded in all its facets."

In the autumn of 1869 Grantzow again wrote to Perrin. "A few words now about the questions you ask me regarding my reappearance in Paris", she began. "I agree with you completely in this matter, and also find that the ballet I had begun to study in Paris is not entirely suitable for me, considering that Saint-Léon has told me that he has completed it in quite another way than he would have done if he had been working with me. Apart from that, it will probably be necessary for you to give it during this winter, and I definitely have nothing against that."

Adèle Grantzow had quite recovered by then, and made her reappearance in St. Petersburg in Saint-Léon's new ballet, *Le Lys*. The choreographer was not deceived by the rapturous acclamations that greeted her return. "She still has charm and much intelligence", he told Perrin, "but between ourselves, she no longer has the fine qualities she showed in *Giselle* and the rehearsals of *La Source*." Shortly before the New Year, a further misfortune befell her: she slipped while rehearsing, and pulled a muscle in her left foot. Saint-Léon wrote to Nuitter that her cure would take at least a month or five weeks, and went on to suggest, for her return to Paris: "As a change, could she not be presented under a lively, sprightly aspect, which suits her admirably? Apart from M. Perrin's project, I have two or three little ideas that could be discussed: before her accident, I was beginning to produce *Pâquerette*, in which she plays the part of a roguish peasant. I thought she was very good."

About a fortnight later, on January 28th, 1870, Adèle Grantzow, who was looking forward to dancing in Paris again in the summer, wrote to Perrin. "I already know, through Saint-Léon, that you are kindly thinking of producing a new ballet for my return", she began, "and I am very glad to hear that you have not abandoned this idea and that you no longer plan to have me appear in *La Poupée de Nurnberg*. If you and Saint-Léon decide on the subject of the ballet, please do not fail to give me some details of it." The project that Perrin was considering for her return was a ballet based on some of the adventures of Don Quixote, with a score by Jean Duprato. Giving news of it in March 1870, *L'Entr'acte* remarked: "It will be strange to see our ballerinas in the rôles of Don Quixote and Sancho Panza, as apparently there are to be only *danseuses* in the cast."

This plan, however, came to nothing, for yet another, and graver, misfortune was awaiting Adèle Grantzow. A few days after she had danced in St. Petersburg on the last day of the Carnival season, she was lying critically ill with typhus fever.

For three weeks her life was in danger. In April her sister
informed Mme Dominique that she would soon be well enough
to make a private visit to Paris to see her friends, but the
following month Adèle herself wrote to Perrin from Hanover
to tell him that she had changed her plans. "It would have
been so painful", she said, "to find myself inactive before a
stage I love so much."

But the cruellest misfortune was still to come. In 1877,
shortly after becoming engaged to a Prussian cavalry officer,
she unwisely allowed an unqualified practitioner to treat a rash
on her calf. He failed to take proper antiseptic precautions, and
almost at once blood poisoning set in. The doctors did their best
to prevent its onset and, in a desperate attempt to save her life,
decided to amputate. But the pain she had endured had left her
very weak, and shortly after the operation, at half-past six in the
evening of June 7th, she who very nearly became the first
Swanilda died in the Augusta Hospital, Berlin.

Giuseppina Bozzacchi was only fifteen when Perrin selected
her to play the leading rôle in the new ballet. She was born
in Milan on November 23rd, 1853, the daughter of a skilled
bronze-founder, and, through her mother, the granddaughter
of the celebrated Dr. Rasori. It soon became evident that she
possessed unusual gifts. "At four years of age she would imitate
with the greatest accuracy the aerial postures and graceful
attitudes of the flying angels over the head of the Virgin Mary
in the Church of San Paolo. The manner in which this extraordinary vocation was first discovered is curious. Her canary
had escaped from its cage, and while others were lamenting its
loss, the little creature, with the grace and agility of a fairy,
had jumped through the window on to the leads, and was
beheld, to the great terror of the neighbours, running lightly
along the edge of the parapet, soon to bring back the canary
in triumph; and while the mother was giving way to a fit of
hysterics, the little warrior of the drama, all unconscious of
the danger, was coolly replacing the ragged boots she had
taken off for her aerial expedition."

Giuseppina began to attend dancing lessons in 1862, and
within a few months had attracted the notice of Amina
Boschetti, the prima ballerina of the Scala, who was shortly

leaving for Paris to dance at the Opéra. Encouraged, perhaps even persuaded, by Boschetti, who was anticipating a long engagement, the Bozzacchi family settled their affairs in Milan and emigrated to Paris. There Boschetti introduced Giuseppina to Mme Dominique, and for a time paid for her lessons. But after a few months Boschetti returned to Italy. Mme Dominique, however, had been quick to recognize Giuseppina's exceptional promise, and was by then already giving her individual attention. She knew that Giuseppina's family was very poor, and some time in 1865, considering that her pupil had acquired sufficient command of technique, she arranged an audition before Perrin and Saint-Léon. The two men were astonished at the child's talent, and to enable her to complete her training, Perrin at once offered her a six-year engagement with a stipulation that she was not to dance in public during the first two years. Giuseppina's father, though suffering from pneumonia, left his sick-bed to sign the contract on his daughter's behalf. "His pale smile told me", Perrin remembered afterwards, "that his end would be the sweeter for carrying with him a hope."

But for this engagement, Giuseppina would have been forced to give up attending Mme Dominique's classes and to seek work in one of the smaller theatres, for on her father's death shortly afterwards, her mother was left almost destitute, with five children, three of them infants, to support. The family were now dependent on Giuseppina's small salary and an allowance granted by the Société Italienne de Bienfaisance de Paris. As though he foresaw her future triumph, Perrin watched over Giuseppina with an almost paternal solicitude: he paid her school fees, and in July 1868, thinking she needed a change of air, arranged for her to spend a month in the country at Bois-Colombes.

Early in 1869, while Delibes was in Italy searching for a dancer to take the leading part in Saint-Léon's new ballet, Perrin remembered Giuseppina. He and Saint-Léon—and, on his return, Delibes too—visited Mme Dominique's class daily to observe the child's progress. Then one day Perrin informed Giuseppina of his decision that she was to bear the responsibility of creating this rôle for her début. Beaugrand, who was sharing the lesson, concealed her bitter disappointment and warmly congratulated Giuseppina, of whom she was very fond.

Giuseppina announced the good news to her benefactor, the Vice-President of the Société Italienne de Bienfaisance, on May 4th. "I am very happy", she wrote, "and I want you to be the first to receive the good news that M. Perrin, who has been so kind to me for nearly two years, is not content with paying for my schooling, but has just engaged me as an artiste, at a salary of 6000 francs a year. I shall have for my début a leading rôle at the Opéra, a creation, in about March. Before anything else, I beg you to convey my gratitude to the Société Italienne and the Consul, who have been so charitable towards a poor family in distress. If there had not been a good soul like you to protect me like this, God knows what would have become of us. As soon as possible after my début, I will see if I can summon all my resources—and it is my greatest wish to do so—to reimburse the Society for the whole of the sums it has up to now so generously granted me. That is not all. I renounce, as from to-day, the monthly allowance it has made me since February 15th, 1868, and I shall be very proud if one day, thanks to the future that the Opéra allows me to foresee, I can show my gratitude for so much kindness by inscribing myself, in the humble measure of my efforts, among the benefactors of the Société Italienne de Bienfaisance de Paris."

That summer, Saint-Léon pressed on rapidly with the rehearsals, as Eugène Coralli's reports to Perrin bear witness:

"May 3rd. To-day at one o'clock, M. Saint-Léon begins rehearsing with Mlle Bozzacchi.

"May 16th. Saint-Léon still in the Foyer with Bozzacchi.

"May 24th. This morning, everyone was rehearsed in Saint-Léon's ballet, the two scenes being finished.

"June 24th. M. Saint-Léon rehearsed the second act of his ballet yesterday.

"July 15th. This morning, M. Saint-Léon is rehearsing the third scene of his ballet in the Foyer.

"August 19th. M. Saint-Léon is to rehearse the whole of his ballet to-day and all the week."

Although the public's interest in the forthcoming ballet was maintained by constant announcements of its imminent production, Perrin had decided that it should not be given until Giuseppina was quite ready for the ordeal that lay before her, and certainly not before March 1870. Having been in rehearsal for two summers, the work was most thoroughly prepared by the end of August 1869, when Saint-Léon had to return to St. Petersburg.

.   .   .   .   .   .

That winter the flow of letters between Saint-Léon and Nuitter was resumed.

"Keep me well informed about M. Perrin's arrangements for the new ballet", wrote Saint-Léon on November 3rd. "A good opportunity has turned up for me in Vienna, and I am keeping five or six weeks free for whenever M. Perrin may need me for the rehearsals of the *ensemble* and corrections. I shall be available from February 1st, and consequently at his disposal. But the most important work must be prepared, and I must be given a fortnight's notice. Delibes is probably not working? Hurry him. . . . Do not rehearse too much, and if M. Justament wishes to take on this boring task, I can only be grateful to him."

On December 11th: "You leave me entirely without news of M. Perrin's arrangements. But probably nothing is settled yet. Will M. Perrin need me apart from the production of *Coppélia*? . . . Russia has never bored me more than it does now. I have decided not to extend my engagement, which ends next season. The weather this year is so terrible that, for my health, I have always to stay at home when I have finished my rehearsals."

Nuitter replied that Perrin wished Saint-Léon to arrange a *divertissement*, to the music of Weber's *L'Invitation à la valse*, for a revival of *Le Freychütz*. "I shall be leaving on the 27th", wrote Saint-Léon on January 13th, 1870. "If I can gain one or two days, I will take advantage of them by making the journey more leisurely. As soon as I arrive, I shall know M. Perrin's decision concerning the cuts in the ballet, and at about the same time I will set to work on *L'Invitation à la valse*. This delicious piece is a charming scene to arrange, following the musical idea very exactly. The music reveals or indicates the action. I am very pleased that M. Perrin is giving me the opportunity of doing it. . . . I learnt of Mérante's appointment [as *premier maître de ballet*] with great pleasure; he is an intelligent and able artiste and a charming comrade. Perhaps he will be able to help M. Perrin fill the gaps which Coralli pointed out to me. . . . *À bientôt*, my dear friend. . . . A little more patience, and I shall be hearing the whistling of the harmonious locomotive."

On January 18th: "I answer your letter of January 10th to tell you to leave to Mérante the provisionary choice of three girls to replace Morando, Ricois and Nini, for on my arrival I want to glance over everything to get a personal impression. Changes can be made afterwards, if necessary. . . . Get hold of Delibes, so that everything is ready on my arrival and I can attend to the changes, great or small, that have to be made."

Saint-Léon arrived in Paris at the end of January, and the rehearsals of the new ballet were resumed and continued into the spring. There was a brief delay in April, when the choreographer fell ill, but the work was then nearly ready, and soon afterwards the two dress rehearsals were arranged to take place on the evenings of Saturday and Sunday, May 21st and 22nd, and the first night on Wednesday, May 25th.

Saturday's dress rehearsal, devoted mainly to shortening the ballet's final scene, was held before a very small number of specially invited guests. The Minister of Fine Arts, Maurice Richard, was present, and so were the Administrator and the Vice-President of the Société Italienne de Bienfaisance, to whom Perrin had written: "You, who share with me the paternity of our dear *débutante*, must be among the first to be able to judge her marvellous progress."

Saint-Léon had ·the happy idea of reviving an old tradition of the Opéra that had long fallen into disuse, and when the curtain rose and Giuseppina saw the orchestra for the first time—until then they had rehearsed only among themselves— he took her by the hand and with a few kindly words presented her to the musicians.[1] The salvo of applause that burst from the orchestra pit and echoed round the huge, deserted auditorium was to be her earliest memory of the great Opéra stage.

At the second dress rehearsal, to which a number of journalists, *abonnés* and guests were admitted, *Le Freychütz* and *Coppélia* were played straight through and timed; it was hoped to

---

[1] Although Perrin, in his funeral oration over Giuseppina's grave, stated that this presentation was made by Saint-Léon, the *Paris Journal* at the time reported that it was made by Gevaërt, the *directeur de chant*.

compress the two works, which were to be given together and
entailed six changes of scenery, into a duration of four and a
quarter hours—a hope that was not in fact fulfilled, for the
first performance lasted for nearly five hours. Two working
lights served to illuminate the stage. In the wings on one side
stood Saint-Léon, cane in hand, his eye following every
movement, while opposite was Sacré, the chief machinist,
watching over the manipulation of the sets. Delibes sat at an
upright piano in the middle of the orchestra pit, and on his
right stood Deldevez, the deputy conductor. Perrin, followed
by the faithful and inseparable Nuitter, was hurrying from
one part of the house to another to judge the effect of the
spectacle. When the rehearsal was over, everyone went home,
tired but confident, to await the first performance on the
Wednesday, three days later.

Coppélia had now reached its final form, and the manuscript
scenario, which had been duly approved, was sent to the
printers, together with a list of the cast selected for the first
performance.[1] Nuitter had been inspired by one of Hoffmann's
tales, *Der Sandmann*, but the resemblance between this and the
scenario of *Coppélia* went no further than the name and vocation
of Coppélius; the macabre fantasy had given place to a light
comedy, whose charm lay in the simplicity of its construction.
For the principal effect of the ballet, Nuitter relied on a scene
in which a human being assumes the guise and imitates the
actions of a mechanical doll, a situation affording great scope
for the choreographer. While working on this scenario, Nuitter
had also been collaborating in writing the libretto for
Offenbach's *La Princesse de Trébizonde*—produced at the Bouffes
in December 1869—into which he introduced a somewhat
similar situation.

He set the first act of *Coppélia* in the square of a small town
in Galicia. To the left, back-stage, is Swanilda's house, painted
in bright colours like all the others except one—that of
Coppélius, whose bolted door and barred windows bear a
sinister aspect in contrast. Seeing Coppélius's daughter,
Coppélia (Irma Bourgoin), reading by a window, Swanilda

---

[1] The cast list given in the printed scenario, which is repeated in parentheses
in the *résumé* of the plot that follows, differed slightly from that of the first night.
Élise and Adèle Parent were then unable to appear, and were replaced at short
notice by Marie Pallier and Héloïse Lamy respectively.

(Bozzacchi) tries in vain to attract her attention, and is about to knock on the door of the house in her annoyance, when she hears a noise within. Coppélius (Dauty) appears at a lower window. At the same time, Swanilda sees her *fiancé*, Frantz (E. Fiocre), whom she suspects of a secret admiration for Coppélia, and concealing herself, watches him bow to her rival, who bows stiffly back. Swanilda then notices Coppélius leering from his window, and angrily wonders whether he is plotting to lure Frantz into his house. She disguises her feelings and runs into the open, chasing a butterfly. Frantz sees her, and catching the insect, stabs it with a pin and triumphantly attaches it to his collar, only to be reproached by Swanilda for having killed it. She then accuses him of having deceived her, and refuses to listen to his explanations. At that moment the Burgomaster (E. Cornet) arrives, followed by a crowd of people, both young and old, whom he invites to a festival to inaugurate a bell presented to the town by the lord of the manor. Suddenly strange noises are heard from Coppélius's house, and a reddish light glows behind the windows. The fear of the girls is soon allayed when someone [1] explains that it is only crazy Coppélius at his forge. Seeing Swanilda, the Burgomaster tells her that the lord of the manor is giving dowries to several engaged couples who are being married the next day, and invites her to wed Frantz. She replies by relating the story of an ear of corn which reveals all secrets. She picks an ear; Frantz can hear nothing from it, but a friend tells her that he can hear its message distinctly. Swanilda angrily breaks the ear, telling Frantz that all is over between them. Frantz sadly walks away, and while the health of the lord of the manor is being toasted, Swanilda and her companions dance a *thème slave varié*, after which everybody joins in a *czardas*. Night falls, and the crowd disperses. Coppélius then emerges from his house, locking the door behind him. He is at once set upon by a band of youths, from whom he at length manages to escape. Swanilda reappears, saying goodnight to her companions. One of the girls finds Coppélius's key, which he has dropped in his skirmish with the youths. Swanilda is tempted to use it to see her rival, but she hesitates. Then, seeing Frantz in the shadow of the trees, her jealousy returns, and she and her companions

---

[1] Although the scenario does not indicate it, the person who gives this explanation is Frantz's mother, Nettchen. This rôle was created by Mlle Aline.

enter the mysterious house. Frantz creeps across the square with a ladder, which he leans against the wall of Coppélius's house. As he begins to climb, he hears Coppélius returning in search of his key, and nimbly jumping to the ground, makes his escape.

The first scene of the second act takes place in Coppélius's workshop. Placed round the room are several automatons: an old white-bearded Persian reading a volume at a table (Ganforini), a menacing negro (a lifeless figure), a cymbalist sitting on a cushion (Lavigne, a young boy), and a large Chinaman with a dulcimer (Petit). Nervously, Swanilda and her companions enter the room by a staircase at the back. Then, plucking up courage, Swanilda draws back a curtain at the side and reveals Coppélia. She soon finds that the object of Frantz's admiration is nothing more than a mechanical doll. All fear is gone now, and the girls dance merrily, operating the mechanism of the figures. Suddenly they are interrupted by the return of Coppélius. They all escape, except Swanilda, who, unseen by Coppélius, hides behind the curtain that conceals Coppélia. Having, as he thinks, rid his house of intruders, Coppélius sees Frantz entering through the half-open window at the back. He allows him to enter, and seizes him as he creeps towards Coppélia's alcove. Frantz tries to make his way back to the window, but the old man bars his way and demands an explanation. Frantz admits that he is in love, and Coppélius invites him to take wine with him. He pours out two glasses, offers one to Frantz and, unobserved, throws away the contents of the other. Frantz tries to stagger towards Coppélia, but slumps over a table in a stupor. With a gesture of triumph, Coppélius consults a book of magic, and then wheels Coppélia to the table. He makes as though to draw out the living force from Frantz and transfer it to the doll, which moves, at first mechanically, but later, with the application of more magic, becoming more and more human until finally it might really be a woman. Coppélius is beside himself with delight, but soon discovers that his creation has become dangerously capricious. He tries to calm her by giving her first a mantilla and then a tartan scarf, with which she dances a *manola* and a *gigue*, but this is only a temporary expedient. In desperation, he pushes her back on to her pedestal, and wheels her into the alcove. Frantz is now awakening. Coppélius orders him to leave. Suddenly the tune that accompanies the movements of the automatons is heard: Swanilda, who has been impersonating Coppélia all the time, has set the doll in its awkward motion. Before she and Frantz make their escape,[1] she starts two more going. Coppélius realizes that he has been fooled, and falls senseless among his automatons, which continue their movements as though deriding their master's grief.

The last scene is set in the grounds of the manor. The bell stands at the back of the stage, behind an allegorical car on which the various players who are to take part in the festival are grouped. After the blessing of the bell, the priests are presenting the betrothed couples—among whom are Swanilda and Frantz, now reconciled—to the lord of the manor (F. Mérante), when Coppélius arrives, angrily complaining. Swanilda offers to pay for the damage with her dowry, but the lord of the manor stops her and throws Coppélius a purse. The signal is then given for the festival to begin. The bent figure of Time hands his hour-glass to a young bell-ringer (L. Mérante) and commands him to animate the players. The *divertissement* begins.

(1) *Valse des heures*. The Hours of Morning.

(2) *L'Aurore*. Dawn (Fonta) appears surrounded by flowers, and the Hours of Morning dance round her.

(3) *La Prière*. Prayer (A. Mérante) blesses the new day and rises into the heavens.

(4) *Le Travail (La Fileuse)*. At the command of the bell-ringer, the Hours of Morning and Dawn give place to the Hours of Day. It is the time for work: a spinner (Villiers) and harvest-women (Pallier, A. Parent) begin their tasks.

(5) *L'Hymen (Noce Villageoise)*. The procession of Hymen (Ribet), bearing her torch, approaches. Accompanied by Cupid (Biot), she presides at a village wedding.

(6) *La Discorde et la Guerre*. This happy scene is followed by the appearance of Discord (L. Marquet), bringing in her wake War (Montaubry, Rust). Arms are unsheathed, and a fiery glow lights the darkened sky.

(7) *La Paix*. Peace (E. Parent) appears, carrying an olive branch. All is calmed. *Danse de fête, pas seul* by Bozzacchi.

---

[1] Although no mode of exit is specified in the scenario, Paul de Saint-Victor, in his review in *La Liberté* (May 30th, 1870), twice mentioned that Swanilda and Frantz made their escape through the window at the back and down the ladder.

(8) *Galop Final*. The Hours of Evening and of Night, and two
   follies (Stoïkoff, Invernizzi) appear, leading the procession of Pleasure (Bozzacchi). The final *ballabile* is
   danced by the whole company.

Coppélia had undergone many developments during the
many months of preparation. Its title had been finally decided
upon only shortly before the ballet was produced; in its early
stages it was called *La Poupée de Nurnberg*, and although it was
occasionally referred to as *Coppélia* during 1869, another title,
La Fille aux yeux d'émail, which eventually became the sub-title,
was being considered in the winter of 1869–70. There had been
uncertainty, too, as to the name of the principal character:
first she was Olympia, then, in the autumn of 1869, she became
Antonia, then Nani, and only in the spring of 1870 was she
finally baptized as Swanilda.

Saint-Léon's skill at adapting national dances and weaving
them into his ballets was turned to good account in the *czardas*
in Act I, which repeated the success he had obtained with the
hongroise in *Néméa*. He had hoped to infuse some authentic
Hungarian fire into this dance, and had written to Nuitter in
September 1869: "One of these days you will receive a card
of mine which will be brought to you by one named Bekefy,
a dancer of Hungarian and Slav *pas*—in short, of *pas de genre*.
He is not a bad mime, and is gay enough in comic things.
There is a shortage of men in the ballet personnel; perhaps
use could be made of him. If he comes, please speak to
M. Perrin about him. I do not think he will ask for much, and
he has *chic*, which our own Zephyrs have not, in *pas slaves*. . . .
I was forgetting—as a *danseur noble*, not strong.' Bekefy was
not engaged, but the *czardas* was received none the less warmly.
It was danced, wrote Gautier, "with a verve and energy that
reminded us of the great evenings in St. Petersburg. . . . An
unusual success for a *pas d'ensemble*."

The *divertissement* in the last scene, which was first to be
shortened and later, in 1872, omitted altogether, was planned
on a large scale and included, as well as the action, groups
performed by children: sleeping peasants, praying peasants,
harvesters and hay-makers, a nocturnal procession, and
peasants being attacked by soldiers.

The expense of mounting *Coppélia* was not unusually large,

the final account, which excluded normal overheads and salaries, being summarized:

Copying the music	2,474.10	francs
Rehearsals	2,104.70	,,
Properties	251.00	,,
Costumes	29,523.12	,,
Scenery	3,293.12	,,
TOTAL	37,646.04	,,

As the figures show, this relatively small cost was achieved by economies in scenery. Only one new set had been designed—that of the second scene, Coppélius's workshop, which was by Despléchin and Lavastre; for the first and last scenes respectively, the sets for *Le Roi d'Yvetot* and Act II, Scene 1, of *L'Étoile de Messine* were taken from store and touched up by Cambon. Nor were all the costume designs original: Swanilda's first costume, for instance, was made from the sketch for Zina Mérante's costume in the 1863 revival of *Giselle*.

. . . .

On the Wednesday evening, May 25th, 1870, a distinguished audience assembled in the Opéra to witness the first performance of *Coppélia*. In the boxes could be seen Camille Doucet, the academician . . . the Turkish Ambassador . . . Paul Daru, President of the Jockey . . . the Duc de Persigny, a close friend of the Emperor . . . the Earl of Craven . . . Alfred Musard, the popular orchestra conductor, and his beautiful American wife, her dress glinting with diamonds. In the amphitheatre was a gathering of theatrical personalities: Mme Gueymard, Marie Sass, Rosine Bloch, Bernardine Hamakers of the Opéra . . . Aimée Desclée, who had recently created the title-rôle of *Froufrou* . . . Zulma Bouffar of the Variétés . . . Adeline Plunkett and her sister, Eugénie Doche . . . Ernestine Urban, then *prima mima* of the Théâtre Italien. Among the gentlemen in the orchestra stalls, to which ladies were not admitted, were Nigra, the Italian Ambassador . . . the son of Théophile Gautier . . . Flotow, the composer of *Marta* . . . Edmond About, the author . . . Charles Garnier, the architect of the new Opéra.

This evening marked the last visit of Napoleon III to the Opéra. The Imperial Box was empty when, at half-past seven, the orchestra struck up the overture to *Le Freychütz*; and the second act of the opera was well under way when the Emperor, who was noticed to be in particularly good spirits, appeared. As soon as the Imperial party arrived, the leader of the *claque*, following the usual custom, stood up and shouted, "*Vive l'Empereur!*" His cry was taken up by his men and a large proportion of the audience, but one section, more intolerant than the rest, resented this interruption, and their angry cries of "*sh!*" were heard plainly throughout the house.

Saint-Léon's *divertissement*, *L'Invitation à la valse*, had been inserted in the third act of *Le Freychütz*, the leading parts being taken by Louis Mérante and Léontine Beaugrand. "Mérante is an intrepid and graceful dancer", commented Jouvin, "and Mlle Beaugrand 'vocalizes' vigorously with her feet. Her dancing is forceful, correct, and, where necessary, *athletic.*"

During the interval between the opera and the ballet the Emperor entered a small box, adjoining the Imperial Box and overlooking the stage from behind the curtain, and from there, unobserved, watched the stage being set for the first act of *Coppélia*. His intention had been made known beforehand to Perrin, who purposely engaged Giuseppina and the Italian Ambassador in conversation in full view of the little box. The Emperor only rejoined the Empress when the order was given for the rising of the curtain.

The success, both of the new ballet and of the new dancer, was immediate and unequivocal. Choreographically, *Coppélia* was considered to be one of Saint-Léon's best works, remarkable in particular for the originality and elegance of the *pas d'ensemble*, while Delibes' melodious score met with an acclamation that was to be confirmed by the test of time. The ballet's one failing was the length and irrelevancy of the final *divertissement*. Many of the boxes and seats were empty when the curtain finally rang down, and in consequence Perrin ordered this scene to be shortened still further for the second performance.

Seldom had a *débutante* been received so enthusiastically as was Giuseppina Bozzacchi on this first performance of *Coppélia*. In the very suddenness of her triumph, she seemed at a loss to acknowledge the tumultuous ovation that greeted her. She faced the audience smiling, her head held high with pride, having quite forgotten in the intoxication of the moment the conventional *révérence* that Mme Dominique had taught her; and when the final curtain had fallen and she came to take her first call with Eugénie Fiocre, she paid no attention to the Emperor, who was applauding her warmly, until her partner took her by the hand and presented her to the Imperial Box. In the second scene, the audience had insisted on her repeating the *gigue*, after which Dauty, who was playing Coppélius, had led her forward to bow, first to the public, then to the Emperor. Her triumph affected her as it might a child: she was happy, excited, bewildered, and in the interval, when many gentlemen made their way to the Foyer de la Danse to pay homage to her, they found her laughing and playing with her friends of the *corps de ballet* as though nothing had happened. When the performance was over, she was taken to the Imperial Box and presented to Their Majesties.

Giuseppina appeared younger than her sixteen and a half years. She was a small person, delicate and supple in build, with expressive, intelligent features, still childlike in their prettiness, illumined by two large black eyes gleaming like gems against her smooth, pale complexion. She danced with the assurance of a ballerina of many years' experience, tireless, betraying nothing of the toil of the class-room. Although her style was perhaps still not fully formed, many critics were carried away by her freshness, her artlessness, her precocious talent. "Mlle Bozzacchi is quite simply a little marvel", said one; she "will be a Carlotta Grisi", prophesied another; Mlle Bozzacchi, added yet another, "has quite dried the tears of those old balletomanes who bewailed Carlotta Grisi and would not be consoled". She was a pupil of Mme Dominique, who had formed Emma Livry, and the greatest compliment of all came from Escudier, who wrote: "La Bozzacchi dances with as much grace as Emma Livry, and with more naïvety." Like Livry's, Giuseppina's style was noble and chaste, a true product of the classical French school, as opposed to the more gymnastic Italian school; there was a moderation in her movement which she observed, wrote Albert de Lasalle, "to the point where she truly dances, and does not leap about and do all those dangerous *cabrioles* which have become fashionable these last few years". Her *pointe* work was rapid, precise, firm, yet delicate; her agility and lightness gave an unusual brilliance to her *parcours*; her steadiness in *temps d'aplomb* was remarkable, her *tacqueté* of a perfect finish. She was only found a little wanting in elevation and *ballon.*

She danced as though for pleasure, not only with her feet, but with her arms, her eyes, her whole person. Amédée Achard noticed her hands particularly. "Mlle Bozzacchi", he wrote, "has dancing hands, expressive hands, hands that are alive, that thrill, quiver, and do not fall lifeless amid the folds of muslin, but play an active and intelligent part in the dialogue of her miming."

While as a dancer she had acquired the best qualities of the French school under the tuition of Mme Dominique, her Italian temperament had enabled her to develop into a strong mime, comprehending the essence of the rôle and unafraid of expressing herself with passion. In the *pas de la paille* in the first act, wrote Gautier, "her charming face expresses in turn uneasiness, joy, anger and love, with extremely delicate shading, according to the confidences of the ear of corn." The second scene, in which she imitates the doll, afforded her a great opportunity to display her talent. "The *danseuse* rises", described Charles Yriarte, "and with that stiffness peculiar to Nuremberg toys, performs the jerky, unknowing gestures of an automaton. Then, little by little, by an artifice of the plot, the dry, metallic, automatic movement loses its stiffness, and by a gradation that is a masterpiece of miming, passes from the immobility of a statue to the vivacity, the lightness, the whirling of the liveliest and most supple dancer." "She must be seen playing the doll", added Saint-Victor, "first, imitating a statue, and then darting out of this stiff envelope, like a butterfly from its chrysalis, and filling the stage with her aerial leaps. In all this second scene, she gives the impression of a dainty, frolicsome little fairy entering a sorcerer's laboratory, bringing light and disorder, filling it with her tricks and her malice, and then flying out through the open window."

By her side, François Édouard Dauty was creating the rôle of Coppélius at the age of sixty-two. Off the stage he always looked very sad and serious, and was often being mistaken for the *curé* of the Madeleine, whom he greatly resembled; but once he assumed a rôle, he became completely transformed. "M. Dauty makes a good caricature out of the character of Coppélius", wrote Francisque Sarcey. "His buffoonery is very funny and has the rare quality of being distinguished." Like more than one member of the original cast of *Coppélia*, he was not to survive another twelve months; he died at his home, No. 14 Rue de Moscou, during the last days of the Commune, on May 11th, 1871.

.　　　.　　　.　　　.　　　.

On Friday, May 27th, Giuseppina danced in *Coppélia* for the second time, and, it was said, gave an even better performance than her first. At the third performance the following Monday, she was beginning to show signs of fatigue, but there was then a brief respite—until the Friday—before her. The demand for seats for the fourth performance was so great that several rows of the pit had to be transformed into orchestra stalls.

Giuseppina's sudden success was not unnaturally resented by some of the less fortunate and less talented members of the *corps de ballet*. One hot summer afternoon, as Perrin was sitting in his office with the windows open and the shutters closed, he overheard several of Giuseppina's companions discussing her in the courtyard below. One of them remarked that she hoped she would break her leg, and when, a minute later, Giuseppina arrived, welcomed her with a kiss. Shortly afterwards Giuseppina entered Perrin's room. "Come here, my child", he said, taking his handkerchief from his pocket. "Let me wipe away the stain from your cheek."

Others were more generous, for Giuseppina remained unspoilt by the adulation that was now being lavished upon her. Within a few weeks of her début, somebody had adapted the song of the Turcos, the Algerian infantry, and soon everyone was singing the words:

> *Le chic exquis*
> *Par Bozzacchi*
> *Acquis,*
> *Elle le doit à qui?*
> *À Domini,*
> *À Madame Domini!*

Even the formidable orchestra was charmed by Giuseppina's simplicity and lack of affectation, and presented her one day with a magnificent bouquet of white flowers as a token of their admiration. In return, Giuseppina gave each musician a photograph of herself, on which she had written: "To M. —— of the Opéra orchestra, a souvenir of *Coppélia*. G. Bozzacchi."

One of her first thoughts after her triumph had been to send the Société Italienne de Bienfaisance a donation of 100 francs in gratitude for its help to her in the past, and to promise more when her salary permitted. The letter that accompanied this sum, and also that which she had written in May 1869, were read at the Society's annual general meeting on June 3rd, which removed all doubts as to their authenticity that had been raised by their impeccable style: the letters were genuine, although undoubtedly she had received guidance in composing them, for her command of French was very limited.

Nigra, the Italian Ambassador and the Honorary President of the Society, was the first person outside the management of the Opéra to be officially told, at the end of June, that Giuseppina had been given a new contract. This contract bound her to the Opéra for a period of five years as *première danseuse*, doubling her salary to 12,000 francs for the first year, with rises to 15,000, 18,000 and 24,000 francs at the end of the first, second and third years. Despite this increase in their income, however, the Bozzacchi family still found life very difficult. There were numerous debts to pay, and the first monthly sum of 1000 francs received by Mme Bozzacchi for her daughter only served to pay off the most pressing of these. Perrin came to their aid with a timely loan of 500 francs. Economies were still necessary. Though exhausted after the performance, Giuseppina nearly always covered the few hundred yards to her home in the Passage Saulnier on foot to save a cab fare. It was only after her ninth appearance on June 24th, during which she had accidentally slipped and fallen during the *gigue*, that she was at last persuaded, for once, to break this self-imposed rule.

A fortnight after the first night of *Coppélia*, Saint-Léon again fell seriously ill, and was advised by his doctor to spend a month at a spa. Before he left, he invited Giuseppina to stay at his country house in Enghien during his absence, telling her that his servants would be at her disposal. She accepted his offer with joy, and within a few days was installed in the house with her mother and a married sister and her baby. On her finger was a diamond ring which Saint-Léon had given her as a souvenir of her triumph.

In the early days of July the news broke that a Prussian prince had been offered and had accepted the crown of Spain, and the long pent-up feeling of exasperation at the conceit and growing ambition of Prussia found violent expression in France. The Prussophobe Foreign Minister, the Duc de Gramont, spoke in the Chamber of his country's duty to preserve its interests and its honour, and his cry was eagerly taken up: stirring calls filled the newspapers, and the *Marseillaise* was sung in the streets. Tension between the two countries was mounting rapidly to crisis pitch; the clouds of war were gathering.

Few could believe that Prussia would go so far as to risk armed conflict, and signs of her yielding in the face of France's firm determination were constantly being sought. After Giuseppina had danced in *Coppélia* for the twelfth time on July 8th, it was hopefully reported that "the presence of Count Solms, the Prussian *chargé d'affaires*, was in itself a presage that lightened the 'dark clouds'. Furthermore, the amiable diplomat reassured his anxious friends by looking at La Bozzacchi through his opera-glasses. When, in the last scene, La Bozzacchi *tacqueté'd* the *pas de la paix*, his friends once again watched Count Solms, who, with a slight inclination of his head and the glimmer of a smile, seemed to be replying, 'But yes . . . peace, peace!'"

Such optimism was unfortunately unjustified, for Bismarck was playing his hand relentlessly and unscrupulously in Berlin, plotting to create a situation in which France would have no choice but to declare war on Prussia. By July 19th he had succeeded; on that day the fatal declaration was made. A few days later, a sick Emperor left his capital for the last time to place himself at the head of his soldiers. Cheering crowds accompanied the battalions as they entrained for the frontier, and soon the first *communiqués*, optimistic in tone, were being placarded on the walls of Paris.

Up to the outbreak of war Giuseppina had appeared in *Coppélia* fourteen times in seven weeks, and Perrin decided that she should now take a rest. *La Muette de Portici* was therefore announced to take its place, with Eugénie Fiocre as Fenella and Laure Fonta dancing in the *pas de l'Uccellatore*. By the time that *Coppélia* returned to the bill, on Friday, August 12th, the war situation had become suddenly critical. On the previous

Sunday, rumours of a great victory announced at the Bourse the day before were belied by a proclamation giving the bad news of defeats at Wissembourg, Frœschwiller and Forbach. There had been demonstrations against the régime on the Tuesday, and a new Cabinet had been formed on the Wednesday. Worse news was to follow. Early in the morning of September 4th it was learnt that Marshal MacMahon's army of 80,000 men had surrendered at Sedan, and that the Emperor was a prisoner in German hands. That afternoon, the Empress-Regent escaped the clutches of the mob clamouring outside the Tuileries, and began her flight into exile.

A few days before, on Wednesday, August 31st, Giuseppina had danced in *Coppélia* for the eighteenth and last time, before the Opéra was closed for the duration of the war. Then, late in the evening of Friday, September 2nd, Saint-Léon had a sudden heart attack in a little *café-divan* he was in the habit of frequenting in the Passage de l'Opéra. He was dead before his friends could bring him back to his home in the Rue de Laval. His funeral took place a few days later in the Lutheran church in the Rue Chauchat. Perrin and Jules Perrot were among the mourners, and Delibes, playing the organ, intro- duced an excerpt from the score of *Néméa* as the coffin was being borne out of the church on its journey to the Montmartre Cemetery.[1]

The Germans completed the investment of the capital on September 18th. Paris became an armed camp almost over-night. The railways were no longer running, and all available rolling stock was being converted into temporary dwellings for the refugees who were streaming into the city from the neighbouring countryside. Long lines of horses, field guns, ammunition limbers and *mitrailleuses* filled the Tuileries Gardens, where crowds gathered daily to watch the gunners drilling. A cartridge factory was improvised in the Halles; rooms were set aside in the Théâtre Français for the reception of wounded; everywhere men were to be seen carrying rifles. Despite an attempt at control, food prices soared as such delicacies as beef and mutton, and later even dogs and cats, grew scarce; in the middle of November a sewer rat at three

---

[1] On October 19th, 1881, the remains of Saint-Léon, his mother and his father were removed to Père-Lachaise. A concession for five years was purchased, on the expiry of which, as no further payment was made, the remains were removed to the *fosse commune*.

francs was a bargain! As winter drew on, shortage of fuel
was added to the Parisians' hardships; the supply of gas was
cut off, and when the first snow came in November there was
a frenzied felling of trees in the city.

Giuseppina had been begged to leave Paris before the
German ring had closed, but she preferred to remain in the
beleaguered city with her family. Many of her comrades
stayed, too, and though no salaries were being paid by the
Opéra, continued to attend classes. As the winter drew on,
many arrived famished and blue with cold, and their numbers
began to diminish as some fell ill with bronchitis or pleurisy.

One day in November the actress Marie Colombier visited
the class in which Giuseppina was working. The unhappiness
of the little Italian girl created a painful impression on her.
That same evening, Charles Bocher, an *abonné* of the Opéra,
dined at her apartment. Haunted by the memory of Giuseppina,
Marie described the class she had watched, and Bocher told
her that the child's despair was due not only to the shattering
of her hopes by the war but also to the straitened circumstances
to which she and her family had been reduced. Marie's heart
bled at the thought of the misery which Giuseppina was
suffering, a misery which to some extent her own sister, a
colleague of Giuseppina's, might have shared, were she not
safe in the country. Determined to do all she could to help,
Marie went next day to the Passage Saulnier, where, on the
fifth floor of No. 20, the Bozzacchi family lived: "a dark
apartment in a sad house", she described it afterwards. For
the sake of her sister, Marie offered to lend Giuseppina whatever
she might need. Giuseppina was touched by this unexpected
kindness, but declined the offer, for the Italian Embassy had
just heard of her family's plight and come to their assistance.

Shortly afterwards, on Sunday, November 20th, Giuseppina
felt unwell and was put to bed. Two days later the seriousness
of her condition could no longer be doubted. Insufficiently
nourished, her delicate frame had been unable to withstand
the rigours of the siege, let alone resist the ravages of smallpox.
Perrin was sent for, and came at once to see her, bringing a
doctor with him. But the fever was too far advanced for any
hope of recovery to be held; and at half-past eight on the
morning of her seventeenth birthday, November 23rd, 1870,
Giuseppina died.

It had been her last wish that the presents she had received after her début should be buried with her, and these were placed by her body in the coffin. She was buried on the 25th. The funeral procession left the Passage Saulnier shortly before midday. Annette, Dorina and Élisa Mérante held the cordons of the pall, and a large crowd of mourners followed the hearse to the Church of Saint-Eugène—Perrin, Nuitter, the octogenarian Auber, noblemen, *abonnés*, stage-hands, journalists, artistes. The coffin was taken into the church and placed before the High Altar while Low Mass was said. It was covered with a profusion of white flowers, among which were a bouquet and crown made of orange-blossom and a crown bearing a star with the inscription, *Giuseppina Bozzacchi, Étoile de l'Opéra.* When the short ceremony was over, the coffin was borne out of the church to the strains of a funeral march improvised on the organ by Delibes, in which could be recognized several melodies from *Coppélia.*

The procession continued its journey to the Montmartre Cemetery, where someone had planted three rows of white marguerites around the open grave. After prayers had been said, and a *De Profundis* chanted by three male singers of the Opéra, Perrin stepped forward to deliver the funeral oration.

"Already more than once", he began, "have I had the mournful duty of bidding, on your behalf, the last farewell to those who have been dear to you. But never have I felt my heart racked with a deeper emotion. The grim times through which we are passing certainly spare us no suffering. Anguish, tears, shame have become our daily bread. Yet now, amid these public misfortunes and this incessant and vast mourning, the cruellest and most unforeseen of deaths, the death of this child who was only just beginning to live, overwhelms us with a sorrow more acute than all the others. Those who have done their work, who have lived their lives, can pass away and disappear. That is the hard law, but the inevitable law—the expected arrest of nature. . . .

"Alas! within two months we have accompanied both master and pupil to their last resting-place. But the man had struggled for years against suffering, while the child succumbed to the first attack of a terrible malady, struck down like a reed snapped in a thunderstorm. Poor, dear child! All the brilliance of her youth, her budding beauty, that blossoming of all gifts and all charms . . . are buried for ever in this pitiless coffin. . . .

"May these flowers", he concluded, "these last pale flowers of this fateful year, blooming on our invaded soil beneath our besieged ramparts, lie close and whisper our farewell. These pure emblems of candour, youth and innocence can be no more chaste, no more immaculate, than was the charming being who is to-day no more than a memory, and who bore the name—Giuseppina Bozzacchi."

Their hearts heavy with sorrow, the mourners then parted and went their ways. They had attended the close of the Romantic Ballet; they had buried a hope. For when, the following summer, the Opéra opened its doors again, things were very different. New faces had taken the place of the old: Perrin was no longer at the head; Saint-Léon was mourned and sadly missed; Marie Taglioni was to be seen no more in the Rue Richer; and the days of the opera house in the Rue Le Peletier—the scene of so many glories of the Romantic Ballet—were numbered, for soon it was to be superseded by Garnier's palatial new building on the Boulevard. And who knows but that the greatest loss of all did not lie in the *fosse commune* of the Montmartre Cemetery, beneath a simple wooden cross, which, not three years later, was to be found neglected among the weeds, its proud inscription, *Étoile de l'Opéra*, barely decipherable—a monument to the fickle and ungrateful memory of man.

APPENDIX A

PREMIERS MAÎTRES DE BALLET, RÉGISSEURS DE LA DANSE, AND
PROFESSEURS DE LA CLASSE DE PERFECTIONNEMENT AT THE PARIS
OPÉRA BETWEEN OCTOBER 1847 AND SEPTEMBER 1870

PREMIERS MAÎTRES DE BALLET

(1847). J. Coralli [1]
1850. Saint-Léon
1853. Mazilier
1860. L. Petipa
1868. Justament
1869. Mérante

RÉGISSEURS DE LA DANSE

1847. J.-B. C. Desplaces
1848. Coulon
1850. Châtillon
1855. Berthier
1867. E. Coralli
1870. Pluque

PROFESSEURS DE LA CLASSE DE PERFECTIONNEMENT

(1847). Coulon
1851. Saint-Léon
1853. Gosselin
1860. Marie Taglioni

---

[1] The last ballet arranged by Jean Coralli was *Ozaï*, in April 1847. He continued as titular *premier maître de ballet* until the end of May 1850, although the burden of his functions was borne by Mazilier, Perrot and A. Mabille.

APPENDIX B

The periods given immediately after their names are those during which they were dancing as *sujets*, engagements solely as *maître de ballet* or teacher being ignored.

Dates of birth and death indicated with a † have been verified from certificates.

Beaugrand, Léontine, 1861–80.
    b. Paris, April 26th, 1842.   *d.* Paris, May 27th, 1925.
Beretta, Caterina, 1855–57.
    b. Milan, December 8th, 1839.   *d.* Milan, January 1911.
Besson, Mathilde, 1853.
Bogdanova, Nadezhda, 1851–55, 1865.
    b. Russia, 1834.   *d.* Russia, September 15th, 1897.
Boschetti, Amina, 1864.
    b. Milan, 1836.   *d.* Naples, January 2nd, 1881.
Bozzacchi, Giuseppina, 1870.
    b. Milan, November 23rd, 1853.   *d.* Paris, November 23rd, 1870.†
Cerrito, Fanny, 1847–55.
    b. Naples, May 11th, 1817.†   *d.* Paris, May 6th, 1909.†
Clavelle, Hortense, 1857.
Cucchi, Claudina, 1855–58.
    b. Milan, March 20th, 1838.   *d.* Milan, March 10th, 1913.
Dor, Henriette, 1867.
    b. 1844.   *d.* Neuilly-sur-Seine, March 1886.
Dumilâtre, Adèle, 1840–48.
    b. Paris, June 30th, 1821.   *d.* Paris, May 4th, 1909.†
Emarot, Célestine, 1845–57.
    b. Dijon, March 18th, 1824.   *d.* Paris, October 7th, 1892.
Fabbri, Flora, 1845–51.
    b. Florence.
Ferraris, Amalia, 1856–63.
    b. Voghera, 1830.   *d.* Florence, February 8th, 1904.
Fiocre, Eugénie, 1864–75.
    b. Paris, July 2nd, 1845.   *d.* 1908.
Fioretti, Angelina, 1863–70.
    b. 1846.   *d.* Milan, July 1879.
Fonta, Laure, 1863–81.
Forli, Regina, 1852–55.
Friedberg, Katrine, 1858.

Fuoco, Sofia, 1846–50.
    b. Milan, January 16th, 1830.   *d*. Carate Lario, June 4th, 1916.
Grantzow, Adèle, 1866–68.
    b. Brunswick, January 1st, 1845.   *d*. Berlin, June 7th, 1877.
Grisi, Carlotta, 1841–49.
    b. Visinida, June 28th, 1819.†   *d*. near Geneva, May 20th, 1899.
Guy-Stéphan, Marie, 1840–41, 1853–55.
    b. 1818.   *d*. Paris, August 21st, 1873.
Karlitski, Isabelle, 1856.
Legrain, Victorine, 1852–57.
Livry, Emma, 1858–62.
    b. Paris, September 24th, 1842.   *d*. Neuilly-sur-Seine, July 26th, 1863.†
Maria [Jacob], 1837–49.
    b. *c*. 1818.
Marquet, Louise, 1851–79.
    b. Tours, 1830.   *d*. Paris, December 22nd, 1890.†
Mérante, Annette, 1866–77.
Mérante, Zina, 1857–63.
    b. Moscow, 1832.   *d*. Courbevoie, September 13th, 1890.†
Muravieva, Martha, 1863–64.
    b. Russia, July 11th, 1838.   *d*. Russia, April 27th, 1879.
Petipa, Marie, 1861–62.
    b. St. Petersburg, February 27th, 1836.   *d*. Novocherkassk, April 5th, 1882.
Pitteri, Giovannina, 1859.
Plunkett, Adeline, 1845–52, 1855–57.
    b. Brussels, March 31st, 1824.   *d*. Paris, November 8th, 1910.†
Priora, Olimpia, 1851–54.
    b. Venice, June 26th, 1836.
Richard, Zina (*see* Mérante, Zina)
Robert, Élisabeth, 1843–55.
    b. *c*. 1823.
Rosati, Carolina, 1853–59.
    b. Bologna, December 13th, 1826.   *d*. Cannes, May 1905.
Salvioni, Guglielmina, 1864–67.
Sanlaville, Marie, 1864–69, 1872–89.
Taglioni, Louise, 1848–57.
    b. Naples, March 13th, 1823.   *d*. Cutrofiano (Lecce), April 1893.
Urban, Ernestine, 1863–64.
Vernon, Marie, 1862–64.

Beauchet, Magloire, 1851–64.

    d. Paris, May 17th, 1875.

Berthier, Francisque Garnier, 1847–67, 1871–74.

    b. Lyons, 1813.   *d.* Paris, December 27th, 1875.

Chapuy, Alfred, 1855–66.

    b. Bastide (Gironde), August 29th, 1829.   *d.* Brussels, June 2nd, 1871.

Kshesinski, Felix, 1862.

    b. Russia, November 17th, 1823.   *d.* Russia, June 16th, 1905.

Mazilier, Joseph, 1830–48.

    b. Marseilles, 1797.   *d.* Paris, May 19th, 1868.†

Mérante, Louis, 1848–87.

    b. Paris, July 27th, 1828.†   *d.* Courbevoie, July 17th, 1887.†

Perrot, Jules, 1830–35, 1849.

    b. Lyons, August 18th, 1810.†   *d.* Paramé, August 24th, 1892.

Petipa, Lucien, 1839–62.

    b. Marseilles, December 22nd, 1815.   *d.* Versailles, July 7th, 1898.

Saint-Léon, Arthur, 1847–52.

    b. Paris, September 17th, 1821.†   *d.* Paris, September 2nd, 1870.†

Segarelli, Domenico, 1856–58.

    b. Naples, August 3rd, 1820.   *d.* Turin, March, 1860.

BALLETS FIRST PERFORMED AT THE PARIS OPÉRA BETWEEN OCTOBER 1847 AND SEPTEMBER 1870

Date of First Performance	Title of Ballet	Description	Author of Scenario	Choreographer	Composer	Stage Designers	Costume Designer	Principal Dancers	Number of Performances	Time in Repertory	Average Receipts over First 10 (or Less) Performances
20 Oct. 1847	La Fille de marbre	BP, 2a 3s	Saint-Léon, after Deshayes Dumanoir	Saint-Léon	[Costa,] Pugni	Cambon, Thierry	Lormier	Cerrito; Saint-Léon	20	1847–49	8,254.58 fr.
16 Feb. 1848	Griseldis, ou les Cinq sens	BP, 3a 5s	Mazilier	Mazilier	Adam	Cambon, Thierry	Lormier	Grisi; L. Petipa	14	1848	4,721.68 "
21 Aug. 1848	Nisida, ou les Amazones des Açores	BP, 2a 3s	Deligny	A. Mabille	Benoist	Philastre, Cambon, Thierry	Lormier	Plunkett, Maria; L. Petipa	19	1848–49	2,481.44 "
20 Oct. 1848	La Vivandière	BP, 1a	Saint-Léon	Saint-Léon	Pugni	Despléchin, Séchan, Dieterle	Lormier	Cerrito; Saint-Léon	90	1848–72	3,483.98 "
19 Jan. 1849	Le Violon du Diable	BP, 2a 6s	Saint-Léon	Saint-Léon	Pugni	Despléchin, Thierry	Lormier	Cerrito; Saint-Léon	50	1849–52	5,682.00 "
8 Oct. 1849	La Filleule des fées	BF, 3a 7s	Saint-Georges	Perrot	Adam, Saint-Julien	Cambon, Thierry (Prologue and Act 1); Despléchin (Act 2) Machines: Sacré	Lormier, H. d'Orschwiller	Grisi; L. Petipa, Perrot	22	1849–52	Figures not available
22 Feb. 1850	Stella, ou les Contre-bandiers	BP, 2a 4s	Saint-Léon	Saint-Léon	Pugni	Cambon, Thierry	Lormier	Cerrito; Saint-Léon	32	1850–52	4,766.74 fr.
15 Jan. 1851	Pâquerette	BP, 3a 5s	Gautier	Saint-Léon	Benoist	Despléchin, Cambon, Thierry	Lormier, Marchal	Cerrito; Saint-Léon	9	1851	5,022.27 "
24 Nov. 1851	Vert-Vert	BP, 3a 4s	Leuven	Mazilier, [Saint-Léon]	Deldevez, J. B. Tolbecque	Cambon, Thierry	Lormier	Priora, Plunkett; Saint-Léon	17	1851–52	3,978.65 "
29 Dec. 1852	Orfa	BP, 2a	Trianon	Mazilier	Adam	Cambon, Thierry	Lormier	Cerrito, Bogdanova; L. Petipa	51	1852–60	6,857.60 "
21 Sep. 1853	Aelia et Mysis, ou l'Atel-lane	BP, 2a	Mazilier	Mazilier	Potier	Cambon, Thierry (Act 1); Despléchin (Act 2)	Lormier	Priora, Guy-Stéphan; L. Petipa	14	1853–54	6,854.40 "
11 Nov. 1853	Jovita, ou les Boucaniers	BP, 3s	Mazilier	Mazilier	Labarre	Despléchin (Sc. 1); Cambon, Thierry (Sc. 2) Machines: Nolau	Lormier	Rosati; Mérante, L. Petipa	39	1853–59	6,269.75 "
31 May 1854	Gemma	B, 2a 5s	Gautier	Cerrito	Gabrielli	Rubé, Nolau	Lormier	Cerrito; Mérante, L. Petipa	7	1854	5,348.53 "
8 Jan. 1855	La Fonti	B, 2a 6s	[Deligny]	Mazilier	Labarre	Martin (Act 1); Cambon, Thierry (Act 2)	Lormier	Rosati; Mérante, L. Petipa	24	1855	5,936.88 "
23 Jan. 1856	Le Corsaire	BP, 3a 5s	Saint-Georges	Mazilier	Adam	Martin (Sc. 1, 2); Despléchin (Sc. 3, 5); Cambon, Thierry (Sc. 4) Machines: Sacré [1867 revival: Cambon, Despléchin, Rubé, Chaperon, Lavastre Machines: Sacré]	Albert	Rosati; Segarelli	81	1856–68	1867 revival 8,174.56 fr.
11 Aug. 1856	Les Elfes	BF†, 3a 4s	Saint-Georges	Mazilier	Gabrielli	Nolau, Rubé (Sc. 1); Despléchin (Sc. 2); Martin (Sc.3); Cambon, Thierry (Sc. 4)	Albert	Ferraris; L. Petipa, Segarelli	37	1856–61	5,654.87 "
1 Apr. 1857	Marco Spada, ou la Fille du bandit	BP, 3a 6s	[Scribe]	Mazilier	Auber	Cambon, Thierry (Sc. 1, 4, 5); Despléchin (Sc. 2); Nolau, Rubé (Sc. 3) Machines: Sacré	Albert, Lormier	Rosati, Ferraris; L. Petipa	27	1857–59	8,036.23 "

Date of First Performance	Title of Ballet	Description	Author of Scenario	Choreographer	Composer	Stage Designers	Costume Designer	Principal Dancers	Number of Performances	Time in Repertory	Average Receipts over First 10 (or Less) Performances
26 Nov. 1860	Le Papillon	BP, 2a 4s	Saint-Georges	Marie Taglioni	Offenbach	Martin (Act I, Sc. 1); Despléchin (Act I, Sc. 2); Nolau, Rubé (Act II, Sc. 1); Cambon, Thierry (Act II, Sc. 2)	Albert	Livry; Mérante	42	1860-62	7,128.43 fr.
25 Mar. 1861	Graziosa	BP, 1a	Derley	L. Petipa	Labarre	Cambon, Thierry	Albert	Ferraris; Chapuy	65	1861-72	6,626.98 „
29 May 1861	Le Marché des Innocents	BP, 1a	M. Petipa	M. and L. Petipa	Pugni	Cambon, Thierry	Albert	Marie Petipa; Mérante	88	1861-71	6,065.92 „
20 Nov. 1861	L'Étoile de Messine	BP, 2a 6s	Foucher	Borri	Gabrielli	Despléchin (Sc. 1, 2, 5); Thierry (Sc. 3); Martin (Sc. 4); Cambon (Sc. 6)	Albert	Ferraris; Mérante	37	1861-63	7,367.21 „
6 July 1863	Diavolina	BP, 1a	Saint-Léon	Saint-Léon	Pugni	Cambon, Thierry	Lormier, Albert	Muravieva; Mérante	52	1863-74	6,582.66 „
19 Feb. 1864	La Maschera, ou les Nuits de Venise	BP, 3a 6s	Saint-Georges	Rota	Giorza	Cambon, Thierry; Despléchin (Act III)	Albert	Boschetti; E. Fiocre; Mérante	25	1864-65	7,226.37 „
11 July 1864	Néméa, ou l'Amour vengé	BP, 2a	Meilhac, L. Halévy	Saint-Léon	Minkus	Despléchin, Lavastre	Lormier, Albert	Muravieva, E. Fiocre; Mérante	53	1864-71	7,202.80 „
28 Dec. 1865	Le Roi d'Yvetot	BP, 1a	Marquis de Massa	L. Petipa	Labarre	Cambon, Thierry	Albert	Fioretti, Fonta, E. Fiocre; Mérante	10	1865-66	6,000.32 „
12 Nov. 1866	La Source	B, 3a 4s	Nuitter	Saint-Léon	Delibes, Minkus	Despléchin, Lavastre (Sc. 1, 2, 4); Rubé, Chaperon (Sc. 3)	Lormier, Albert	Salvioni, E. Fiocre; Mérante	73	1866-76	6,750.37 „
25 May 1870	Coppélia, ou la Fille aux yeux d'émail	B, 2a 3s	Nuitter	Saint-Léon	Delibes	Cambon (Sc. 1, 3); Despléchin, Lavastre (Sc. 2)	Albert	Bozzacchi, E. Fiocre; Dauty	717* to 31·12·1973	1870– (still in repertory)	8,401.08 „

ABBREVIATIONS: B = Ballet; BF = Ballet-Faery; BFt = Ballet-Fantastique; BP = Ballet-Pantomime. a = acts; s = scenes.

In calculating the average receipts over the first ten or less performances, benefit performances (for which the prices were usually increased) have been ignored.

* Includes 47 performances of only one scene. Excludes 64 performances of Descombey version between 1966 and 1971.

APPENDIX D

OPERA DIVERTISSEMENTS FIRST PERFORMED AT THE PARIS OPÉRA BETWEEN OCTOBER 1847 AND SEPTEMBER 1870

Date of First Performance	Title of Opera	Composer	Choreographer	Principal Dancers	Remarks
26 Nov. 1847	*Jérusalem*	Verdi	Mazilier	Fuoco, A. Dumilâtre, Plunkett, Fabbri	
16 June 1848	*L'Apparition*	Benoist	A. Mabille	Caroline; Théodore	
6 Nov. 1848	*Jeanne la folle*	L. Clapisson	A. Mabille	Maria, Fuoco, Robert, L. Taglioni	
16 Apr. 1849	*Le Prophète*	Meyerbeer	A. Mabille	Plunkett, Robert; L. Petipa, Théodore	
6 Dec. 1850	*L'Enfant prodigue*	Auber	Saint-Léon	Plunkett, Robert	Plunkett played the mime rôle of Lia
16 May 1851	*Zerline, ou la Corbeille d'oranges*	Auber	Mazilier	Fabbri, Plunkett, Robert, Emarot; L. Petipa, Beauchet	
6 Aug. 1851	*Les Nations* (cantata)	Adam	Saint-Léon	Fabbri, Robert, Emarot, Caroline, Nathan, L. Marquet, Lacoste, Pierron, Savel	
23 Apr. 1852	*Le Juif errant*	Halévy	Saint-Léon	L. Taglioni, Bogdanova, Legrain; Mérante	*Le Berger Aristée et les abeilles*
2 May 1853	*La Fronde*	Niedermeyer	L. Petipa	L. Taglioni, Bogdanova, Forli; Mérante, Beauchet, Minard	
18 Oct. 1854	*La Nonne sanglante*	Gounod	L. Petipa	Robert, Bogdanova, Forli, Legrain; Mérante	
13 June 1855	*Les Vêpres siciliennes*	Verdi	L. Petipa	Beretta, Cucchi, Legrain, Nathan	*Les Saisons*
27 Sept. 1855	*Sainte-Claire*	Ernst, Duke of Saxe-Coburg-Gotha	Mazilier	Rosati, Plunkett, Beretta, Cucchi, Forli; Beauchet	
12 Jan. 1857	*Le Trouvère*	Verdi	L. Petipa	Cucchi, Z. Richard, Poussin, Schlosser; Mérante	
21 Sept. 1857	*Le Cheval de bronze*	Auber	L. Petipa	Ferraris, Caroline; Mérante	
17 Mar. 1858	*La Magicienne*	Halévy	Mazilier	Z. Richard; Mérante	*Les Échecs*

Date of First Performance	Title of Opera	Composer	Choreographer	Principal Dancers	Remarks
4 Mar. 1859	Herculanum	David	Mazilier	Livry; Mérante	
7 Sept. 1859	Roméo et Juliette	Bellini and Vaccaj	Mazilier	Z. Richard, Pitteri; Mérante	
9 Mar. 1860	Pierre de Médicis	Poniatowski	L. Petipa	Ferraris, L. Fiocre; Mérante, Coralli	Les Amours de Diane
9 July 1860	Sémiramis	Rossini	L. Petipa	Savel, Villiers, Beaugrand; Beauchet	Additional music by Carafa
13 Mar. 1861	Tannhäiser	Wagner	L. Petipa	Rousseau, Stoïkoff, Troisvallets	Les Grâces
28 Feb. 1862	La Reine de Saba	Gounod	L. Petipa	Livry, Z. Richard; Chapuy	
28 Dec. 1863	Moïse (revival)	Rossini	L. Petipa	Fioretti, Vernon, Fonta, Beaugrand, Baratte	
3 Oct. 1864	Roland à Roncevaux	Mermet	L. Petipa	Fonta, Fioretti, Pilatte; Rémond	
28 Apr. 1865	L'Africaine	Meyerbeer	Saint-Léon	L. Marquet, Morando; E. Cornet, Pluque	
2 Apr. 1866	Don Juan (revival)	Mozart	Saint-Léon	Fioretti, Beaugrand, E. Fiocre	Ballet des roses
11 Mar. 1867	Don Carlos	Verdi	L. Petipa	Beaugrand, A. Mérante, Ribet, L. Marquet; Mérante	Ballet de la reine; la Peregrina
9 Mar. 1868	Hamlet	Thomas	L. Petipa	Fioretti, E. Fiocre	La Fête du printemps
3 Mar. 1869	Faust	Gounod	Justament	Fioretti, Fonta, E. Fiocre	
7 Mar. 1870	Robert le Diable (revival)	Meyerbeer	Saint-Léon	Fonta	
25 May 1870	Le Freychütz (revival)	Weber	Saint-Léon	Beaugrand, A. Mérante, Gozelin; Mérante, Rémond, Friant	L'Invitation à la valse (arr. Berlioz)

APPENDIX E

Dance Activities at other Parisian Theatres between October 1847 and September 1870

Théâtre de L'Ambigu-Comique

Divertissements were occasionally introduced into the dramas produced at this theatre. Among the dancers who appeared here were Léon Espinosa, Mme Adèle Monplaisir, Rachel and Maria Francesco, and Clara, Amalie and Rosa Price.

Théâtre des Bouffes-Parisiens

24 June 1856. *Les Bergers de Watteau, divertissement* by Mathieu and Placet. Cast included Mariquita, Clara and Rosa Price.

Théâtre Impérial du Chatelet

Many of the faeries and spectacles produced here contained *divertissements* arranged by Honoré. Victorine Legrain appeared in *La Poudre de Perlinpinpin* (September 4th, 1869).

Théâtre Impérial du Cirque

Carlo Blasis produced two *divertissements* here in 1860, one in *L'Histoire d'un drapeau* (17 Jan.), the other *Une Fête à Versailles* in *Le Cheval fantôme* (27 Apr.).

Théâtre Déjazet

19 May 1860. Cristina Mendez and Spanish dancers.
7 Mar. 1861. Aladar Bekefy and Hungarian dancers.
28 May 1861. *Le Diable amoureux* and *Le Retour du matelot*, English *divertissements* by J. Milano. Cast included J. Milano, Clara and Barbara Morgan, Fanny Brown.

Théâtre des Fantaisies-Parisiennes

29 Apr. 1867. *Rumbo y Calia*, Spanish ballet in 6 scenes. Cast included Mariquita.

Théâtre des Fleurs, Pré-Catelan

3 June 1857. *Nella*, ballet-pantomime with chorus by C. Bridault and Duchâteau, music by Pilati. Cast included Irma Aymé, Paul Legrand, and Petra Cámara and Spanish dancers.
7 July 1857. *La Naïade*, ballet-pantomime in 2 acts with chorus by T. Julian, C. Bridault and Duchâteau, music by Pilati. Cast included Irma Aymé, Paul Legrand, and Petra Cámara and Spanish dancers.

17 June 1858.   *Claribella*, children's ballet in 4 scenes by Katti
  Lanner. Danced by 36 Danish children.
17 June 1858.   Rafaela Montero and Spanish dancers.
21 June 1859.   Cristina Mendez and Spanish dancers.

THÉÂTRE DES FOLIES-CONCERTANTES, later DES FOLIES-NOUVELLES

16 Jan. 1855.   *Le Possédé*, ballet-pantomime in 1 act by Brunel,
  music by Hervé.
5 July 1855.   Antonio Ruiz and Spanish dancers.
15 Jan. 1856.   *Le Joli régiment*, ballet-pantomime by Hervé. Cast
  included Mlles Z. Colinet, Antonia Salvador;
  Victoriano Piedra.
8 Apr. 1857.   Señora Romeral and Spanish dancers.

THÉÂTRE FRANÇAIS

19 Aug. 1862.   Revival of *Psyché*, by Corneille and Molière, with
  a ballet by Adrien. In the ballet: Hippolyte
  Mazilier (nephew of Joseph), Marie Dumilâtre
  (niece of Adèle), Héloïse Lamy.

THÉÂTRE DE LA GAÎTÉ

5 July 1856.   *L'Oiseau de paradis*, faery in 5 acts and 10 scenes by
  Masson and Gabriel, choreography by Massot.
  Marie Guy-Stéphan played an important dancing
  rôle.
21 July 1865.   *Le Paradis perdu*, drama (revival), included a
  divertissement by Alexandre Fuchs, *Les Filles d'Ève*,
  in which Lauretta Lanza appeared. Fuchs'
  action in affixing his wife's maiden name of
  Taglioni to his own on the bills involved him
  in a quarrel with Paul Taglioni.
18 July 1867.   *L'Ours et le Pacha*, vaudeville, included a *divertissement* by Fuchs in which Manuela Perea (La Nena)
  appeared.

THÉÂTRE DU GYMNASE-DRAMATIQUE

13 May 1851.   Petra Cámara and Spanish dancers.
2 June 1853.   Petra Cámara and Spanish dancers.
3 June 1854.   Manuela Perea (La Nena) and Spanish dancers.
25 July 1864.   *Don Quichotte*, play by Sardou, included dances
  arranged by Rota to music by Giorza.

THÉÂTRE ITALIEN

25 Feb. 1851.   Carolina Rosati made her Paris début as Ariele in
  Halévy's opera, *La Tempesta*. The rôle had been
  created by Carlotta Grisi in London the previous
  summer.

18 May 1857.   Nadezhda Bogdanova and her brother, Nicolai Bogdanov, danced a *pas de deux* at the benefit of Signorina Picchiottino, an Italian actress appearing with Adelaide Ristori.

26 Apr. 1865.   *Don Zeffiro*, ballet in 1 act by Saint-Léon, music by Pugni. Cast included Ernestine Urban and Émile Gredelue.

18 Nov. 1865.   *Il Basilico*, ballet in 1 act by Tréfeu and Saint-Léon, music by Graziani. Cast included Ernestine Urban, Mlle Rossi, Mme Pougaud-Mège, MM. Gredelue, F. Mérante.

19 Feb. 1866.   *Gli Elementi, divertissement* in 1 act by Saint-Léon, music by Pugni. Cast included Mmes Gredelue-Mérante, Pougaud-Mège, Mlles Rigl, Diani.

19 Mar. 1866.   *La Fidanzata valacca*, ballet in 1 act by Saint-Léon and Nuitter, choreography by Saint-Léon, music by Graziani and Mattiozzi. Cast included Ernestine Urban, Mme Pougaud-Mège, Mlle Diani, MM. Gredelue, F. Mérante, Mège.

THÉÂTRE LYRIQUE

22 Jan. 1853.   *Le Lutin de la vallée*, opera-ballet in 2 acts and 3 scenes by Saint-Léon, music by E. Gautier, verses by Carré and Alboize. Dancing cast included Saint-Léon, Marie Guy-Stéphan, Julie Lisereux, Marie Millet, Josephine Kohlenberg.

22 Oct. 1853.   *Le Danseur du roi*, opera-ballet in 2 acts and 3 scenes by Saint-Léon, music by E. Gautier, verses by Alboize. Dancing cast included Saint-Léon, Nathalie Fitzjames, Adèle Nathan, Julie Lisereux, Rosalie Lilienthal, Maria Godefroi, Emilia Arányváry, Mlle Yella, Rosalie Lequine.

6 Feb. 1854.   *Les Étoiles*, opera-ballet in 1 act and 2 scenes by Clairville, choreography by Barrez, music by Pilati. Dancing cast included Alfred Chapuy and Lucile Lemonier.

22 Oct. 1861.   *Le Neveu de Gulliver*, opera-ballet in 3 acts, libretto by Boisseaux, music by Lajarte, choreography by Adrien. Dancing cast included Hortense Clavelle.

THÉÂTRE IMPÉRIAL DE L'ODÉON

27 Apr. 1862.   *La Flor de Sevilla*, with Anita Montes, Lola Melea, Mariano Camprubí and Alemany.

OPÉRA-NATIONAL

6 Mar. 1848.   *La Jardinière et son seigneur*, ballet-pantomime in 1 act by Labie, choreography by Lerouge, music by Pilati. Cast included Mlle Soldini.

Théâtre du Palais-Royal

7 June 1854.   Josefa Vargas and Spanish dancers.

Théâtre de la Porte-Saint-Martin

18 July 1848.   *Tableaux aériens*, ballet.

2 Dec. 1848.   *Trois Filles à marier*, ballet in 1 act and 2 scenes by Ragaine.

27 Aug. 1849.   *L'Étoile du marin*, ballet in 2 acts and 4 scenes by Lerouge, music by Morel. Cast included Mlles Camille, Thierry, Léon Espinosa.

1 Dec. 1849.   The Viennese Children, under the direction of Josephine Weiss.

30 Jan. 1855.   *Idalia, ou la Fleur inconnue*, ballet in 2 acts and 3 scenes by Bretin and Cazzoletti, music by Scaramelli. Cast included Flora Fabbri, Josephine Kohlenberg, Maria Hennecart, M. Mège.

2 June 1855.   *La Perla de Madrid* and *La Maja de Sevilla*, ballets by Antonio Ruiz and José Archez. Cast included Concepción and Dolores Ruiz.

9 July 1856.   Petra Cámara and Spanish dancers.

24 Dec. 1856.   *La Esmeralda*, ballet in 2 acts and 5 scenes by Perrot, music by Pugni. Cast included Maria Scotti (Esmeralda), Rosita Comba (Fleur de lys), M. Paul. The first and only Paris production of Perrot's famous ballet.

22 Apr. 1858.   *Yanko le bandit*, ballet-pantomime in 2 acts by Théophile Gautier, music by Deldevez, choreography by Honoré. Cast included Mlles Battaglini, Coustou, Guichard, Cérésa, M. Honoré.

2 Oct. 1859.   *Le Jockey du diable*, ballet in 1 act by Espinosa. Cast included Léon Espinosa, Adèle Monplaisir, Petra Cámara.

9 Oct. 1859.   *Le Carrousel, divertissement* by Espinosa. Cast included Léon Espinosa, Adèle Monplaisir, Petra Cámara.

Many of the dramas and faeries produced at this theatre also contained *divertissements*. Other dancers who appeared here during the years 1847 to 1870 included Giuseppina Bossi, Mlle C. Bottali, Noëmie and Judith David, Félicie Delan, Carlotta De Vecchi, Rachel and Maria Francesco, Clara Galby, Virginie Magne, Mariquita, Zina Mérante, Rafaela Montero, Mlle Westmaël. Among the choreographers who worked for this theatre were Adrien, Léon Espinosa, Charles Honoré, Henri Justament and Pinzetti. Fanny Génat, who had been a dancer at the Opéra, appeared here as an actress in Foucher's *Le Carnaval de Naples*, in 1863.

THÉÂTRE DES VARIÉTÉS

Nov. 1847.	Hungarian dancers.
2 May 1856.	Cristina Mendez and Spanish dancers.
9 June 1860.	*La Fille du Diable*, vaudeville fantastique, included a pastoral ballet by Barrez. Judith Ferreyra (1837–68) played the part of Diavoline. One scene pictured a ballet at the Opéra as seen from the wings, with the audience in the background.
13 June 1865.	Petra Cámara and Spanish dancers.
26 Apr. 1868.	*La Comédie bourgeoise*, an *à-propos* in song and dance, ended with a *ballet des pifferari*, arranged by Justament and danced by Zina Mérante, Mariquita, M. Bertottot, etc.

THÉÂTRE DU VAUDEVILLE

7 Sept. 1864.	Mariano Camprubí and Dolores Juanita Serral and Spanish dancers.

APPENDIX F

BIBLIOGRAPHY OF PRINTED SOURCES FOR THE HISTORY OF THE
PARIS OPÉRA BALLET, 1847–70

ANON. *Biographie de M. et Mme Fanny Cerrito-Saint-Léon de l'Opéra.* (Paris, 1850.)

ANON. *More Uncensored Recollections.* (London, 1926.)

ABRAHAM, ÉMILE. *Les Acteurs et les Actrices de Paris.* (Paris, 1861.)

BEAUMONT, CYRIL W. *Complete Book of Ballets.* (London, 1937.)

BEAUMONT, CYRIL W. *A Miscellany for Dancers.* (London, 1934.)

BERNAY, BERTHE. *La Danse au théâtre.* (Paris, 1890.)

BICKNELL, ANNA L. *Life in the Tuileries under the Second Empire.* (London, 1895.)

BOCHER, CHARLES. *Mémoires.* (Paris, 1907.)

BOIGNE, CHARLES DE. *Les Petits mystères de l'Opéra.* (Paris, 1857.)

CASTIL-BLAZE, F. H. J. *L'Académie Impériale de Musique.* (Paris, 1855.)

COLOMBIER, MARIE. *Mémoires.* (Paris, 1898–99.)

DELDEVEZ, E. M. E. *Mes Mémoires.* (Le Puy, 1890.)

DU CAMP, MAXIME. *Souvenirs d'un demi-siècle.* (Paris, 1949.)

DUPEUTY, ADOLPHE. *Où est la femme?* (Paris, 1864.)

FOURCAUD. *Léontine Beaugrand.* (Paris, 1881.)

GONCOURT, EDMOND and JULES DE. *Journal des Goncourt.* (Paris, 1887–96.)

HALÉVY, LUDOVIC. *Carnets.* (Paris, 1935.)

HERVEY, CHARLES. *The Theatres of Paris.* (Paris and London, 1846.)

JAPY, GEORGE. *Adèle Granzow.* (Paris, 1868.)

JOLLIVET, GASTON. *Souvenirs de la vie de plaisir sous le Second Empire.* (Paris, 1927.)

KARSAVINA, TAMARA. *Theatre Street.* (London, 1930.)

LAJARTE, THÉODORE DE. *Bibliothèque musicale de l'Opéra.* (Paris, 1878.)

LEMERCIER DE NEUVILLE, LOUIS. *Les Figures du temps. Marie Petipa.* (Paris, 1861.)

LÉO. *Amina Boschetti.* (Paris, 1864.)

L'ÉPINE, QUATRELLES. *Une Danseuse française au XIXe siècle. Emma Livry.* (Paris, 1909.)

LEVINSON, ANDRÉ. *Marie Taglioni (1804–1884).* (Paris, 1929.)

LIFAR, SERGE. *Carlotta Grisi.* (Paris, 1941.)

LOLIÉE, FRÉDÉRIC. *La Fête impériale.* (Paris, 1912.)

MAUGNY, Comte ALBERT DE. *Souvenirs du Second Empire.* (Paris, 1889.)

MOYNET, GEORGES. *La Machinerie théâtrale. Trucs et décors.* (Paris, 1893.)

MOYNET, J. *L'Envers du théâtre.* (Paris, 1873.)

NÉRÉE-DESARBRES.   *Sept ans à l'Opéra.*   (Paris, 1864.)

NEWMAN, ERNEST.   *The Life of Richard Wagner.*   (London, 1933–47.)

PALIANTI, L.   *Petites archives des théâtres de Paris.   Souvenirs de dix ans. Théâtre Impérial de l'Opéra.*   (Paris, 1865.)

PROD'HOMME, J. G.   *L'Opéra (1669–1925).*   (Paris, 1925.)

ROYER, ALPHONSE.   *Histoire de l'Opéra.*   (Paris, 1875.)

SAINT-LÉON, ARTHUR MICHEL.   *De l'État actuel de la danse.*   (Lisbon, 1856.)

SAINT-LÉON, ARTHUR MICHEL.   *La Sténochorégraphie.*   (Paris, 1852.)

SALA, GEORGE AUGUSTUS.   *Paris Herself Again.*   (London, 1879.)

SCHNEIDER, LOUIS.   *Offenbach.*   (Paris, 1923.)

SCUDO, PAUL.   *L'Année musicale.*   (Paris, 1861 and 1862.)

SOUBIES, A.   *Soixante-sept ans à l'Opéra en une page.*   (Paris, 1893.)

VAILLAT, LÉANDRE.   *La Taglioni.*   (Paris, 1942.)

VIEIL ABONNÉ, UN (pseudonym: Paul Mahalin).   *Ces Demoiselles de l'Opéra.*   (Paris, 1887.)

VIEL-CASTEL, Comte HORACE DE.   *Mémoires sous le règne de Napoléon III (1851–1864).*   (Paris, 1883–84.)

VIZENTINI, ALBERT.   *Derrière la toile.*   (Paris, 1868.)

WOLZOGEN, ALFRED VON.   *Ueber Theater und Musik.   Historisch-Kritische Studien.*   (Breslau, 1860.)

X.Y.Z.   *Le Nouvel Opéra.   Le monument, les artistes.*   (Paris, 1875.)

ZED (pseudonym: Comte Albert de Maugny).   *Le Demi-monde sous le Second Empire.   Souvenirs d'un sybarite.*   (Paris, 1892.)

ZED.   *La Grande vie à Paris.*   (Paris, 1889.)

Борисоглебский, М.   Материалы по истории русского балета.   (Leningrad, 1938.)

Плещеев, А. А.   Наш Балет, 1673–1899.   (St. Petersburg, 1899.)

Слонимский Ю.   Мастера балета.   (Leningrad, 1937.)

Худеков, С. Н.   История танцев.   (Petrograd, 1915.)

NEWSPAPERS AND PERIODICALS

L'Artiste.
L'Art Musical.
Le Constitutionnel.
Le Coureur des Spectacles.
The Court Journal (London).
L'Entr'acte.
Le Figaro.
La France Musicale.
Le Gaulois.
L'Illustration.
Journal des Débats.
Le Journal des Théâtres.
Journal Officiel.
Le Journal pour rire (later *Journal Amusant*).
La Liberté.
Le Ménestrel.
Le Monde Illustré.
Le Moniteur Universel.
Le Nain Jaune.
L'Opinion National.
Paris Journal.
Le Pays.
La Presse.
La Revue et Gazette Musicale.
Le Théâtre.
The Times (London).
L'Univers Illustré.
La Vie Parisienne.

INDEX

Ballets and *divertissements*, operas and operettas, and plays and other dramatic spectacles, are listed under general headings. Opera-ballets are listed under Ballets or Operas, according to which component was predominant.

271